P9-EES-224

DATE DUE			
Faculty 2-23			
FE 27 '03			
MR 17 '03			
MR 31 '03			

813
MOG

Mogen, David.

11086

Ray Bradbury.

BLAIRSVILLE HS LIBRARY

818379   09266B

Ray Bradbury

Twayne's United States Authors Series

Warren French, Editor

Indiana University

TUSAS 504

Ray Bradbury
Photograph © 1984 by Thomas Victor

Ray Bradbury

By David Mogen

Colorado State University

Twayne Publishers
A Division of G.K. Hall & Co. • *Boston*

Ray Bradbury

David Mogen

Copyright © 1986 By G.K. Hall & Co.
All Rights Reserved
Published by Twayne Publishers
A Division of G.K. Hall & Co.
70 Lincoln Street
Boston, Massachusetts 02111

Copyediting supervised by Lewis DeSimone
Book production by Elizabeth Todesco
Book design by Barbara Anderson

Typeset in 11 pt. Garamond
by P&M Typesetting, Inc., Waterbury, Connecticut

Printed on permanent/durable acid-free paper
and bound in the United States of America

Library of Congress Cataloging in Publication Data

Mogen, David, 1945—
  Ray Bradbury.

  (Twayne's United States authors series; TUSAS 504)
  Bibliography: p. 173
  Includes index.
  1. Bradbury, Ray, 1920–   —Criticism and
interpretation. I. Title. II. Series.
PS3503.R167Z77   1986   813'.54   86-11972
ISBN 0-8057-7464-5

Contents

About the Author

David Mogen received his B.A. (cum laude) from Columbia University and his Ph.D. from the University of Colorado in Boulder, where he specialized in American literature. He is now associate professor of English at Colorado State University, where he teaches a variety of courses, including science fiction, literature of the American West, and American Indian literature.

Dr. Mogen has published a book on the frontier theme in American science fiction, *Wilderness Visions*, which will be followed by a companion volume, *New Frontiers, Old Horizons*. He is currently editing two anthologies of original criticism on frontier mythology in American literature, *Frontier Gothic* and *The Frontier Experience and the American Dream*. He has published critical articles on subjects ranging from Henry James to American frontier gothicism to science fiction, in publications including *American Literary Realism*, *Genre*, and *Twentieth-Century Western Writers*.

Preface

Ray Bradbury provides an unusually complex subject for a book of this type, both because of his multifaceted career and because his life is so interwoven with his artistic creations. Though he is known primarily as a science-fiction and fantasy writer, and though indeed he has produced a large and impressive body of fiction in these genres, he has been prolific in many other areas as well: he has written extensively in a medium I call "autobiographical fantasy," most notably in his two Green Town novels, *Dandelion Wine* and *Something Wicked This Way Comes*; published an anthology of detective fiction and a detective novel, *Death Is a Lonely Business*; produced a large quantity of essentially realist fiction throughout his career; written treatments and screenplays both for major movie productions and for numerous television and radio productions, and also had many of his own works translated into film; written and produced his own drama, published two major volumes of plays, and written lyrics for several musical performances; written verse throughout his career, and published three volumes of poetry. Interspersed throughout these activities he has also written countless articles and reviews, granted numerous published and unpublished interviews, and appeared frequently on talk shows, panels, and in lectures.

The sheer volume and diversity of Bradbury's creative work is complicated further by the complex ways in which his art reflects and interprets his own life. Bradbury discovered early in his career that his best prose symbolically interprets personal experiences, that he could bring exotic subjects to life as metaphors for things we know. Thus, Bradbury's creations often transform his personal experience in oblique but sometimes surprisingly direct ways. "Green Town" transforms real memories of Waukegan, Illinois, into a myth symbolically representing the ceremonial life of a vanished era. Yet "Mr. Electrico," who might appear exclusively the product of fantasy, similarly transforms into a gothic symbol a very real traveling showman, who actually did present his strange show in an electric chair as part of a "seedy two-bit carnival," who actually told twelve-year-old Ray Bradbury that he would "live forever" and that in a previous life Bradbury had died in his arms in Ardennes forest.[1] Properly impressed, Bradbury wove this strange childhood encounter into the carnival of evil in *Something Wicked This Way Comes*, just as he transformed the local Waukegan barber into an alien vampire in "The Man Upstairs," and transformed himself into the murderously precocious infant of "The Small Assassin." Transforming fact into fiction, Bradbury weaves myth and fantasy out of both commonplace and bizarre experiences in his own life.

Bradbury's career does not divide into clearly distinct stages, and because he primarily writes short pieces, one cannot accurately describe his achievement by concentrating on his major novels. Throughout his career he has consistently produced material in a wide variety of genres, for a variety of media. Thus, any interpretation of his creative work must proceed thematically rather than strictly chronologically, for Bradbury's central themes structure all his work, however different the genres and media. Yet though his career does not divide into clearly distinct periods, Bradbury has shifted in emphasis over the years—from science fiction and fantasy in the forties and early fifties, to film work and the Green Town stories in the mid-fifties and early sixties, to drama and poetry in the late sixties and seventies, to detective fiction in the eighties. Though Bradbury has worked in many forms during all these somewhat arbitrarily designated periods, they do in a general way describe the pattern of his development.

To describe this diverse achievement, I have organized the chapters thematically, yet ordered them in a pattern that roughly follows the chronology of Bradbury's development. Thus, the first chapter on fiction treats his "weird" tales, a type of story that helped establish Bradbury's reputation early in his career; and the final chapters before the conclusion treat his detective fiction and his major work in other media and other genres, to which he has devoted much of his energy since the early sixties. To provide a clear foundation from which to interpret his creative works, the study begins with three background chapters—a chapter on biography, a chapter outlining the controversy surrounding Bradbury's mainstream reputation as the "uncrowned king of science fiction,"[2] and, finally, a chapter on Bradbury's literary style, which provides the foundation for the genre analysis that follows. The chapter on weird fiction precedes four chapters on science fiction—two thematic studies of short stories, and one each on the major science-fiction novels, *The Martian Chronicles* and *Fahrenheit 451*. The following chapter treats Bradbury's two Green Town novels, *Dandelion Wine* and *Something Wicked This Way Comes*, as opening and concluding a unified myth about "growing up with the country." And subsequent chapters survey Bradbury's achievement in realist fiction and detective fiction as well as in film, drama, and poetry. The concluding chapter evaluates Bradbury's overall achievement in this prolific and diverse career.

This interpretation of Bradbury's life and work benefits profoundly from the bibliographical information and critical insight provided by earlier studies. Anyone seriously interested in Bradbury's career must certainly share the sentiments expressed in Bradbury's introduction to William F. Nolan's invaluable book-length bibliography, *The Ray Bradbury Companion* (1975):

> Looking over the prodigious job done by William F. Nolan causes me to think the following things:
> I'm glad I didn't have to do the research.
> I'm glad that I have written every day of my life for forty years in order to make this kind of trouble for Bill Nolan.[3]

But Nolan's massive bibliographical work is complemented by several other major works which provide biographical background, critical insight, and updated bibliographical material. Craig Cunningham's "oral autobiography" in UCLA's Special Collections (1961) provides a fascinating overview of Bradbury's early career in his own words. Joseph D. Olander and Martin Harry Greenberg's anthology of critical essays, *Ray Bradbury* (1980), combines some excellent criticism on major themes in Bradbury's fiction with helpful bibliographical material. Wayne L. Johnson's *Ray Bradbury* provides a readable and informed account of Bradbury's life and work, as well as some particularly interesting background information about the real Waukegan behind the Green Town myth. And Gary K. Wolfe's extended essay on Bradbury in *The Dictionary of Literary Biography* (vol. 8) provides a perceptive description and evaluation of Bradbury's achievement. I hope this volume succeeds in integrating the best insights from these earlier studies into my own interpretation of Bradbury's significance.

I am especially grateful to Ray Bradbury himself for his friendly, helpful assistance. When I informed him back in 1979 that I was beginning research for this book, he agreed to a two-day marathon interview at his office and home in Los Angeles to provide background source material. In the summer of 1980, accompanied by colleague and friend Mark Siegel from the University of Wyoming, I recorded a ten-hour conversation with Bradbury ranging over everything from his earliest memories to his current projects. My two-hundred page transcript of that interview has proved a helpful and interesting source, which I believe adds an important personal dimension to this study of Bradbury's life and work. Since he is a superb talker—self-assured, eloquent, and often witty—interviewing Bradbury proved both valuable and delightful.

My gratitude extends also to William F. Nolan (Bradbury's bibliographer and a prolific writer himself) and to Bruce Francis, collectors of Bradbury's work, both for their hospitality and for providing access to materials that would otherwise have been difficult to obtain. Willis McNelly provided encouragement at a crucial point in my writing, and he also convinced me of the need for an extended treatment of Bradbury's style, which appears in this study as chapter three. And Mark Siegel has helped shape my thinking about Bradbury over the years, from his participation in the initial background interview to his comments on the completed manuscript.

Finally, I thank Georgia State University for supplying research assistance during my first year of gathering materials for this book as well as Colorado State University, which provided funds for acquisition of materials, travel to the California interview, and typing the interview transcript and final book manuscript. The Special Collections library at the University of Nevada, Reno, provided copies of difficult-to-locate materials. My thanks as well to Susan Baylen, Marcia Davis, and Marcia Lukes for contributing their research expertise and typing skills to the success of this project.

David Mogen

Colorado State University

Chronology

1920   Born, 22 August in Waukegan, Illinois; third son of Leonard Spaulding Bradbury and Esther Marie Moberg Bradbury (twin older brothers, Leonard and Samuel, were born in 1916, but Samuel died in 1918, so that Ray grew up as the younger of two brothers).

1926   Birth of younger sister, Elizabeth; family moves to Tucson in fall.

1927   Elizabeth dies of pneumonia; family returns to Waukegan in May.

1928   Discovers science fiction in *Amazing Stories*.

1931   Begins writing first stories by hand on butcher paper.

1932   Father, laid off his job as telephone lineman, moves family to Tucson again; Ray performs as amateur magician at Oddfellows Hall and American Legion, secures air time on radio station KGAR to read comics to children on Saturdays.

1933   Family returns to Waukegan; Ray visits Century of Progress exhibit at World's Fair in Chicago.

1934   Again looking for employment, father moves family to Los Angeles; Ray becomes "live audience" for the Burns and Allen radio show.

1937   Scriptwriter, producer, and director of the *Roman Review* at L.A. High School; enters the Los Angeles Science Fiction League.

1938   First short story, "Hollerbochen's Dilemma," printed in *Imagination!*, an amateur fan magazine; graduates from high school.

1939   Publishes *Futuria Fantasia*, his own fan magazine; attends World Science Fiction Convention in New York; joins Laraine Day's drama group, Wilshire Players Guild.

1941   Attends Robert Heinlein's weekly writing class; first paid publication, "Pendulum" (coauthored with Henry Hasse) in *Super Science Stories*.

1942 Gives up job selling papers to write full-time; writes "The Lake," the story in which he feels he first discovered his distinctive style.

1945 Breaks through into "slick" magazine publications; travels to Mexico; "The Big Black and White Game" selected for *Best American Short Stories*.

1947 Marries Marguerite McClure; publishes first book, *Dark Carnival*; "Homecoming" selected for O. Henry Awards *Prize Stories of 1947*; becomes client of literary agent Don Congdon.

1948 O. Henry Award for "Powerhouse"; "I See You Never" selected for *Best American Short Stories 1948*.

1949 First daughter born; selected by the National Fantasy Fan Federation as the "best author of 1949" in science fiction and fantasy.

1950 *The Martian Chronicles*; rave review by Christopher Isherwood in *Tomorrow*.

1951 *The Illustrated Man*; second daughter born.

1952 Writes extended treatment for *It Came from Outer Space*; "The Other Foot" selected for *Best American Short Stories*.

1953 *The Golden Apples of the Sun; Fahrenheit 451;* travels to Ireland to spend six months writing the screenplay for John Huston's *Moby Dick*.

1955 *Switch on the Night* (children's book); *The October Country;* third daughter born.

1957 *Dandelion Wine;* father dies.

1958 "The Day It Rained Forever" selected for *Best American Short Stories;* fourth daughter born.

1959 *A Medicine for Melancholy.*

1962 *Something Wicked This Way Comes; R is for Rocket.*

1963 Academy Award nomination for *Icarus Montgolfier Wright;* first collection of drama, *The Anthem Sprinters.*

1964 *The Machineries of Joy; American Journey,* his film history of the nation, opens at the New York World's Fair; produces *The World of Ray Bradbury* in Coronet Theatre in Los Angeles.

1965 Produces second major theater production in Los Angeles, *The Wonderful Ice Cream Suit; The World of Ray Bradbury* has brief, unsuccessful run in New York; "The Other Foot" selected for *Fifty Best American Short Stories: 1915–1965.*

1966   *Twice 22; S is for Space;* Truffaut's *Fahrenheit 451* released; mother dies.

1967   *Dandelion Wine* staged as musical drama at Lincoln Center; collection of Irish plays, *The Anthem Sprinters,* produced at Beverly Hills Playhouse.

1968   Wins Aviation-Space Writers Association award for "An Impatient Gulliver above Our Roots," science article in *Life Magazine.*

1969   Film of *The Illustrated Man* released; *I Sing the Body Electric!* published; *Christus Apollo,* cantata, performed at UCLA.

1970   "Mars Is Heaven!" selected for the Science Fiction Hall of Fame by the Science Fiction Writers of America.

1972   *The Wonderful Ice Cream Suit and Other Plays; The Halloween Tree.*

1973   First collection of poetry, *When Elephants Last in the Dooryard Bloomed.*

1975   *Pillar of Fire and Other Plays.*

1976   *Long after Midnight.*

1977   *Where Robot Mice and Robot Men Run Round in Robot Towns* (second poetry collection); receives a Life Achievement Award at the World Fantasy Convention.

1980   *The Stories of Ray Bradbury;* receives a Gandolf Award as "Grand Master" at the Hugo Award Ceremonies.

1981   *The Haunted Computer and the Android Pope* (third poetry collection).

1982   *The Complete Poems of Ray Bradbury.*

1984   Film of *Something Wicked This Way Comes* (screenplay by Bradbury) released; *A Memory of Murder* (collection of early mystery stories); receives the Jules Verne Award; awarded the Valentine Davies Award by the Writers Guild of America for his work in cinema.

1985   *Death Is a Lonely Business.*

Chapter One

The Life behind the Myth: From Green Town to the Future

The key to understanding Bradbury's life is, logically enough, the episode that opens his most overtly autobiographical book, *Dandelion Wine*. Trembling with fear and anticipation, Douglas Spaulding waits that fine summer day for something to spring from the surrounding forest. When it does, the atmosphere of gothic tension becomes rhapsodic, celebrating a fervent awareness of the most primal fact—consciousness of life itself.

And at last, slowly, afraid he would find nothing, Douglas opened one eye.

And everything, absolutely everything was there.

The world, like a great iris of an ever more gigantic eye, which has also just opened and stretched out to encompass everything, stared back at him.

And he knew what it was that had leaped upon him to stay and would not run away now.

I'm alive, he thought. [1]

Actually, this episode metaphorically depicts an experience that began much earlier in Bradbury's youth, a sensation of helpless, feverish immersion in life, both ecstatic and fearful, which seems to have descended upon him during infancy. Indeed, Bradbury believes he remembers the trauma of birth itself, the first shock of infant awareness. "I have what might be called almost total recall to the hour of my birth. I remember suckling, circumcision, and nightmares-about-being-born experienced in the crib in the first weeks of my life. I know, I know such things are not possible . . . but I saw, I heard, I knew." [2] The grotesque and frightening implications of such intense infantile awareness are explored in one of his weird fables, "The Small Assassin," which depicts just such a preternaturally conscious infant as filled with pain and rage for the suffering of birth. He finally gets retribution by calculatedly murdering his mother. Perhaps fiction's only malevolent thug in diapers, the murderous infant in "The Small Assassin" suggests that Bradbury's youthful impressionability had a frightening dimension, expressed in the dark, weird tales that were his first truly quality fiction. But this same heightened awareness is also the wellspring of his creativity, which he identifies with a capacity to fall madly in love with many things at once. He feared death because he might miss the next Tarzan episode in the *Chicago Tribune*, or the carnival, or *Fantasia*. Though *Dandelion Wine* presents his early experience in pastoral imagery—immersion in "the bee-fried air, by God, the bee-fried air"[3]—Bradbury's overtly autobiographical reminiscences speak primarily of media events, the wonderful trash that enchanted American youth in the twenties and thirties. "Out of this grand trash heap of recollection, the impact of Chaney, Douglas Fairbanks, Edgar Allan Poe when I was eight, Buck Rogers at nine, Tarzan at ten, and all the science fiction magazines from those same years, my fevers grew and towered and compelled me . . . the sort of impulse that only some small hyper-active boys can know."[4] Or, as he phrased it more recently, "I feel I've always had enough brains to run out in the rain without an umbrella and get drenched."[5]

Background: From Waukegan to Los Angeles (1920–38)

Bradbury's reminiscences, both written and oral, all emphasize this sense of being drenched in experience from birth. Born to a middle-class family in Waukegan, Illinois, in 1920, he remembers his "typical" middle-American youth as a constant fever of anticipation of things to come. His immersion in popular culture began at three, when he was "profoundly affected"[6] by viewing Lon Chaney's *The Hunchback of Notre Dame* from his mother's knee. From then on many of his most moving experiences were encounters with a wide variety of entertainment media: books, comics, movies, theater, museums, magic-shows, circuses. A chronology of key events in Bradbury's life compiled by his bibliographer, fellow-writer, and friend William F. Nolan, indicates that Bradbury considers these encounters among the formative experiences of his life. The middle-American childhood he mythologized in *Dandelion Wine* was an accumulation of enthusiasms he has never abandoned: a book of fairy tales when he was five; the Oz books at six; *Amazing Stories* (the first science fiction magazine) at eight; Edgar Rice Burroughs at nine; the town library at ten; Blackstone, the Magician, at eleven; Jules Verne and the radio series *Chandu, the Magician* at twelve.

Initially, writing was merely a spontaneous extension of Bradbury's appetite for imaginative entertainment. By the time he was twelve he had begun writing Buck Rogers stories on his new toy-dial typewriter, and he had also developed a habit of trying to type out scripts of *Chandu, the Magician* episodes. And in 1932 his first extended foray as a writer was inspired by his frustration as a reader. Having finished Edgar Rice Burroughs's *The Gods of Mars*, which concludes with the heroine trapped in a "sun prison" awaiting John Carter's rescue, he and a friend were inspired to write the sequel they were impatient to read:

> I couldn't wait the year until the next book came out, and what is more, even when the book came out I couldn't afford it, and the libraries didn't carry them. They were not considered right for children. It was a long way to my next birthday and Christmas; so that's why I sat down with my friend, Bill Arno, and why we got out a roll of butcher paper and wrote and illustrated a sequel to *The Gods of Mars* in which I figured out a way of her surviving the year and escaping the sun prison. I launched right into the novel-writing business at the start of my career.[7]

In 1932 the Depression helped end the Waukegan boyhood Bradbury has mined so extensively in his writings. His father lost his job as a telephone lineman and took the family out West to Tucson, where a job selling chili bricks sustained them for a year. After two years of moving back and forth between Illinois and Arizona, looking for work, he finally moved the family to Los Angeles in 1934. Bradbury loved the city from the first, and he has lived there ever since. He passionately defends its cultural life, which is uniquely in tune with his own interests and temperament. Indeed, he has endowed both his "home towns," Waukegan and Los Angeles, with decidedly mythical qualities, representing a spectrum of the values he holds most dear. He transformed Waukegan into his fictional "Green Town," a symbol of the Norman Rockwell values of pre-Depression smalltown America; but he also cherishes Los Angeles as the preeminent city of the future, the vital center of the media activity that has always enthralled him. Depicting Los Angeles as a fusion of Zen wis-

dom, glamorous imagery, and Disneyland playfulness, Bradbury exu-
berantly celebrates his second home as "the land of the hummingbird,
the paradox implausible, the illusion that must be seen to be be-
lieved."[8] In Bradbury's mythos, the community values of Green
Town (representing the best of the American past) and the creative
vitality of Los Angeles (which shapes and anticipates the future) both
are defined by contrast to the poisonous self-consciousness of Eastern
culture:

> We [Angelenos] have learned the great secret along the way from surf to
> mountains: you don't have to look busy to be busy. You don't have to scowl
> and pout and paw the turf and summon ghosts of Jung and seances of
> Freud. . . . The guy trotting on the red beach at sunset, yelling, may well
> be a biochemist from down the Coast, guiltless and free as the sandpipers,
> capable of abandoning forever the analytical couches of his New York . . .
> past. He may be lugging Camus under one arm, but James Bond is tucked
> inside Camus, with Shakespeare snugged inside of Bond, and B.C., The Wiz-
> ard of Id, and Peanuts used as bookmarks for all.[9]

Though he loved Los Angeles from the first, Bradbury suffered a
painful adolescence there which he remembers with bemused chagrin.
Unlike his older brother Skip, an athlete who became one of the
"muscle-people,"[10] Bradbury remembers himself during this period as
a caricature "dreamer," helpless to defend himself in the jungle of adolescence. Plagued with the title "four-eyes" because of his glasses,
verbally precocious but physically and emotionally insecure, he was
the "James Thurber boy," one of the "milktoasts" with the look of
the "startled doe or fawn" which invites harassment from more aggressively insecure peers. After two years of torment he finally learned
to defend himself when he turned on his "particular albatross," an
"American-Armenian boy" who would "spit and pour ink on my
books through the ventilating holes in my locker. I took this sort of
torture until I was sixteen. . . . Suddenly, one day I was mad, and I
turned on him and clobbered him. I didn't win the fight, but I got
a couple of wonderful blows in. On that day of all days, the revelation
came to me, that when you hit other people on the nose, then they
begin to leave you alone. Well, it was a little too late; I was a writer
by then."[11]

Perhaps partially to forget his ignominious life in school halls during these years, Bradbury devoted his free time to searching for stars.
Exhilarated to find himself living so near the entertainment center of

the world, he instantly embarked on an often-manic quest to meet his radio and film heroes in the flesh:

> The second day we were in L.A. I walked two blocks to the corner of Western and Pico and asked the news-seller, "Which way to MGM?"
> He pointed West. I started off. "Hey, you nut," cried the news-seller. "You can't *walk* there from here! It's ten miles!"
> "Then," said I, "I'll rollerskate."[12]

"I was one of Them," Bradbury observes of these adolescent years. In "W. C. Fields and the S.O.B. on Rollerskates," a humorous but poignant reminiscence about his first years in Los Angeles, he evokes the particular sadness and ecstasies of these years as a fan, when he was one of "the Strange Ones. The Funny People. The Odd Tribes of autograph-collectors and photographers. The Ones Who waited through long days and nights, who used other people's dreams for their lives."[13] But if the reminiscence is partially about the frantic emptiness of such lives, it also depicts the energy that eventually took him from the fringes of the entertainment world to its center.

He may have been only a fan, but he was an unusually innovative and successful fan, the kind of crazy kid whose enthusiasm seems to have inspired affection as well as tolerance from the stars he pursued. W. C. Fields called him a "little sonofabitch" as he signed his autograph book, one of the great moments of his career in fandom. He simply walked up and introduced himself to George Burns and Gracie Allen, and as a result he and a friend were the first live audience for their nationally broadcast radio show. He wrote comic skits for Burns and Allen every week, and his first pay as a writer was for a short piece they used to close out one show.[14] With a bemused incredulity like that he must have evoked from some of his idols, Bradbury recalls the curious contradictions he embodied, when his insecurities in some areas impelled him to feverish originality in others:

> I was a combination of coward and brassy chutzpah kid. I can't figure out how I could actually get around to being as nervy as I was. Because when it came to other parts of my life I was terrified—terrified of girls and that whole thing boys go through, when they want to be loved and there's just no way.
> But when it came to hanging around Hollywood, boy, I spoke up. I used to ride around in Louella Parson's limousine when she wasn't working . . . her chauffeur took me on errands. And when she found out I got kicked out,

but for awhile there I was living high on the hog. We'd pull up at stop signs and people would look in the back of this limo to see who was there, and it was Ray in the ninth grade of junior high school, wearing his torn denims.[15]

Bradbury's high school writing career was a combination of success and discouragement. The yearbook his senior year described him as "headed for literary distinction," yet the encouragement he had received was hardly unqualified. He himself describes most of his early writing as "dreadful," and two of his writing teachers who remained lifelong friends seem to have concurred. They reacted to his efforts with respectful distaste, with praise for his style but consternation at his choice of subject. "On my very first story, which was a dreadful gangster story of violence and brutality, she put, 'Simply dreadful, but you can write.' "[16] And he recalls with a more bitter sense of irony that he was the only student in the fiction class who did *not* get a story printed in the high school short story anthologies. The reason given was more infuriating than the rejection itself. "The only person in the class who went on and became a writer, myself, was excluded because of the science fiction subject matter. The space age was still a long way off in some never-never land of tomorrow."[17] Sharing the frustration of many science-fiction writers of his generation, Bradbury would later express similar exasperation at the mainstream literary establishment for refusing to recognize science fiction as a legitimate modern art form.

Though Bradbury recalls his high school years as "the most unhappy years of my life,"[18] they ended on a positive note. By the time he graduated in 1938 he had effectively channeled his energies in both writing and drama. After saving lunch money to acquire a $10.00 typewriter in 1937, he began contributing reviews and humorous sketches to the school paper. Arriving at tryouts for the annual "Roman Revue" talent show equipped with scripts and a repertoire of voices he had developed practicing to be a radio announcer, he established himself as "not only . . . an announcer, but also as a director, as a sound effects man, and as a scriptwriter."[19] Indeed, his debut as student director, producer, and scriptwriter was so successful he debated for two years whether to devote himself to writing or to theater. But more important than anything that happened in school, perhaps, was his discovery of the Los Angeles Science

Fiction League, a fan organization which introduced him to professional writers such as Robert Heinlein, Henry Kuttner, Leigh Brackett, Jack Williamson, and Edmond Hamilton, and which finally provided him a community which shared his enthusiasms and understood his ambitions. "I think these people saved my life in a way. They helped give me direction at a time when I needed it and . . . when I needed encouragement."[20]

Becoming a Popular Writer (1939–49)

Once he decided what he wanted to do, Bradbury made a remarkably efficient transition from being an enthusiastic high school graduate to being an established professional writer with a distinctive style. His circumstances were modest. Initially he worked as a newspaperboy, and throughout this period he lived with his parents. But when the mundane business of making a living was over his life was filled with exciting new adventures and enterprises. In 1939 he edited four issues of his own fan magazine, *Futuria Fantasia*, and wrote much of the material for it himself. He attended the first World Science Fiction Convention in New York, where he acted as an agent for artist-friend Hannes Bok, placing some of his work with *Weird Tales* (the magazine that would feature Bradbury's own first quality writings in the mid-forties). He joined a threater group led by actress Laraine Day, in which he wrote drama, acted, and flirted briefly with pursuing a life in theater. But by 1940, decisively embarked on his writing career, he had installed his typewriter in his modest "office" in a tenement near his newspaper route, where he devoted as much time as he could to becoming a professional writer.

Bradbury has discussed the process by which writers find an individual voice in numerous forums, and his observations on the subject are based directly on his own experience in the early forties. The keynotes to success, he emphasizes, are simple but demanding: energy, discipline, and genuine enthusiasm and love. With these, you simply work through problems and make discoveries, seeking out help when you genuinely need it. Through the Los Angeles Science Fiction League he met professional writers, several of whom generously offered him advice, encouragement, and criticism. He read everything he could find about the process of writing and was especially influenced by Dorothea Brande's *Becoming a Writer*, which suggested free-association techniques that helped him make contact with his subconsciousness. But, most important of all, he established a routine. He wrote. In 1941, the first year he committed himself fully to a career in writing, he wrote a story a week, a level of production he has tried to maintain ever since. Only three of the fifty-two stories were published, but he feels he could not have written the publishable stories without the experience and self-knowledge gained writing the others. In later years he attempted to formulate what he learned in an essay titled "Zen and the Art of Writing,"[21] which suggests that the source of artistic inspiration is "love," and that love in an artist manifests itself through work. The Zen paradox is that such work cannot be self-conscious or forced, since an artist's work is really a form of play, which must be relaxed as well as disciplined.

Before Bradbury found his own voice, however, he went through an apprenticeship period during which he imitated the styles of others, sometimes consciously, sometimes unconsciously. Though he was publishing regularly in fanzines and nonpaying markets as early as 1940, Bradbury did not discover his characteristic style and subject matter until 1942, when he wrote "The Lake," the first of his weird stories anchored in his own experience. He did begin making sales during his first years of full-time writing: one in 1941, two in 1942, eleven in 1943, eighteen in 1944—when he was beginning to be recognized as an interesting new voice in science fiction and fantasy. Because of his success, by 1943 he was able to quit his newspaper job and devote himself to writing full-time. But he himself distinguishes between the "conventional" stories he wrote during this period and the stories that were distinctively his. Ironically, when he did find his voice some of the pulp editors rejected the new material because it was too unusual. But by then he had enough confidence to begin looking for new markets.[22]

Bradbury's transition from apprentice to professional author to original artist was manifested in his changing relationships with established writers. Initially, he was a promising novice in need of criticism and advice, who sought out and received both. In 1940 Robert Heinlein helped place his first professional piece, a humorous sketch for a West Coast magazine named *Script*, for which he was not paid. And Bradbury credits Henry Kuttner for giving him the two most important pieces of advice he ever received. Kuttner told him to stop writing "purple" or he'd stop reading his stories. And he told him to shut up:

> He came in one day and said, "Ray, do me a favor." I said, "What?" He said, "Shut up." I said, "Why do you say that?" He said, "You go around telling your ideas all the time and you blow the energy, you give away the passion that should go into your writing. So if you're not careful you're going to throw your career right out the window and you'll never write another story." So he scared me and he was right. It's the best advice I've ever had. That was thirty-eight years ago, and I've never discussed an unwritten story since.[23]

Of all the writers he knew, Henry Kuttner and Leigh Brackett were most important as personal influences, and two incidents involving them dramatize the beginning and the end of his apprenticeship period. In 1942 Kuttner actually wrote the ending for "The Candle," Bradbury's first sale to *Weird Tales*: "I started out in *Weird Tales* with a conventional story called 'The Candle' and the ending was written by Henry Kuttner. I couldn't solve the ending. I was clumsy. So Hank said, 'For God's sake, here. Give me your typewriter.' He typed out the last two hundred words, as I recall. And they're still in the story."[24] During this time he also met weekly with Leigh Brackett at "Muscle Beach," where they read and criticized each other's writings for the week. "She'd play volleyball down there and read my dreadful stories. . . . And I'd read her beautiful little excursions off to Mars and around the universe, and I'd just weep with frustration because I wasn't as good as she was. And I imitated her style."[25] But in 1944, after he had begun to write quality fiction of his own, Brackett asked him to take over in an emergency and finish her space-opera novella, "Lorelei of the Red Mist." When he successfully finished the piece for her, they both recognized and celebrated the fact that he had finally mastered her style after discovering his own:

> Leigh had to work on a film—I think it was *The Big Sleep*—and she called me and said, "Do me a favor and finish it for me." And I said, "Well, what the hell. Let me read it." And I sat down and in about a week I finished it and brought it to her. And she said, "You sonofabitch. You got it. You got me." And I said, "Yeah, I've been around you forever. If I can't imitate you by now I'll just give up." And people cannot tell when they read that story where she leaves off and where I begin. I have trouble finding the exact spot myself.[26]

By 1947, gaining recognition as one of the most interesting talents to emerge from the science fiction and fantasy magazines, Bradbury was already beginning to attract an audience outside the genre. His fantasy stories had been a major attraction in *Weird Tales* for years. Since the publication of "King of the Grey Spaces" in 1943, he had brought a fresh new style into science fiction. His first book, *Dark Carnival* (a collection of early weird stories, as the title suggests), came out in October. "The Meadow," a radio drama, was selected for *Best One-Act Plays of 1947–1948.* "Homecoming" was selected for the O. Henry Awards *Prize Stories of 1947.* And in addition to establishing himself professionally he also completed a major transition in his personal life. On 27 September 1947 he married Marguerite Mc-Clure. Perhaps as a symbolic gesture to affirm that his apprenticeship was long over, he burned "a million words of his 'bad writing' "[27] the day before his wedding. Indeed, as the decade ended, many of the seemingly unrealizable dreams of Bradbury's youth had become reality. He had been selected as the best author in science fiction and fantasy by the National Fantasy Fan Federation in 1949; he was a happily married father (of the first of four girls); and he was the one author in the science fiction and fantasy field to consistently place stories in the relatively prestigious and high-paying "slick" magazines.

Major Achievements (1950–85)

During the forties Bradbury defined his style and established his reputation in science fiction and fantasy. But these successes merely prepared the way for his major breakthrough in the fifties and sixties, when he became the first author from the genre magazines to capture a mainstream audience and to receive consistently favorable recognition from mainstream critics. Much of his best fiction was written during this period, including his five major novels. This new stage in Bradbury's career began with the publication of his two science-fiction novels, *The Martian Chronicles* (1950) and *Fahrenheit 451* (1953), both of which received unprecedented praise from mainstream critics (who at this time habitually ignored science fiction completely), though reaction within the science-fiction community itself was ambivalent. *Dandelion Wine* (1957) established him as a bestselling author in a new genre, fantasy based on his Waukegan boyhood, which he continued to explore in *Something Wicked This Way Comes* (1962). His one novel of the seventies, *The Halloween Tree* (1972), is an educational fantasy for juveniles. In the eighties Bradbury has moved into new fictional territory by publishing *Death Is a Lonely Business* (1985), a detective novel.

Throughout his career Bradbury has published short-story anthologies, which contain much of his finest work. (He is preeminently a short-story writer; indeed, two of his novels, *The Martian Chronicles* and *Dandelion Wine*, consist of short pieces woven into a dramatic pattern.) But most of Bradbury's fiction was written by the mid-sixties, as the publication dates of his anthologies indicate: *Dark Carnival* (1947); *The Illustrated Man* (1951); *The Golden Apples of the Sun* (1953); *The October Country* (1955); *A Medicine for Melancholy* (1959); *R is for Rocket* (1962); *The Machineries of Joy* (1964); *The Vintage Bradbury* (1965); *S is for Space* (1966); *Twice 22* (1966—a collection of two earlier anthologies); *I Sing the Body Electric* (1969); *Long After Midnight* (1976); *The Stories of Ray Bradbury* (1980—his selection of the best stories of his career); *Dinosaur Tales* (1983); and *A Memory of Murder* (1984—a collection of early mystery stories). Much of the material in the later anthologies was written early in his career.

Prolific as Bradbury's output of fiction has been, he has written extensively for other entertainment media as well. He produced some radio drama during the forties, but he decided then to concentrate on fiction until he felt ready to write for the movies. After he established his reputation in fiction he began taking occasional work as a scriptwriter in the fifties, beginning with an elaborate treatment for *It Came from Outer Space* in 1953. And in 1953 another of his longstanding dreams came true when John Huston, his idol for years, asked him to do the screenplay for *Moby Dick*. Though his personal relationship with Huston ended bitterly after Huston insisted on half-credit for a screenplay he didn't help write,[28] the experience took Bradbury to Ireland (the inspiration for numerous stories and plays in years to come) and to the center of the film industry which had always fascinated him. Since then he has not only accumulated numerous scriptwriting credits in television and film, but he has also written a number of screenplays which have never been produced—though some of his projects are finally being translated into film, not always in forms of which Bradbury approves: he wrote a screenplay for *The Martian Chronicles* as early as 1960, but was not consulted meaningfully on the television production in 1980, which he feels was boring and passionless; he is much more enthusiastic about *Something Wicked This Way Comes* (1984), which is based on a screenplay he wrote himself and which was produced by a studio he admires. Since the mid-sixties, Bradbury has been especially active in drama and poetry. In the sixties he finally returned to the theater, where he has been enthusiastically involved as writer and producer, adapting his own works to the stage. Though most of these productions have been successful on the West Coast, his one New York production was a short-lived disaster. Nevertheless, he feels his drama has been extremely successful at the grassroots level, in high school and college productions, and he hopes it will continue to gain in popularity. Bradbury has been publishing poetry since 1936, when he was still in high school, but he did not publish his first volume of verse until *When Elephants Last in the Dooryard Bloomed* appeared in 1973, followed by *Where Robot Men Ran Round in Robot Towns* (1977) and *The Haunted Computer and the Android Pope* (1981), now collected in *The Complete Poems of Ray Bradbury* (1982). Though he has increasingly devoted his energies to poetry in recent years, his verse has not been favorably received.

Both in expository writing and in speech, Bradbury has expressed himself in numerous formats throughout his career: in articles, introductions, book reviews, personal reminiscences, and interviews. Especially since the sixties, when he became an established media personality as well as a well-known author, he has been increasingly active both as an essayist and as a participant in colloquia, interviews, and talk shows: thus, he wrote a series of articles on the implications of space age technology for *Life* and *Playboy* (and received an Aviation Space Writers Association Award in 1968); he was interviewed on British television during the moon-landing in 1969; he participated with Arthur C. Clarke, Carl Sagan, and others in a published panel discussion, *Mars and the Mind of Man*, in 1971. He has also integrated his writing abilities with his lifelong love of music, resulting in a musical comedy production of *Dandelion Wine* (1967), a production of his cantata, *Christus Apollo* (1969), and a production of *Madrigals for the Space Age* (1973), for which he wrote the lyrics. He even has hopes to stage his radio drama, *Leviathan 99*, as an opera (a *literal* space opera), or as a wide-screen space epic on film, or as both. In love with museums since childhood, he designed the film *American Journey* for the United States Government Pavilion at the World's Fair in 1964. And he helped design Spaceship Earth for Disney World, a project he originally conceived with Disney (another of his heroes). Over four million copies of *The Martian Chronicles* have now been sold, and Bradbury has become the world's most widely anthologized author, with selections in over 1200 anthologies.

As even this brief summary of Bradbury's activities of the last forty years demonstrates, he has in some ways remained, throughout his career, very much the boy he wrote of in *Dandelion Wine*—pursuing all his dreams at once, planning feverishly to cram all his projects into one fleeting summer, one lifetime. But now he dashes from the typewriter to the movies to the theater to museums to re-create his own dreams in new forms, as well as to absorb those of others. He is much more an optimist in his sixties than he was in his thirties, but the sheer intensity of his experience seems never to have faded, from his nightmares in the crib about the horror of birth to his ecstasy the night we finally landed on Mars, when he "stayed up all night with my friends at the jet-propulsion lab—to dance around and cry and laugh, like a bunch of boys . . . in a New Year's Eve that's gonna last forever."[29] When asked at the age of sixty how he would like to be remembered a hundred years from now, he didn't speak of particular works but of his general sense of life, the exhilaration and occasional dread of being constantly drenched in experience, which he has expressed in so many forms:

I hope . . . to be remembered as a lover of the whole experience of life. And I think it's all in my writing, but you've got to read it all to get that. And if you could write that on my tombstone, you know: "Here's a teller of tales who wrote about everything with a great sense of expectancy and joy, who wanted to celebrate things . . . even the dark things because they have meaning." Then I would be content with that. But no specific things beyond that—just the joy of being alive for another day, and being able to celebrate a particular sense of that day that you didn't celebrate the day before.[30]

Chapter Two

Bradbury and the Critics: Between Two Worlds

The history of Bradbury's literary reputation is an intriguing, often paradoxical, drama of itself. As the first genre writer emerging from the pulp magazines to capture a mainstream audience, he has had the best of two worlds—an enthusiastic popular following, and eloquent praise from major figures in the literary establishment. Indeed, this may be the source of the Bradbury mystique, the special (and to some, quite irritating) role Bradbury has assumed, as the celebratory voice of the space age: more than any other modern American author, he has bridged the gap between popular culture and highbrow culture. Hailed by *Time Magazine* in 1953 as the "Poet of the Pulps," he has become a kind of unofficial poet laureaté of America in the twentieth century, attempting to capture the terrors and delights of the space age in downhome cadences and imagery. Yet, for all his success, Bradbury has also been a highly controversial writer. And, surprisingly, the most severe criticism of his work has come from the science-fiction community, rather than from the mainstream literary establishment. Though he may be the world's best-known science-fiction personality, Bradbury's reputation within the science-fiction community itself has always been ambivalent.

The controversy about the value of Bradbury's contribution to science fiction may appear to concern a relatively trivial question of labeling—especially since Bradbury himself has resisted (with good reason) being labeled a "science fiction writer." But in fact such arguments invariably have been linked to fundamental value judgments about Bradbury's most highly regarded works. Within science fiction circles the term "science fiction" is often implicitly an honorific, so that to deny the label to an author's work implies either his ignorance or intellectual and artistic superficiality.

The brief entry under "Ray Bradbury" in *A Reader's Guide to Science Fiction* (1978) is characteristic of the way Bradbury's science-fiction reputation has been treated within the field. "Ray Bradbury is a bit of a problem," the editors observe, before they go on to describe the discrepancy they perceive between his public image and his reputation within the field. "While to many people outside the field of science fiction, his is one of the first names that comes to mind when science fiction is mentioned, many aficionados will argue as to whether he is a science fiction writer at all." Though this might be left as a mere debate over labels, the argument really extends into aesthetics as well, as is indicated by the *Guide's* subsequent description of Bradbury's science fiction as "stylized" play, and by its perfunctory dismissal of what is generally considered his most impressive work: *"The Martian Chronicles* do not make a whole greater than the sum of the parts." A parenthetical observation that his writings might be more appropriately labeled "anti-science fiction" perpetuates a criticism directed at him throughout his career, that his values and philosophy are fundamentally opposed to the ethos of true "science fiction."[1]

Since his major breakthrough in the 1950s, Bradbury's distinctive style has elicited both admiration and impatient hostility, especially from within a science-fiction community at once proud of his success, doubtful of his credentials as an authentic science-fiction writer, and resentful of his public role as a science-fiction prophet who has risen above his origins. Academic criticism—of which there has been surprisingly little, until very recently—tends to circumvent such controversy, partially by placing Bradbury's work in a larger tradition of American fantasy writing which includes, but is not limited to, American science fiction.

Discovery by Mainstream Writers and Reviewers

Though by 1949 he was already highly successful in the genre publications (with the exception of John W. Campbell's *Astounding*), though he was consistently placing stories in the "slick" magazines, Bradbury's real breakthrough to a mainstream audience began in 1950, when Christopher Isherwood raved about *The Martian Chronicles* in *Tomorrow* magazine.[2] Isherwood's tone of delighted discovery anticipated the tone of numerous mainstream reviewers in years to come (when most mainstream critics were still startled to discover quality writing in a "subliterary" genre)—all were enamored to find that at least some of the books decorated with rocket ships and bug-eyed monsters contained writing they immediately recognized as good.

Isherwood's analysis of *The Martian Chronicles'* literary virtues would be elaborated with varying degrees of emphasis throughout Bradbury's subsequent career: the novel suggested that other unexpected treasures might be discovered in hitherto unpromising territory, that "the best of this new generation of science fiction writers are sensitive and intelligent"; yet Bradbury's achievement is partly that he escapes limitations identified with the science-fiction medium, for Isherwood clarifies that his enthusiasm should "not suggest . . . that Ray Bradbury can be classified simply as a science-fiction writer, even a superlatively good one"; indeed, he really belongs to an American fantasy tradition going back to Poe, and "he already deserves to be measured against the greatest master of his particular genre"; his science-fiction settings are there for artistic, not mechanical, reasons, for "his interest in machines seems to be limited to their symbolic and aesthetic aspects"—clearly, to Isherwood, an aesthetic virtue; his novel is a thoroughly *American* parable; and finally, most importantly, his style is vivid and powerful, rendering even the most dreadful subjects beautiful. "The sheer lift and power of a truly original imagination exhilarates you, almost in spite of yourself. So I urge even the most squeamish to try Mr. Bradbury. His is a very great and unusual talent."[3]

In years to come Bradbury would garner similar praise from numerous other mainstream writers and reviewers, many of them major literary figures. His work was praised by Aldous Huxley and Gerald Heard (who also became personal acquaintances). He was singled out by J. B. Priestley as an example of a new breed of science-fiction writer, "still sparsely represented," singular for "being genuinely imaginative and having some literary merit."[4] Clifton Fadiman wrote a glowing preface for *The Martian Chronicles*, as did Gilbert Highet for *The Vintage Bradbury*. Orville Prescott described him in the *New York Times* as "the uncrowned king of the science fiction writers, a young author whose fanciful imagination, poetic prose, and mature understanding of human character have won him an international reputation."[5] Angus Wilson praised *The Martian Chronicles* as a major contribution to fiction in English. "For those who care about the future of fiction in the English language it is, I believe, one of the most hopeful signs of the last twenty years."[6] And Kingsley Amis saluted him as "the Louis Armstrong of science fiction"[7] in characteristically diffident style: "Another and much more unlikely reason [besides his 'would-be-poetical badness'] for Bradbury's fame is that, despite his tendency to dime-a-dozen sensitivity, he is a good writer, wider in range than any of his colleagues, capable of seeing life on another planet as something extraordinary instead of just challenging or horrific, ready to combine this with strongly-held convictions."[8]

As Amis's reference to Bradbury's more limited colleagues suggests, Bradbury's sudden elevation to the pantheon of original modern artists had ambiguous implications for the reputation of science fiction as a whole. If he was usually interpreted as evidence that science fiction might be virgin literary territory, filled with natural wonders as yet unseen by civilized man, he was also the basis for numerous invidious comparisons. Thus, a reviewer in *Antioch Review* described Bradbury as among "a small handful [along with Theodore Sturgeon and Frederic Brown] out of hundreds in the field" who "give the form what distinction it has single-handed, carrying on their backs the copyists, the sensation-mongers. . . . The demands of the market force them to serve as focal points for swarms of lesser talents."[9] Singled out by *Time* as the "poet of the pulps" whose voice is "raised against the mechanization of mankind,"[10] he was often praised for virtues that seemed suspiciously contradictory to the very spirit of science fiction. To many in the science-fiction community the brilliance mainstream reviewers ascribed to Bradbury reflected ambiguously on his background: sometimes the illumination seemed to reveal other neglected treasures; sometimes it seemed only to highlight the surfaces of drab machinery.

Science-Fiction Critics: The Case against Ray Bradbury

Like other genre writers of the time, Bradbury began publishing in the pulp magazines amidst the enthusiastic admiration and criticism of fandom, in which debating the merits of aspiring and established authors was inextricably part of a voracious appetite for personal information about favorite authors. By 1945, when he wrote a personal column for *Weird Tales*, Bradbury was no longer an aspiring novice but an established favorite author, a bit uncomfortable in his new role: "There isn't much a writer can say about himself that he hasn't already said in his story."[11] As is only natural in a milieu that encourages such feelings of personal kinship between writers and readers, Bradbury's unprecedented rise to fame resulted in fannish elation and adulation, so that by 1949 he was hailed in *Famous Fantastic*

Mysteries as "a youth with the stature of an old master," "the fair-haired boy of fantasy." Beneath his portrait, surrounded with harrowing images derived from his early stories, the magazine celebrates what is clearly the triumph of one of its own: "The greatest original writer the fantasy field has produced in modern times, Bradbury has won international recognition with his reprintings in the O. Henry Memorial Awards and Best American Short Stories. His works have been dramatized on the radio and translated into Spanish."[12]

Perceiving him as the "fair-haired boy" from their magazines who made it in the big time, most of the gang from his old neighborhood (to adopt a ghetto metaphor peculiarly appropriate to the history of American science fiction) were delighted both by Bradbury's personal success and because the prestige of science-fiction and fantasy writing in general seemed enhanced. A 1953 entry in *Current Biography* suggests the excitement his "discovery" generated among much of the magazine audience: "One result of Bradbury's achieving a wider audience is that while distinguished critics are 'discovering' him and suggesting that he is too good to be called a science fiction writer, the science fiction fans, who hail Bradbury as among their best, are pointing with pride to his work as an example of what science fiction can produce."[13]

In the 1950s, when Bradbury's discovery was still an ongoing drama, many science-fiction publications continued to express excitement about Bradbury's achievement, interpreting his success as a breakthrough for the entire science-fiction field. Sam Sackett hoped he would help remove the "stigma" from science fiction: "Ray Bradbury . . . has perhaps more chance than any other of escaping the stigma which attaches itself to the practitioners of his art."[14] *Thrilling Wonder Stories* greeted *The Golden Apples of the Sun* with the observation that "science fiction readers can take heart from the fact that hardened reviewers, enchanted by the author's poetic prose, are giving science fiction more than a passing nod."[15] Chad Oliver feared that science-fiction readers might lose critical perspective because of their gratitude for Bradbury's contributions to the field: "Ray Bradbury is such a superlatively good writer, and most of us are so grateful to him for what he has done for science fiction literature, that we tend to become critically blinded by the halo of his brilliance."[16]

But though the predominant tone of mainstream reviewers in this period was one of delighted discovery, Chad Oliver need not have worried that the science-fiction world would be blinded to Bradbury's limitations. Many science-fiction reviewers were sceptical about Bradbury's sudden rise to fame. Partly, this simply reflected an appetite among fans for debate. Thus, the first issue of the *Journal of Science Fiction* featured Edward Wood's "The Case Against Ray Bradbury," which vigorously, if somewhat incoherently, argues that there might be some hope for "a writer who is now reaping vast amounts of uncritical and generally unwarranted praise," but only "if he can achieve a firmer writing discipline before his present dazzling success overwhelms him"—all of which leads up to Wood's devastating parting shot: "Some day he may even write some science fiction."[17] The case against Ray Bradbury was not made fully articulate, perhaps, until two fellow science-fiction writers turned critics, Damon Knight and James Blish (writing as William Atheling, Jr.), began their ironic evaluation of Bradbury's reputation and talents. Between them, they defined a pragmatic yet literate standard of critical discourse for a field that had lacked one. They sought to establish consistent critical principles, and Bradbury's science fiction, which seemed to violate them, consistently evoked their exasperation mingled with grudging respect. Even his best work appeared to violate their basic premise (that of John W. Campbell)—that good science fiction is based on knowledgeable scientific extrapolation and cannot be inconsistent with known science. Yet they acknowledged Bradbury's emotional impact. Respecting his obvious virtues as a stylist and craftsman, they also called attention to his stylistic excesses and marveled at his growing reputation as America's foremost science-fiction writer.

To both Knight and Blish, Bradbury was a peculiarly effective anomaly whose influence could be destructive to science fiction's central artistic and philosophical values. Blish felt that, as a "scientific blindworm," Bradbury was "in certain respects . . . bad for the field," though he conceded that "in the face of such artistry, it's difficult to care."[18] Knight had similar reservations about Bradbury's use (or abuse) of science, likening him to Richard Matheson in his "ignorance and mistrust of science," and labeling his ironic science fiction "anti-science fiction."[19] More than that, the title of his essay on Bradbury, "When I Was in Kneepants," suggests the deeper thrust of his criticism—that Bradbury's lyricism, no matter how emotionally effective, is fundamentally escapist and childish: thus, Bradbury's attitude toward science is really a child's fear of machines; his style, when not braced with horror, is so "syrupy" it is "sickening" to mature taste; his "one subject" is childhood, and, in a blast at the mainstream

writers who helped establish Bradbury's reputation, Knight observes
that "learned opinion to the contrary, Bradbury is not the inheritor
of Poe, Irving, or Hawthorne . . . his . . . is the voice (a little
shriller) of Christopher Morley and Robert Nathan and J. D. Sal-
inger."[20]
   Though Blish and Knight were perhaps most articulate in expressing ambivalence about Bradbury's influence on science fiction, they
have not been alone, especially in their insistence that he is "anti-
science." Anthony Boucher, in many respects an admirer of Bradbury's work, could also burst out in exasperation at his "need to attack a science, a technology, and a civilization which he is unwilling
to understand."[21] L. Sprague and Catherine Cook de Camp describe
his fiction as written from "a sentimental or anti-scientific point of
view," though they describe the results as "gems of mood and feeling."[22] Ambivalence within the field was perhaps best expressed in
Damon Knight's image, representing Bradbury's reputation as a
"huge, brightly-colored bubble" to which " 'serious' critics reacted
with rapture." But to many science-fiction readers with a view from
inside the bubble, it was apparent that such reviewers were distracted
by gaudy surfaces, that their joyful "discovery" of Bradbury left them
as ignorant as before about the nature of science fiction. "Inside the
bubble we get a clearer and more distorted view. Although he has a
large following among science-fiction readers, there is at least an
equally large contingent who cannot stomach his work at all; they say
he has no respect for the medium; that he does not even trouble to
make his scientific double-talk convincing; that—worst of all—he
fears and mistrusts science."[23]
   Though Bradbury's reputation is hardly the controversial subject in
the 1980s that it was in the 1950s, the subject can still elicit powerful reactions, perhaps exacerbated in the last decade by Bradbury's
media role as the official voice of science fiction. But if an older generation of critics expressed respectful impatience with that reputation,
at least one representative of a later generation, Thomas M. Disch,
finds nothing at all in Bradbury's career to respect. Reviewing *The
Stories of Ray Bradbury*, Bradbury's selection of the one hundred finest
stories of his career, Disch used the *New York Times* (a forum in which
Bradbury was once heralded as an exciting and original new talent) to
ridicule both his reputation and his artistry.
   Disch's evaluation is an unqualified indictment. Mocking the Bradbury "Reputation" as pure media puffery, he portrays Bradbury as a

mindless mannikin performing celebratory incantations. "Ray Bradbury is America's Official Science Fiction Writer, the one most likely to be trotted out on State occasions to give a salute to, as he puts it, 'our wild future in space.' " And he quotes from some of Bradbury's more unfortunate prose to demonstrate that his style belongs with Rod McKuen's poetry, Kahil Gabran's philosophy, and Norman Rockwell prints as examples of American kitsch.[24] Disch never mentions the stories that have established Bradbury's true reputation over the years—a reputation that was not granted at state functions, after all, but resulted from millions of readers enjoying and sharing his books. Three decades after his "discovery," the case against Ray Bradbury has finally been prosecuted without reservation, without admission of evidence for the defense.

Perhaps the history of Bradbury's science-fiction reputation contains an ironic moral about "progress," like so many of his early science-fiction stories. When Bradbury was first enthusiastically reviewed in the *New York Times*, science fiction had been regarded by mainstream publications as beneath notice. Who would have thought, back then, that a fellow science-fiction writer would one day have the opportunity to write reviews for the *New York Times*, only to dismiss the life work of the genre's "fair-haired boy" with withering scorn?

In Bradbury's Defense: Metaphor, Theology, and Tradition

Though Bradbury has never publicly responded to specific criticisms of his science fiction, he has certainly made clear that he is not, in any obvious sense, "anti-science," anti-technology, or anti-progress, as his critics have insisted. Indeed, his basic views on these subjects are clearly on record as early as 1953, when he explained them in the *Nation:* as a science-fiction writer he is fascinated by new technologies and optimistic about their potential, both because they are symbols of our desires and because they function as extensions of our senses which open us up to new dimensions of experience. "It is both exciting and disconcerting for a writer to discover that man's machines are indeed symbols of his most secret cravings and desires, extra hands put out to touch and reinterpret the world."[25] And certainly, in the decades since, he has forcefully and directly expressed his faith in our ability to use science to shape a better future, in the compelling need to migrate from earth to fulfill our destiny in the larger universe. Indeed, as Disch's sarcasm suggests, Bradbury's media role as the science-fiction voice of our time is overtly celebratory. No one has been a more fervent public advocate for investing in scientific research, for opening up the space frontier, for the importance of science fiction and science together to prepare us for the future. The persistent notion that Bradbury is "anti-science" is in part a tribute to the ironic power of his early science fiction, which combines futuristic satire with vivid nostalgic imagery. Often, the effect is to contrast deeply human values of an idealized past with sterile gadgetry of the future. But in this Bradbury only participates in an ironic, satirical science-fiction tradition which goes back at least as far as H. G. Wells's "The Time Machine" and which includes much of the best writing in the field, by writers as diverse as Aldous Huxley, Frederic Pohl, and Ursula K. Le Guin. The message of such fiction, as Bradbury has reiterated throughout his career, is to warn about the consequences of misusing the new powers science and technology create, not to retreat into fantasies about Green Town or life in the wigwam or the cave. And Bradbury insists he is trying to prevent horrible futures, not predict them: "Not that we won't be able to adjust to any problems met at home or abroad in the solar system of 1999. But I do think our adjustment will derive in part from our practicality in both entertaining ourselves with science fiction and looking to our answers now."[26]

Bradbury's actual fiction is perhaps more disturbing and ambiguous than this tidy explanation implies, but it is clear that he, like H. G. Wells and John W. Campbell himself (in "Twilight"), often writes most powerfully about nightmares he believes we can avoid. In addition, Bradbury's image as a nostalgic escapist has not been perpetuated exclusively by misunderstandings about the intent of his fiction. It has also been perpetuated by details of his lifestyle, which have acquired a symbolic import that enhances the ironic thrust of his fiction. Thus, the fact that Bradbury will not drive a car or ride in planes has been interpreted to mean he rejects modern technology—though he is enthusiastic about trains, modern transit systems, and rockets. His earlier horror at the destructive impact of telephones and television seem to affirm his rejection of modern communication and entertainment media—though he is a lifelong, unabashed movie addict and a connoisseur of radio drama and comic strips.

Something of a showman, as is evident in his abiding passion for theater, Bradbury has obviously enjoyed his public role as a curiously paradoxical science-fiction personality, articulating his loves and hates in personal essays, interviews, and talk shows. But his public image is clearly consistent with the spirit of his science fiction: both in his art and in his lifestyle he communicates a vigorous response to the technological wonders that surround us. He has never rejected science or technology. Rather, he affirms that in the alternately exhilarating and frightening delirium of future shock we must not lose contact with basic passions, with love and hate. Science fiction's value is precisely that it combines both speculative thought and emotional impact, helping us to interpret changes in our environment as well as to recognize our own fears and desires.

But there may be a more fundamental reason why science-fiction critics have implied so frequently that Bradbury's values conflict with the ethos of science fiction: Perhaps to science-fiction writers and fans who are most comfortable with the John W. Campbell tradition of science fiction, Bradbury values science and the promise of the future for the wrong reasons. He appears a romantic, a sentimentalist. He values rockets and robots because they are extensions of our "souls," and he uses the word "soul" constantly, without blushing.

Though Bradbury has demonstrated that he can write accurately about the nuts and bolts of technology when he chooses,[27] his real interest has never been in rocket machinery itself but in the new emotional and spiritual vistas it opens to us. As Isherwood suggested in his initial "discovery" of Bradbury, "his interest in machines seems limited to their symbolic and aesthetic aspect."[28] But while to Isherwood this implies Bradbury's artistic priorities are in order, to critics such as Knight and Blish it implies he lacks a crucial extrapolative dimension that anchors science fiction in reality, which distinguishes Heinlein's fantasies from moonshine.

Fundamentally, Bradbury's science-fiction mythos is theological, which may be what many science-fiction critics react to when they label him "anti-science." Bradbury's science does not seem to them like "real" science. To Bradbury, however, science fiction can imaginatively adapt still-powerful religious symbols to the implications of scientific knowledge. Indeed, to him this fusion of essentially religious emotion and scientific imagery is a primary source of the "sense of wonder" generated by the best science-fiction writing and films.[29]

But to a science-fiction tradition that identifies the scientific outlook
with hardheaded materialism, this "spiritual" dimension in Bradbury's work is suspect, either a perpetuation of old superstitions, or
false rhetoric, or both. As Russell Kirk argues, distinguishing Bradbury's "moral imagination" from the central Wellsian science-fiction
tradition, Bradbury's fiction, though much less doctrinaire than that
of C. S. Lewis, projects similar religious concepts which are much
"out of fashion" with the spirit of the times—certainly, with much
of the science fiction audience: " 'Soul,' a word much out of fashion
nowadays, signifies a man's animating entity. That flaming spark the
soul is the real space traveller in Bradbury's stories. 'I'm alive!'—that
exclamation is heard from Waukegan to Mars and beyond, in Bradbury's fables."[30]

Though Bradbury is not affiliated with any organized religion,
though his "theology" is a highly metaphorical articulation of his individual sense of wonder, he himself defends his artistic practice in
theological terms, while also suggesting that the science-fiction tradition represented by his critics limits both the speculative and the expressive possibilities of science fiction:

> When we write our science fictions we're dealing with ideas, and they
> don't have to be scientific, necessarily, or they can be very primitively scien-
> tific. But they can also be philosophical, because these scientific things im-
> pinge on our lives. And they can become theological, because suddenly we
> realize that, if we wish, we can embody ourselves in robots and send the
> robots out to space for us. These are extensions of our souls . . . a robot that
> represents your soul's yearning to go out and investigate the universe. And
> so we make do with those mysteries, and that is where the fun comes. . . .
> So what's lacking in a lot of science fiction—and naturally I would say this,
> since I'm defending my own way of perception—is philosophy, and theol-
> ogy, and art history and too many of the things that make being alive and
> wandering through a library fun.[31]

The long controversy over Bradbury's merits as a science-fiction
writer has distorted as many issues as it has clarified. Obviously, even
Bradbury's best science fiction lacks both the detailed extrapolative
dimension and the no-nonsense, world-conquering ethos many
science-fiction readers value. But in part, the controversy results from
limitations in the aesthetic principles applied by reviewers and critics
in the science-fiction field, a discrepancy between theory and actual
practice which makes it difficult for science-fiction critics to evaluate

science fiction that works as art even if it lacks serious scientific extrapolation. Though John W. Campbell undoubtedly brought a new rigor and coherence to science-fiction theory, his emphasis on the importance of "real" science to science fiction tended to ignore the medium's metaphorical potential, which in actual practice has always been at least as important as extrapolation. One result has been inordinate energy expended debating whether Bradbury's scientific "mistakes" invalidate his art, when the "mistakes" exist only to readers who insist on taking Bradbury's science-fiction metaphors literally. As readers have probably always known until they get caught up in theoretical controversy about what science fiction "should" be, *The Martian Chronicles* does not pretend to attempt an accurate portrait of the planet Mars, nor is it concerned with the actual technology of space-colonization; its subject is the contradictory values we project into our next frontier, our struggle to adapt to new environments and to learn the lessons of history.

Since the 1960s, when anthologies designed for classroom use began printing Bradbury stories, less disputatious commentary on Bradbury's fiction has developed. Articles in such journals as *College English* and *English Journal* have focused on the artistry of Bradbury's science fiction, approaching it both through traditional methods of literary analysis and as provocative speculation about present and future problems. As Christopher Isherwood and other mainstream writers perceived, Bradbury's best work is part of an American literary tradition that connects him to the contemporary idiom of mainstream writers in his own era—such as Sherwood Anderson, John Steinbeck, and Ernest Hemingway—as well as to earlier mythopoeic writers like Edgar Allan Poe, Nathaniel Hawthorne, Herman Melville, and Mark Twain. Essentially, this is the perspective assumed by more academic critics, and by the three book-length studies of Bradbury's work: William F. Toupence's *Ray Bradbury and the Poetics of Reverie: Fantasy, Science Fiction, and the Reader,* Joseph D. Olander's and Martin Harry Greenberg's *Ray Bradbury* (an anthology of critical essays), and Wayne L. Johnson's *Ray Bradbury* (a survey of his life and career). From this perspective it may be possible to locate Bradbury's imaginative creations without endlessly rehashing old arguments about whether they come from the past or the future or from sheer fantasy. As a symbol of values from our past that we must adapt to journey with us in space, Green Town exists, of course, in all three.

Chapter Three
"Poet of the Pulps": Literary Influences and the Bradbury Style

Attempts to evaluate Bradbury's literary achievement invariably focus in some fashion on his distinctive style. From the early 1940s, when he first found his literary voice, the excitement and controversy his fiction elicited were directly related to the striking quality of the voice itself. While his science-fiction critics lamented sentimental lapses and the poverty of extrapolation in his fiction, readers and mainstream critics alike were enraptured by the sheer vividness of his prose, by a verbal music that invigorated relatively conventional themes with new life and meaning. Gary K. Wolfe's analysis of Bradbury's achievement for *The Dictionary of Literary Biography* emphasizes paradox, and the most fundamental paradox has to do with relationships between Bradbury's subject matter and his style:

> In a field that thrives on the fantastic and marvelous, Bradbury's best stories celebrate the mundane; in a field preoccupied with the future, Bradbury's vision is firmly rooted in the past—both his own personal past and the past of America. In a popular genre where reputations, until recently, have been made through ingenious plotting and the exposition of scientific and technological ideas, Bradbury built an enormous reputation virtually on style alone.[1]

As Willis McNelly suggests, the distinctive quality of Bradbury's voice is best evoked by a word from the vocabulary of fantasy—"enchantment," suggestive of a verbal gift that, like a sorcerer's spell, magically transforms mundane reality and genre cliché. "Perhaps 'enchantment' is the proper word for Bradbury, enchantment in the sense that he seems to have cast a magic spell on his audience. He delights them, bewitches them, charms them completely with his verbal evocations, with his visions of a timeless past, a provocative future, and a challenging present."[2] Though the impact of the Bradbury style has often been described, most analysis of his work to date has focused primarily on his themes and ideas,[3] which may partially explain the intensity of controversy about the quality of his achievement. One of Bradbury's favorite metaphors for his role as artist derives from his youthful admiration of Blackstone, at a time when he too aspired to be a magician. Eventually, he specialized instead in constructing "magic shows" with words and symbols. But it is virtually impossible to explain the enchantment of a magic show by examining the props themselves: there is nothing intrinsically enchanting in a hat or a rabbit—the magical effect is created by the context in which they appear.

Bradbury and the Art of Writing: The Unconscious, the Intellect, and the Personal Voice

At its best, Bradbury's prose combines influences from a wide variety of writers, as well as from other media—films, radio, and theater. Indeed, when he first set up in business as a writer, Bradbury spent several years in what he calls his "imitative period," sometimes consciously, sometimes unconsciously adopting the tone and manner of writers he admired.[4] He discovered his literary voice when he learned to tap his own experience for subject matter and theme—a process he feels began in 1942 when he wrote "The Lake," a weird story based on memories of a childhood sweetheart. At that point the techniques he admired in other writers became his own, tools he employed to express a personal vision. Paradoxically, imitation was a process that ultimately enabled him to shape the conventions of the pulp magazines—first those of weird fiction, then of science fiction—to express an original sensibility:

> This personal memory is the raw stuff of writers. This is the stuff you go to, if you want to write original weird stories. We're told all this stuff, you know, to go to the literature of Poe, to go to Hawthorne. This is all nonsense. These people dug their own symbols, their own needs, and their own terrors out of themselves, and got it on paper. They didn't get it from anyone else. When I made that magical discovery, then I began to write original weird stories.[5]

Though his "magical discovery" was that his own experience, especially his childhood in Waukegan, was a rich source of artistic material, Bradbury has paid tribute throughout his career to those artists
and art forms that have most strongly influenced him. He often refers
to the importance of "feeding" the imagination. Indeed, as the title
of one of his essays for the *Writer* suggests, "How to Keep and Feed
a Muse," "feeding" is a central metaphor for Bradbury when he dis-
cusses influences of his work.[6] For if he emphasizes the importance of
spontaneity and personal subject matter, he also emphasizes the importance of passionate consumption of the work of others. Strongly
influenced at eighteen by Dorothea Brande's *Becoming a Writer*, his reflections on art ever since have projected her basic model of the artistic process: the "unconscious" is the province of genius and
imagination, which must constantly be "fed" with art works it loves;
the process of writing involves quieting the "conscious" mind so that
the unconscious can express itself; disciplined work habits, though
apparently ego-controlled and willful, actually help to quiet the conscious mind and provide access to the unconscious (an apparent paradox Bradbury associates with Zen); the intellect itself is most useful
as a final editor after the writing is completed. From Brande Bradbury learned both the importance of properly "feeding" the unconscious and of employing free-association techniques to gain access to
it:

> The unconscious should not be thought of as a limbo where vague, cloudy
> and amorphous notions swim hazily about. There is every reason to believe,
> on the contrary, that it is the great home of form; that it is quicker to see
> types, patterns, purposes, than our intellect can ever be. Always, it is true,
> you must be on the watch lest a too heady exuberance sweep you away from
> a straight course; always you must direct and control the excess of material
> which the unconscious will offer. But if you are to write well you must come
> to terms with the enormous and powerful part of your nature which lies be-
> yond the threshold of immediate knowledge.[7]

Bradbury recalls that *Becoming a Writer* "helped change my life," a
tribute that suggests the profound impact of a book that helped him
direct his energies both as a writer and as a reader. Brande's model of
the artistic process helped him integrate his attempt to forge an original style with his enthusiasms for diverse forms of entertainment. Her
emphasis on discipline encouraged him to develop the structured

work habits he has maintained throughout his career. And her free-association writing exercises, derived from her emphasis on the unconscious as the source of creativity, helped him discover his own cadences and imagery.

> She deals with the subconscious and she tells you how to prepare yourself. It's got to be a ritual, like being a monk. There are some good suggestions. She said that at night when you go to bed you should put a piece of paper in the typewriter so your subconscious knows the paper is there. Then put a couple of nouns down on the paper, so that they're laying there during the night. Then you get up to go right to the typewriter—no phone calls, no newspaper, no breakfast, nothing—and sit down and start typing whatever comes into your head. It doesn't have to make any sense. And out of all this madness suddenly a line will come. Maybe you'll write a poem. Or just make a list of nouns: the night . . . the lake . . . the attic . . . the cellar, the wine, the frog. . . . Then you say to yourself, "Okay, I've got all these nouns. What do they mean?"[8]

As the resonance of this brief reverie suggests, such free-association techniques first helped Bradbury integrate his memories of Midwestern boyhood with the conventions of weird fiction.

But if *Becoming a Writer* helped Bradbury tap the poetry of his unconscious, it also suggested a new rationale and new directions for his reading. Brande's primary recommendation to aspiring writers is to *write*, both systematically and spontaneously—advice that Bradbury in turn has emphasized to writers throughout his career.[9] But Brande also recommends a similar process for learning from literary models. Part of mastering the craft of writing is to "learn to read as a writer,"[10] seeking out the best models, imitating and adapting specific points of style and technique. Thus, the unconscious is fed on new materials, while the intellect analyzes strategies and forms. This model of the relationship between the writer as art consumer and the writer as art creator encouraged Bradbury to learn from art forms he already loved, but it also suggested the value of exploring new forms.

Bradbury had always browsed avidly in libraries, but during his apprentice years as a writer he took Brande's advice seriously, learning to read with eye and ear attuned to what might be appropriated for his own purposes. Though he never abandoned his love for the "grand trash heap" of entertainment he absorbed as a child, he also explored those areas of the library which contained highly regarded writers of

the past, as well as contemporary mainstream writing. As he more
clearly defined his goals as a writer, he began to think of his reading
as a self-directed education, an analogy he made overt in the title of
his address to a group of librarians, "How, Instead of Being Educated
in College, I Was Graduated from Libraries."[11] Ultimately, his eclec-
tic enthusiasms as a reader—ranging from Shakespeare to Edgar Rice
Burroughs, from Hemingway to Heinlein—helped him to enrich the
conventions of the genre magazines.

Though his education was to some extent a systematic exploration
of generally recognized masters of his craft, Bradbury's taste has always been dictated by his own instincts rather than by established
reputations. Indeed, as "poet of the pulps" he seems to have enjoyed
his role as a renegade in both camps—as literary stylist to the science-
fiction audience, and as defender of low-brow art to the artistic establishment. His defense of popular culture has been especially fervent,
partially because he believes the unconscious, though it is neither
evaluative nor critical, finally is wiser and more honest than the intellect. The province of instinct rather than reason, the unconscious is a
voracious appetite hungry for images, symbols, and entertainment,
which can utilize the most unlikely debris as props in the artist's
magic show. For if the unconscious is an appetite to be fed, it is also
a repository in which everything has its peculiar value, where nothing
is ever lost. "I think," he observed, "I'm very unusual in that I've
had so many influences, which have all been crammed in and paid off."[12]

Thus, the unconscious is a cellar or, in one of Bradbury's favorite
images, an attic, a crowded storehouse containing children's abandoned toys, broken-down machinery, old letters, dusty books—all of
which have latent meaning if they have been accumulated by instinct
rather than by artificially imposed design. Defending the validity of
his instinctive judgments, Bradbury has enthusiastically paid tribute
to such influences as the Oz books, Edgar Rice Burroughs, the early
science-fiction magazines, Walt Disney, comics, Blackstone, *King
Kong*, and radio drama. Indeed, he seems basically suspicious of evaluative criticism in general (though he doesn't hesitate to express his
impatience with art works he doesn't like), which he identifies with
sterile, self-conscious intellectualism. If New York represents the center of the forces of "intellect," he prefers the vigor of Los Angeles,
where the "unconscious" romps in unabashed pursuit of entertainment.

Literary Influences

However lasting his attachment to his early loves, Bradbury's library education exposed him to a more traditional literary curriculum which was particularly influential during the period, from approximately 1938 to 1945, when he developed his own distinctive style and tone.

Actually, even the "grand trash heap" he read during youth included such items as the fables of Poe and Hawthorne, key nineteenth-century figures in the tradition of mythopoeic American writing which includes Bradbury's own best fiction. Through the early science-fiction magazines he encountered some of the best speculative writing of the nineteenth century—where Poe and Hawthorne were reprinted along with such early science-fiction writers as Jules Verne and H. G. Wells—as well as the emerging generation of genre writers. And he first developed a lifelong passion for Shakespeare in high school. His more rigorous education as a writer involved rediscovering old favorites as well as discovering new ones.

The mythos and style of American Renaissance fiction influenced Bradbury both directly and indirectly. He was directly influenced by Poe's ornate style early in his career, an influence that had both positive and negative effects, since his imitations of Poe's rich verbal embroidery had a tendency to turn purple. "He was splendiforous. He was gem-encrusted. He reminds you at times of the gila monster that crawls up out of a sand pit to lie in the sun and you look at all those bright encrustations on its hide." He consciously emulated Poe, sometimes with awkward results. "I did a lot of imitating of Poe when I was young, and oh God is it horrible. Where he had two 'saffrons' I had six." But until he reread Hawthorne after he had established his own style, he wasn't conscious of the impact of early exposure to stories such as "The Great Stone Face" and "Rappaccini's Daughter": "When I read his stuff later in my thirties I said, 'Jesus, it's my father. It's gotta be my father.' The thing where he creates the little mechanical butterfly—that's so unusual, and that's pure in me, and in that sense I am part Hawthorne."

Bradbury's "Happiness Machine" in *Dandelion Wine* illustrates his taste for whimsical Hawthornean allegory, but Hawthorne's fiction also projects the ambivalent wilderness imagery that structures much of Bradbury's own writing about Green Town and Mars. He recognized his deep affinity with this mythopoeic American tradition when

he wrote the screenplay for John Huston's film of *Moby Dick*. En-
thralled by Melville's prose (though he had some misgivings about
Moby-Dick's structure), he recognized Melville instantly as a "kindred
spirit" sharing a passion for mythic imagery and the rich textures of
Shakespeare: "John Huston read my dinosaur story, 'The Fog Horn.'
And that had Melville in it, even though I'd never read Melville. But
Shakespeare was an influence of mine, and Shakespeare influenced
Melville to write *Moby-Dick*."[13]

Though Bradbury's education led him back to Shakespeare and to
American Renaissance writing, he was especially eager to learn from
his own contemporaries, both in the genre magazines themselves and
in the mainstream realist tradition. An avid reader of the science-fiction and fantasy magazines since his discovery of *Amazing Stories* at
the age of eight, he was also influenced, during his apprentice writing
years, by his active personal relationships with such central figures as
Robert Heinlein, Henry Kuttner, and Leigh Brackett, all of whom
offered advice and exchanged with him manuscripts of work in progress. Thus, while he developed his style Bradbury was in tune, both
as a fan and as an apprentice writer emulating admired models, with
the operative aesthetics of the genre magazines. But he also pored
through annual anthologies of prize-winning short stories. Following
his instincts, he devoured all forms of contemporary writing that cap-
tured his imagination, exploring different textures and techniques,
noting that stylistic qualities he admired could be adapted from one
genre to another. "And I imitated [Leigh Brackett's] style. . . . Hers
was very clean, derived from her love of Hammett and Chandler, and
it shows in her work and sets her apart from most of the other writers
in science fiction—a much cleaner style than most of them had."[14]

This emphasis on the virtue of a "clean" style is also evident in
Bradbury's description of the impact of Hemingway's "clean, really
fresh-water, wonderful style." In general, Bradbury's reactions to
other mainstream writers of the time illustrate a similar attention to
style, sensitivity to texture and cadence accompanied by an eye for
what might be adopted to enrich his own work. "[Steinbeck's] influence was huge too, because from him I learned how to be objective
and yet get everything in. And he was a little richer in texture than
Hemingway. Hemingway was a little too spare. But I admired him
and he was an influence. Faulkner was riper and richer, and I liked
him because of that, but I could only read his short stories. I read all

of Hemingway's novels and short stories. And I read all of Steinbeck's novels and short stories, up to a point. I think I stopped reading Steinbeck around 1946, after 'The Pearl.' From then on something happened to him which no longer pleased me. I felt his style change, his attitude, whatever it was."[15] Other major influences from contemporary mainstream writers included F. Scott Fitzgerald, whom he considered the one "idea writer" of his generation; Thomas Wolfe, whom he regarded, like Henry Miller (but for different reasons), as a "door-opener," an exciting voice for adolescents which loses much of its appeal in maturity; and Sherwood Anderson, whose *Winesburg, Ohio* was a major model for *The Martian Chronicles*.

Bradbury identifies a major shift in his reading interests and in his own style with his discovery of women writers. "I devoured [different writers] and learned from each of them," he observes of his apprentice years. "And then the women writers began to come into my life, through Kuttner: Katherine Anne Porter, Eudora Welty, Edith Wharton, Ellen Glasgow, Willa Cather—all very important. And I think they added to my life what a lot of men writers could use—a softer aspect, a more romantic, sensual, sexual side. I think that we should be combinations; after all, our minds are neither male nor female." Indeed, the influence of these writers appears to be profound, since Bradbury associates them with qualities he himself brought to genre fiction—attention to "style" itself, to atmosphere, tone, and metaphor. "During the time when I was twenty-one or twenty-two through to the age of twenty-six or twenty-seven I read all these women, like Virginia Woolf, who were teaching me style. Women are more frequently stylists. They care about style, about metaphor, more than men do."[16]

In addition to specifically stylistic influences, Bradbury has also been influenced by writers he considers rich in "ideas," writers whom he emulates in some ways and admires from a distance in others. Within science fiction itself he particularly admires Heinlein and Kuttner as "idea writers." Heinlein especially, with his imaginative and detailed extrapolative backgrounds, represents a science-fiction tradition in which Bradbury felt he could never effectively participate. But he also recognized both that his own gifts were different and that much of the predominantly extrapolative science fiction of the time was stylistically bland, lacking the "human" perspective necessary to generate strong emotion. "I very greatly admire people like Heinlein, who have fecund imaginations about scientific ideas. . . . But he is also missing somewhat the humanist view, and without that I don't see any reason to write."[17]

Outside of science fiction itself, Bradbury has also been influenced by "idea" writers from other traditions compatible with his own tastes. In the tradition of British wit, he finds in his favorite writers—Alexander Pope, Thomas Love Peacock, and, especially, George Bernard Shaw—the ability to make ideas entertaining and compelling through humor. His favorite science writer, Loren Eiseley, appeals to him both as a stylist and as a thinker, articulating the romance of scientific ideas through vivid imagery and personal reverie. In his own essays Bradbury uses similar strategies to evoke the poetry of science, though he tends to be much more upbeat than Eiseley, whose most powerful reflections often create a mood of haunting melancholy.

Books and libraries figure prominently in Bradbury's fiction (most overtly in *Fahrenheit 451* and *Something Wicked This Way Comes*), and the literary style he developed reflects his passion for browsing, for "feeding his muse" with a varied and generous cuisine. At its best, his prose style is a rich synthesis of qualities he cherished as a reader. When it is less effective it tends to be sentimental, artificial, and sometimes a bit affected, as though the other voices he admires have not been fully integrated with his own experience. The quality of Bradbury's work varies considerably in this respect, but particularly in the forties and fifties his lyrical gifts brought color and excitement, sensual impact and emotional depth, to the conventions of genre writing. His most astute critics recognized both his limitations and the unique quality of his voice. Like other science-fiction writers of his generation, Judith Merril found her irritation with his mannerisms and sometimes hackneyed themes more than offset by admiration for the sheer magical effect of his style: "I find his sentimentality intolerably sticky at times; his nostalgias are not mine. . . . Bradbury-the-writer seems to step out of his own dreamy attic, onto the main street of the world *I* know. But when he does step out on the street, he does it with style, with integrity, and with the magic of that attic still inside him."[18]

If the magic attic to which Merril refers is Bradbury's "muse," his unconscious, it is an attic whose contents express the various and sometimes eccentric enthusiasms of its owner. Yet the motley collection it contains is shaped by certain basic principles of selection. As Merril's tribute to the special quality of Bradbury's style suggests, his attic is animated by his love of magic, which is one way of defining the common ground in the literary traditions he loves and perpetuates. "He is one of the most skillful 'symbol writers' in the business—and the business he is in is myth-and-magic making."[19]

Varied as are the influences on Bradbury's style, they share certain features—they all participate somehow in the business of "myth-and-magic making." Bradbury has been influenced by H. G. Wells and by Buck Rogers, by the Bible and by Walt Disney. He admires those American mainstream writers whose realism has mythic overtones. But he has always been bored by the detailed novel of manners, whether by Austen, Tolstoy, or James. And irony that does not finally generate a sense of wonder, an exhilaration for life, he finds both boring and distasteful—an attitude that leaves him out of sympathy with most expressions of existentialist philosophy, almost bitter in his rejection of much modernist poetry, absurdist drama, and what he considers reductionist realism in fiction, film, and theater. Both his reading tastes and his writing style communicate a simple conviction that good art, like a good magic show, entertains as it evokes wonder and delight, so that for a time at least we want "to live forever."[20] In words he once placed in the voice of Jules Verne, another of the magicians who entranced him in his youth, meaningful art creates "magic and miracles"[21] in the theater of the imagination, magic shows which stir the eternally youthful unconscious in us all with yearning that ultimately will take us to the stars.

The Bradbury Style and "the Art of the Aside"

As his comments on the influence of other writers suggest, Bradbury defined himself early in his career as a stylist. Gary K. Wolfe observes that "by 1944 Bradbury . . . seemed aware that style was his strong point and became more conscious of developing it."[22] By integrating the themes of genre fiction with the expressive resources of his unconscious, he discovered that his strength as a writer was a flair for striking metaphor and vivid detail, for evoking mood and atmosphere, which reviewers invariably described as "poetic." He also discovered that his style was adaptable to a variety of genres and audiences, that his "magical discovery" of a personal voice resulted in original science fiction and realist fiction as well as evocative weird fantasy. "Bradbury soon discovered that his distinctive poetic style would be more welcomed by *Weird Tales*, a few detective magazines, and eventually the 'slicks' such as *American Mercury, Charm,* and *Mademoiselle,* than by the science fiction magazines he had so avidly read as a teenager."[23]

Bradbury's "distinctive poetic style" partially explains the continuity of his work. Though he has written in a variety of genres throughout his career, his best writing seems all of a piece, no matter how diverse the formats, the settings, the characters, and the central conflicts. Partially, this apparently paradoxical continuity results from certain recurrent themes which inform most of Bradbury's writing. For instance, Green Town and Mars, the most fully realized of Bradbury's settings, may be separated by time and space; but they are fundamentally linked imaginatively, each ironically highlighting the values of the other. It is no coincidence that Bradbury's most famous story, "Mars is Heaven!"[24] depicts American explorers mysteriously and ultimately lethally rediscovering Green Town on Mars, for this ironic relationship between memory and desire is at the core of much of Bradbury's best prose.

This peculiar continuity of Bradbury's work, which incorporates into a distinctive pattern apparently incompatible elements of science and fantasy, autobiography and fiction, has often perplexed critics intent on keeping genre distinctions clear. Yet, as Wayne L. Johnson's description of this "awkward" paradox suggests, the continuity between Green Town and Mars actually helps to explain Bradbury's special imaginative power, his ability to symbolically represent American experience in the mid-twentieth century. "In the world of fiction, and fantastic fiction in particular, Ray Bradbury stands as a somewhat awkward colossus, with one foot amid the tree-lined streets of Green Town, Illinois in the 1920s and '30s, and the other foot planted on the red sands of Mars in the not-too-distant future. Uncomfortable as this position may seem it represents not only the basic thrust of Bradbury's work—from past to future, youth to manhood, Earth to the planets and Mars—but also the actual trend of history for members of Bradbury's generation."[25]

Though the continuity of Bradbury's writing can be partially explained thematically, it is more fundamentally evidence of the distinctive quality of Bradbury's literary style. Once he discovered his voice the "magical" effect he sought was not a product of the particular genre conventions adopted in a given story; rather, the magic was in the style itself, the process whereby a story idea was transformed in the reverie of his unconscious into a tapestry of image and metaphor. Thus, in a reversal of the "feeding" metaphor he employs to describe his reading habits, Bradbury describes his strength as a writer as the ability to flesh out the bare bones of a conception: "If I have one power in my work, I think it is the power to put meat on bones. . . . The plot may not be too much, but I do enjoy the marrow and the gristle, the way I flush [*sic*] out these things."[26]

Actually, as Bradbury learned to flesh out his conceptions with the poetry of his unconscious, he also learned the all-important art of surgery. Before he could add muscle to skeletal structure he had to recognize and remove fatty tissue. Like much genre fiction of the time Bradbury's still-uncollected early stories are, as he is the first to admit, entirely forgettable, standard fare both in style and conception. Even some of the best of his early weird stories were revised when reprinted in *Dark Carnival* in 1947, and the revisions illustrate the craftsmanship that distinguished the apprentice just discovering his own voice from the mature writer. A comparison of the original magazine version of "The Wind" with the opening of the revised version (reprinted in *The October Country*, 1955) illustrates that Bradbury had learned the advantages of a "clean" style. Though the basic conception is strong, the original opening is plodding and cliché-ridden:

John Colt is awake and listening . . .

Moonlight sluiced into his room by the huge triple window fronting the upstairs of the house, fell across his sharp, questioning features.

The wind moved far away in the night, and Colt's lips worked as he listened to it; moving stealthily and mournfully from the sea, approaching the house as surely as mighty horses hooves.

Colt's body shivered, hairs stood upon his neck, and goosepimples clustered on his limbs. He knew why he felt this way. After ten years he could believe nothing else.

He knew the wind was coming toward him—and he slipped from the bed, thrust himself tremblingly into a robe, found carpet slippers and ventured downstairs to await its arrival.

He went to the phone thinking, "This is what I've waited for, calmly at first. Curious. Alert. Sure of most factors. But I don't know how much I can stand. I keep losing my grip, gaining it, and losing it again."

His hand shook as he dialed the call through. "Hello, Herb? This is Colt."

"John—how are you?"

"Not so good. And, like a fool, I dismissed the servants today. I'm alone. . . ."

When he revised the story, Bradbury simply cut the passages of melodramatic and awkward exposition. Applying principles he had learned from Hemingway, among others, he substituted a taut, dramatic dialogue, which evokes emotional intensity rather than describing it:

> The phone rang at six thirty that evening. It was December, and already dark as Thompson picked up the phone.
> "Hello."
> "Hello, *Herb?*"
> "Oh, it's you, Allin."
> "Is your wife home, Herb?"
> "Sure. Why?"
> "Damn it."[27]

But if Bradbury learned the virtues of a "clean" style, the distinctive quality of his prose is most evident in the "poetic" passages in which he fleshed out his plots. If he learned from Hemingway the power in compression and implication, his own mature style characteristically combines such terse dialogue with a technique Bradbury himself refers to as "the art of the aside," cadenzas of imagery and metaphor that embellish his basic theme. Another of his metaphors— referring to flowers rather than flesh, color and texture rather than muscle—suggests the quality of effect he seeks: "In a way, I am the proprietor of a Japanese water flower factory. I make these little paper flowers and bunch them all up together . . . then I put them into a story and they open up in the water."[28] As the metaphor suggests, at its best this technique is the verbal equivalent of a flower blossoming, as the narrative voice pauses to evoke the mood and atmosphere implicit in the plot. (Perhaps inadvertantly, Bradbury's comparison to "paper flowers" also suggests the dangers of this technique, when verbal embroidery becomes artificial, precious, or merely cute.) Actually, assimilating certain aspects of Hemingway's "clean, really fresh-water style" allowed Bradbury to highlight more effectively the lush descriptions his narratives inspired. As the term "art of the aside" implies, his models for this kind of technique begin with Shakespeare himself and include those prose stylists—preeminently Melville— who manage to integrate the rich textures of poetry with narrative.

> So Shakespeare has given me the courage—and Melville—to do the aside, to say, "Goddam, I am going to write an aside." I say to the audience, "I'm going to stop the plot here, okay?" "All right." "And you know what I'm

going to do? I'm going to describe a dinosaur as it's never been described. Now watch this." And then I sit down and write a prose poem about this wonderful creature that comes gliding out of the jungle with its oiled hinges and its mechanisms. It's a Samurai warrior with its armor gilt, you know. It has little watchmaker's hands, and it can pick people up and turn them over like it's gonna repair their works. Except it eats them. It opens its great hinged mouth and all these picket fence teeth and it goes "Aarumph!" and you're gone. And it's got these rolling, ostrich-egg eyes. Yet it walks very delicately balanced. And in the Samurai warrior's mesh, all these coins it wears on its side, you see little insects running around inside between the coins; it's covered with all sorts of bacteria life and slime; it's a walking bark, isn't it? So by the time you're done with my aside, you don't care that I stopped the plot.[29]

Actually, Bradbury's description of the relationship between "aside" and "plot" simplifies what is often a more complex interaction. The specific story to which he refers here is "A Sound of Thunder," and in context this "aside"[30] is crucially important to the story's coherence and overall effect. Just as the aside in Renaissance drama could serve numerous functions at once—to reveal character and inner motivation, to express and comment on the meanings of the action— so too Bradbury's most effective asides both advance the plot and enhance its impact.

This description of the dinosaur in "A Sound of Thunder," for instance, is vitally important both as an element in the plot and as an expression of the story's theme. Since the plot centers on an experienced big-game hunter panicking at the crucial moment and violating the rules of his time-travel safari, the story's coherence depends upon vividly evoking the impact of a firsthand encounter with the king of carnivores, Tyrannosaurus Rex. Though the story's overt theme is a variation of a time-travel paradox—that altering even a minor detail in the past might alter the present from which the time-travelers departed—the story's sense of wonder is primarily generated by the beast itself. Thus, the aside is actually the central climax of the story, which is memorable precisely because it creates such a vivid and overwhelming impression in this key scene. Indeed, this encounter provides the primary appeal of the time-travel plot, which is essentially a vehicle to enable Bradbury and readers who share his passion for dinosaurs to observe firsthand the fabulous beast, with all "its terrors, its incredible beauty." Reminiscing about his lifelong fascination with dinosaurs, he might have been describing the vital principle of this time-travel story, expressed in its climatic aside: "Deep in its

. . . soul, it speaks with the heart of a boy who fell in love with just such beasts and wanted to run and live with them."[31]

One of Bradbury's most sophisticated early stories, "The Next in Line," illustrates the ways the aside can function both to express a psychological theme and to generate an atmosphere of macabre horror. The protagonist, an American woman mesmerized with obsessive dread by the sight of the Guanajuato mummies, helplessly identifies with what she imagines to be their endless silent screams. Here the aside reveals her inner feelings, dramatizes the central image that inspired the story (based on Bradbury's own experience in Mexico in 1945), and implies the psychological dynamics that ultimately cause the protagonist's death:

> Marie's eyes slammed the furthest wall after a back-forth, back-forth swinging from horror to horror, from skull to skull, beating from rib to rib, staring with hypnotic fascination at paralyzed, loveless, fleshless loins, at men made into women by evaporation, of women made into dugged swine. The fearful ricochet of vision, growing, growing, taking impetus from swollen breast to raving mouth, wall to wall, again, again, like a ball hurled in a game, caught in the incredible teeth, spat in a scream across the corridor to be caught in claws, lodged between thin teats, the whole standing chorus invisibly chanting the game on, on, the wild game of sight recoiling, rebounding, reshuttling on down the inconceivable procession, through a montage of erected horrors that ended finally and for all time when vision crashed against the corridor ending with one last scream from all present.[32]

Though this extended description presents the central haunting image that establishes the story's atmosphere of soundless horror, it also establishes the underlying metaphor that expresses Marie's state of mind: to her the mummies are emblems of her own silent anguish, the quiet desperation of her poisonously polite, lethal relationship with her husband. The sexlessness of their "paralyzed, loveless, fleshless loins" parallels her own body image, for even before this encounter she lay awake sleeplessly contemplating the fact that she is "past saving now" because she lacks the "warmth to bake away the aging moisture."[33] The image of her vision "ricocheting" from skull to skull, elaborated through the metaphor of the "ball hurled in a game," expresses her state of mind as it builds to a crescendo of horror. And by paralleling the feverish rhythm of her vision with the imagined "chant" of the "standing chorus," ending with "one last scream from all present," the aside implicitly dramatizes the special horror of her agony and eventual death—that, like these unburied dead, her own inner scream is soundless, unrecognized by the outer world. Thus, the aside focuses the energies and meanings of the plot. Indeed, without this vivid impression of the protagonist's reaction to the mummies, her ultimate death of anxiety and despair would seem merely contrived.

"Rocket Summer," the vignette that opens *The Martian Chronicles*, illustrates some of the functions of the aside in Bradbury's science fiction. Taken literally, it also illustrates a quality that has irritated his science-fiction critics—the use of vivid powers of description to dramatize a scene that is at best implausible scientifically. Indeed, the premise, expressed in the phrase "rocket summer"—that heat from rocket exhausts might drastically and instantaneously transform the climate—is essentially silly if read as serious scientific extrapolation. But if the premise is understood to be metaphorical, it dramatically states the central theme of the book, the ambivalent meanings of the lure of the space frontier, symbolized by the rocket "making summer with every breath of its mighty exhausts":

One minute it was Ohio winter, with doors closed, windows locked, the panes blind with frost, icicles fringing every roof, children skiing on slopes, housewives lumbering like great black bears in their furs along the icy streets.

And then a long wave of warmth crossed the small town. A flooding sea of hot air; it seemed as if someone had left a bakery door open. The heat pulsed among the cottages and bushes and children. The icicles dropped, shattering, to melt. The doors flew open. The windows flew up. The children worked off their wool clothes. The housewives shed their bear disguises. The snow dissolved and showed last summer's ancient green lawns.

Rocket summer. The words passed among the people in the open, airing houses. *Rocket summer.* The warm desert air changing the frost patterns on the windows, erasing the art work. The skiis and sleds suddenly useless. The snow, falling from the cold sky upon the town, turned to a hot rain before it touched the ground.

Rocket summer. People leaned from their dripping porches and watched the reddening sky.

The rocket lay on the launching field, blowing out pink clouds of fire and oven heat. The rocket stood in the cold winter morning, making summer with every breath of its mighty exhausts. The rocket made climates, and summer lay for a brief moment upon the land. . . .[34]

Bradbury's technique in this passage illustrates the highly metaphorical thrust of his science fiction. Like all of Bradbury's asides,
"Rocket Summer" depends for effect upon sheer sensual impact, creating through vivid visual, aural, and tactile detail the sensation of
Ohio winter magically transformed by a "flooding sea of hot air."[35]
Yet even the sensory detail is implicitly metaphorical, since Bradbury
endows the Midwest setting, the rocket itself, and the change of seasons with symbolic associations. The Midwest setting, like Green
Town, is Bradbury's emblem of the American heartland, evoking the
ironic contradictions of the American Dream, past and future. And if
the rocket is the emblem of that future, the unnatural yet curiously
comforting "oven heat" it generates sensually represents its emotional
impact, as it simultaneously transforms reality and reinvigorates dis-
carded dreams.

Metaphorically representing the emotions generated by the emerging space age (T. S. Eliot's term "objective correlative" describes the
overall effect of the entire vignette), "Rocket Summer" dramatizes
the ambivalent implications of the new age through sensual detail.
The dramatic focus of the description, the abrupt change of seasons,
is implicitly a metaphor for future shock. Yet, ironically, it also revitalizes old dreams to reveal the "ancient green lawns" beneath winter
ice. Indeed, the rocket's heat is curiously domesticated, "as if someone had left a bakery door open," as if this symbol of the future somehow could bring back the odors of home cooking from an earlier
time—imagery that anticipates the fervor of the best Martian settlers
(Americans all) to whom homesteading means recovering the values
of Green Town in a new land. Yet the ironic and tragic tensions of
the book are also foreshadowed in the imagery. For if the rocket's heat
reveals green lawns, it also disrupts the natural rhythm of the year.
Winter playthings are "suddenly useless," the "art work" of frost pattern on the windows is destroyed, and snow is transformed into "hot
rain." The impact of the rocket is overwhelming, in ways both exhilarating and sinister, and the ironic repetition of old tragedies is foreshadowed by the biblical cadence and the emphasis on the word
"brief" in the final line: "Summer lay for a brief moment upon the
land. . . ." Thus, Bradbury's aside establishes the tone and the central symbolism of the chronicles that follow.

Another aside, from the first major episode in *Dandelion Wine*, illustrates how Bradbury's style gives a magical aura to metaphorically
depicted autobiography. The book opens with Doug Spaulding's over-

whelming discovery that he is "alive," and Bradbury's description conveys, through sensual detail and metaphor, the quality of the experience:

> "You all right, Doug?" asked Tom.
> His voice was at the bottom of a green moss well somewhere underwater, secret, removed.
> The grass whispered under his body. He put his arm down, feeling the sheath of fuzz on it, and far away, below, his toes creaking in his shoes. The wind sighed over his shelled ears. The world slipped bright over the glassy round of his eyeballs like images sparked in a crystal sphere. Flowers were suns and fiery spots of sky strewn through the woodland. Birds flickered like skipped stones across the vast inverted pond of heaven. His breath raked over his teeth, going in ice, coming out fire. Insects shocked the air with electric clearness. Ten thousand individual hairs grew a millionth of an inch on his head. He heard the twin hearts beating in each ear, the third heart beating in his throat, the two hearts throbbing his wrists, the real heart pounding his chest. The million pores on his body opened.
> I'm *really* alive! he thought. I never knew it before; or if I did I don't remember.[36]

Since the significant event in this episode is Doug's revelation, the effectiveness of the plot depends almost entirely upon Bradbury's abiltiy to evoke vividly his state of heightened awareness. Describing an essentially transcendental experience, the style focuses intensely on immediate sensory details yet generates a sense of interpenetration, in which the boundaries between the self and the world become fluid. The imagery creates a hallucinatory effect, communicating Doug's overwhelming experience of inner vitality as well as his sensation of being immersed in the oceanic currents of life that surround him: the grass "whispered" as insects "shocked the air," paralleling his own preternatural sensitivity to bodily sensations, as he feels each hair on his skin, his heartbeat amplified and multiplied, individual pores opening to the world. But this awareness that his own inner vitality is bathed in the vitality of the forest surrounding him is metaphorically extended to cosmic proportions as well, so that flowers appear as "suns and fiery spots of sky strewn through the woodland," while birds flicker "like skipped stones across the vast inverted pond of heaven," an image that conveys mystical experience in terms appropriate to a Midwestern boy. Thus, through the magic of metaphor, Bradbury links his youthful experience to his mature vision of making

the universe our home. Again, the descriptive aside is not only vital
to the plot but an expression of the central theme of the book itself,
which attempts to capture the transitory magic of the American
Dream as manifested in this last summer of innocence in Green
Town, Illinois.

The peculiar continuity of Bradbury's fiction is due in large part to
the central importance of this technique of the aside, the lyrical cadenza of description which musically expresses the central themes of
the narrative. The distinctive quality of Bradbury's voice is most pro-
nounced in these asides, where central images and symbols are fleshed
out through metaphorical elaboration and sensual detail. Whatever
the overt subject of Bradbury's fiction—be it the terrible beauty of
Tyrannosaurus Rex, the soundless horror of the unburied dead,
"rocket summer" in a Midwest future, or a mystical experience while
berry picking—Bradbury's distinctive tone and style is generated by
the play of associations in his unconscious, that "magic attic" that
stores such a variety of memorabilia and cherished treasures, which
sometimes can be given new life by the mysterious powers of enchantment.

Chapter Four
Weird Tales: The Landscape of October Country

The title of Bradbury's collection of weird stories, *The October Country*, evokes the most powerful metaphor in his early writing. For "October" in this early fiction is both a season of the year and a state of the soul, an atmosphere of sudden winds and dying leaves in which marvelous and monstrous revelations come to lonely people. In 1955, having rewritten some of the twenty-seven early stories from *Dark Carnival* (1947), having combined fifteen of them with four others in the same vein to create the new volume, he recognized he was assembling his "favorite stories from that early work," which his later readers might find "unfamiliar." "For my later readers, *The October Country* will present a side of my writing which is probably unfamiliar to them, and a type of story I rarely have done since 1946."[1] To develop the metaphor of his title he also composed an epigraph, which articulates the themes and atmosphere evoked by the first original Bradbury landscape—neither Midwest summer nor Martian desert, but the season when things ripen and die, when summer has faded and "autumn people" drift like cold rain.

October Country

. . . that country where it is always turning late in the year. That country where the hills are fog and the rivers are mist; where noons go quickly, and midnights stay. That country composed in the main of cellars, subcellars, coal-bins, closets, attics, and pantries faced away from the sun. That country whose people are autumn people, thinking only autumn thoughts. Whose people passing at night on the empty walks sound like rain. . . . (*OC*, epigraph)

Though Bradbury recognized in 1955 that the landscape of October country was no longer his primary setting, his attraction to the gothic is a lifelong passion. None of his childhood enthusiasms was more fundamental than his love of horror and Halloween. If he loved "magic and miracles," he also loved magic and monsters. He remembers being enthralled at the age of three by seeing *The Hunchback of Notre Dame* from his mother's knee, and by the age of six, his love of fairy tales and the world of Oz already established, his "lifelong fascination with horror" was confirmed by seeing *The Phantom of the Opera* and *The Cat and the Canary*.[2] He was afraid of the dark, yet he delighted in hanging upside down from trees in a vampire costume to frighten other children.

The title of Bradbury's children's book, *Switch on the Night*, plays on the ambiguity of this lifelong fascination with the dark. For if darkness evokes an apprehensive longing for light ("Switch on the *light!*"), it also evokes the delicious thrill of entering the unknown, of finally encountering the secret things hidden in the dark crannies at high noon. Bradbury first discovered his own style by indulging his ability to imaginatively "switch on the night," to capture the gothic underside of Green Town's innocent civility. Indeed, his first metaphors for Green Town were not suggested by dandelion wine, which stores the summer sun for winter; rather, they came from places that never see the sun, where hidden passions and obsessions turn monstrous and strange—like the horrible thing preserved in "The Jar," one emblem of the balked love and twisted yearnings of Bradbury's "autumn people." And though he subsequently moved on from the landscape of October country created in his first years as a mature writer, he has occasionally returned to the haunted places he left behind, most notably in *The Halloween Tree* and in *Something Wicked This Way Comes*.

The October Country

As Hazel Pierce recognizes in "Ray Bradbury and the Gothic Tradition," Bradbury's "poetic" abilities helped him integrate traditional gothic themes with his own personal experience and with contemporary life: "Clothing it in the poetry of words, he presents the old darkness fresh and imaginatively modern to us."[3] This effect appears to be generated in part by a technique recommended in Dorothea Brande's *Becoming a Writer*, which suggests free-associating on specific words. Both the titles and the style of many of Bradbury's early weird stories suggest their origin in the free-play of reverie and association this technique encouraged. Many of the titles present a single evocative object: "The Dwarf," "Skeleton," "The Jar," "The Emissary,"

"The Next in Line," "The Crowd," "The Wind," "The Man Upstairs," "The Cistern." Each of the stories creates an eerie context in
which the central object evokes a haunting atmosphere and theme.
The result is a distinctive sombre musical effect, created by what
Gary K. Wolfe describes as "compelling prose poems on themes of
nature and mortality, slightly plotted and stripped of all but essen-
tials of character and setting."[4]

Encounters with death. The first story in which Bradbury
feels he achieved a "quality breakthrough,"[5] "The Lake" (written in
1942), illustrates the distinctively poetic and musical style of his best
weird fiction: the settings themselves evoke an atmosphere of receptive anticipation, and the stories weave through reverie and incident
to revelations either poignantly or grotesquely appropriate. In "The
Lake" the theme is recovery of lost love and lost innocence (a central
Bradbury theme), and the eerie plot itself serves as a metaphor for the
emotional impact of the setting, which reactivates buried and cherished emotions. In the opening description the hero, middle-aged and
reasonably successful in life, finds himself rather deliciously "shut
. . . off from the world" by the lake: "The wave shut me off from
the world, from the birds in the sky, the children on the beach, my
mother on the shore. There was a moment of green silence. Then the
wave gave me back to the sky, the sand, the children yelling. I came
out of the lake and the world was waiting for me, having hardly
moved since I went away" (*OC,* 97).

This opposition between an "other world" (the lake) and the mundane world illustrates a central pattern in these stories, which depict
protagonists who are either enraptured or appalled by encountering
the marvelous. The central figure of "The Lake" is entranced, but his
experience in his "other world" remains private. He returns to the
beach where "Mama" orders him to put on his sweater. The autumn
wind is a bit crisp, and he is suspended curiously between worlds—
the present and the past, his wife and "Mama," the shore and the
lake. If the shore is the "world" it is the world of his youth revisited
in autumn, and autumn is the season of his life. Nowhere is the seasonal metaphor implicit in "The October Country" more overt than
in his early story, which may well have inspired the book's title:

It was . . . the last days when things are getting sad for no reason. The
beach was so long and lonely with only about six people on it. The kids quit
bouncing the ball because somehow the wind made them sad, too, whistling

the way it did, and the kids sat down and felt autumn come along the endless shore.

All of the hot-dog stands were boarded up with strips of golden planking, sealing in all the mustard, onion, meat odors of the long, joyful summer. It was like nailing summer into a series of coffins. One by one the places slammed their covers down, padlocked their doors, and the wind came and touched the sand, blowing away all of the million footprints of July and August. It got so that now, in September, there was nothing but the mark of my rubber tennis shoes and Donald and Delaus Arnold's feet, down by the water curve. (*OC*, 97–98)

The setting has taken him back in time, to the autumn day before he boarded the train that took him west, to his adult life. Once again, he looks up the beach to see "the merry-go-round was hidden with canvas, all of the horses frozen in mid-air on their brass poles, showing teeth, galloping on" (*OC*, 98). Here he will recover his secret past, frozen in mid-stride, like the horses, all his life. In this elegiac atmosphere, entering the autumn of his life, he remembers the twelve-year-old girl who drowned off this same shore when they both were young. When he's finally alone he calls her name. Like other of Bradbury's "autumn people," solitude and the season allow him finally to confront the central trauma of his inner life. "Always before, with the crowd, I hadn't dared to look, to come to this spot and search around in the water and call a certain name. But now—" (*OC*, 98).

He begins a sandcastle and leaves it half-built, as he and Tally used to do. Then he returns again to the "world," to his mother and his wife, only to notice the lifeguard getting out of the boat with "a gray sack in his hands, not very heavy, and his face almost as gray and lined" (*OC*, 98). Before he insists on seeing what's inside he knows she's been found at last. Later he finds another sandcastle, half-built, and he quietly observes "the small prints of feet coming in from the lake and going back out to the lake and not returning" (*OC*, 102). He finishes the sandcastle slowly, then walks away "so as not to watch it crumble in the waves as all things crumble." When he returns to the world this time his wife is "a strange woman named Margaret . . . waiting for me, smiling. . . . (*OC*, 103). Immersed in the lake—emblem of his buried love, his last childhood summer, his memory, his unconscious—he returns estranged to the autumn world in which he lives. Only he knows that the silent ritual on the beach is the magical, ineffably sad, center of his life.

Like many of the stories in this collection, "The Lake" is essentially musical in style and structure—all mood and atmosphere and metaphorically resonant imagery. And its quiet drama of recovery and estrangement defines the central pattern of many of the most haunting tales, which dramatize encounters with death. "The Emissary," though similar in theme, reverses the central roles. The protagonist is a dying young boy (prematurely in the autumn of his life); the buried love is Miss Haight, the young teacher he adored with pure preadolescent fervor, who recently died unaccountably; the "emissary" is "Dog," embodiment of all the boy's lost energy and vitality, who, as the story opens, is the living incarnation of the season: "Martin knew it was Autumn again, for Dog ran into the house bringing wind and frost and a smell of apples turned to cider under trees. In dark clocksprings of hair, Dog fetched goldenrod, dust of farewell-summer, acorn-husk, hair of squirrel, feather of departed robin, sawdust from fresh-cut cordwood, and leaves like charcoals shaken from a blaze of maple trees. Dog jumped. Showers of brittle fern, blackberry vine, marsh-grass sprang over the bed where Martin shouted. No doubt, no doubt of it at all, this incredible beast was October!" (*OC,* 104).

Again, the central effect is created by evocative description, the vivid imagery of the season. Without the "poetry," the story is a simple chiller. Indeed, the ghastly conclusion somewhat violates the story's essentially lyrical tone of elegy. Halloween has passed, Dog has not returned for days (to the sick boy's dismay), and symbols of our annual ceremonial confrontation with death are mouldering themselves: "The last Hallowe'en pumpkins were rotting in trash cans, papier-mache skulls and witches were burnt on bonfires, and ghosts were stacked on shelves with other linens until next year" (*OC,* 109). But Dog does not know the holiday is mere ceremony. In a story in which imagery comes through the medium of a dog, the climactic horror is appropriately communicated through smell. As the boy hears Dog baying in the distance, drawing closer, he ecstatically awaits the reunion. But Dog has been eagerly digging somewhere for days to bring his master his heart's desire, and when he arrives he reeks of "the ripe and awful cemetery earth" (*OC,* 111). Behind him something that should not have been disturbed clumps "painfully" up the stairs. Sometimes buried loves should remain buried.

Though "The Emissary" is in essence a Halloween horror story, concluding with the unnatural stench of the graveyard intruding into a sick boy's room, the central impression the story leaves is not so much the final horror as it is the overwhelming atmosphere of October, the metaphorical resonance of the imagery (influenced in this story perhaps by Bradbury's love of Gerard Manley Hopkins): "But he knew without hearing where Dog had rattled down hills where autumn lay in cereal crispness, where children lay in funeral pyres, in rustling heaps, the leaf-buried but watchful dead, as Dog and the world blew by" (*OC*, 105). This image might describe other of Bradbury's "autumn-people," "leaf-buried but watchful" as the energies of "the world" blow by. "The Cistern," another story in which atmosphere is all-important, opens with "an afternoon of rain, and lamps lighted against the gray" (*OC*, 239). But whereas "The Emissary" begins as a rhapsodic October celebration and ends with horror, "The Cistern" captures in the downpour of rain an ambiguously haunting mood, at once ominous and refreshing.

"The Cistern"'s tonality derives from a fantasy evoked by the object in the title, the fantasy of one of Bradbury's poetically sensitive autumn-people, Anna, who is enraptured at the thought of the watery "other world" into which the cistern opens. The perspective of the normal world is stolidly represented by her sister Juliet, who sews methodically and ridicules her fantasies. But Anna is a talker, swept away by her vision like rain down the cistern, and as she weaves her fantasy it becomes real. Down in that hidden world, suddenly awash with fresh rainwater, is a man, handsome but wasted by illness, accompanied by a young woman, "beautifully, beautifully dead," whose "hair hangs up on the water like a drift of smoke" (*OC*, 242). During dry seasons they lie like autumn leaves, or, even more delicately, "like those Japanese water-flowers, all dry and compact and old and quiet" (*OC*, 243). But when the rains come they float and come gracefully to life in underground rivers, loving "with no worries, very secret and hidden under the earth in the cistern waters" (*OC*, 245). Then she realizes the man is Frank, her lover who died. She does not yet recognize the woman. Juliet mocks her silliness and asks her to help with the sewing. Anna listens to the storm. Juliet awakens later to find the door left open to the rain. She frantically calls into the darkness as "the rain whispered on the street and fell upon the closed lid [of the cistern] all the rest of the night" (*OC*, 247).

To Anna, encounter with the "other world," the world that images her secret desire, brings rhapsodic fulfillment. Or perhaps she is only an overly sensitive, deranged suicide. As Bradbury presents it, however, her vision seems more "real" than Juliet's drab reality. In any case, Anna loves her death. She embraces it like a lover, as she passes through the cistern into a world of fluid grace and fathomless passion. But other sensitive autumn people have less rapturous encounters with the other world. Marie in "The Next in Line" sees her own sterile anguish expressed in the silent screams of the Guanajuato mummies. Mesmerized by this image expressing her own despair, she lies in silent horror in her bed, next to her aloof, controlling husband—representative of the "normal" tourist world which snaps photos and asks curiously about the economics of the mortuary—who sleeps soundly as she dies of fright. She is no paper flower to be rejuvenated by soft rains. Like the mummies, she embodies the soundless horror of the unburied dead.

Though many of Bradbury's stories about death are lyrical and elegiac, they vary considerably in style and tone. "The Scythe" treats death allegorically. Adrift during the Depression (as was Bradbury's family to some extent for several years during the early 1930's), a farmer and his family stumble upon a prosperous farm. The owner has died and willed the property to whomever finds his body, along with the scythe, which bears the motto "Who Wields Me—Wields the World" (*OC,* 177). They move in, live comfortably, and work hard. But the wheat is unnatural. It does not ripen evenly, it rots immediately when it falls, and new shoots immediately replace what is cut. Finally, the farmer realizes he is harvesting human lives, that he is Death himself. When he realizes the stalks representing his family are ripe, he quits. But the house burns down and the bodies of the family lay immobile, neither dead or alive. Finally, in mad grief, he returns to work, rampaging through the fields. The date is 30 May 1938 (*OC,* 188), the Second World War soon ignites, and Death, once a simple family man, "moves on with his scythe, with the light of blind suns and a look of white fire in his never-sleeping eyes, on and on and on. . . ." (*OC,* 190). Though the allegory is not entirely consistent (he somehow reads "their names in the cut grain" [*OC,* 185]), "The Scythe" does create a strong Depression-era setting as well as a powerful and unusual image expressing the impact of the war.

"There Was an Old Woman," on the other hand, treats death whimsically. Indeed, Death here is discomfited and ultimately defeated by the resolute will of Aunt Tildy, who decided early in life she does not believe in death, who knows her own mind, and who simply refuses to die. The "dark young man" and his companions wait patiently with their wicker basket until her tirade is finished, then cart off her body when she is asleep. But, still feisty in spirit if not in flesh, she pursues them to the mortuary, haranguing unmercifully as they attempt to prepare the corpse for the funeral. Finally, in exasperation, they give in. Now she serves coffee to young visitors, shows them her knitted sweaters, and talks. And occasionally, for a special treat, she unfastens "the white lace at her neck and chest" to show "the long blue scar where the autopsy was sewn together" (*OC,* 238). Essentially, the fantastical premise—that her disembodied spirit carries on as relentlessly as ever—is a metaphor for her character. Aunt Tilly is, literally, just too set in her ways, too stubborn, to die.

Grotesques. Another major theme of *The October Country* is the grotesque, a subject that, like encounters with the "other world" of death, has ambiguous implications. "The Dwarf" expresses the paradoxical nature of the theme through artful use of crazy mirrors. The setting is a carnival fun house, the season is blistering mid-summer, and the focus of attention is Mr. Bigelow, a dwarf who comes in late at night to see himself elongated to normal size by his special mirror. The point of view is split. Ralph Banghart, the carny ticket taker, finds the "gink" grotesque and amusing, but he also knows that even for "normal" people "that rollie coaster's the handiest thing to death there is," that the "whole damn carny business's crazy" (*OC,* 3) because it feeds on people's secret passions (a theme that becomes central in *Something Wicked This Way Comes*). But Aimee, Ralph's girl friend, finds herself oddly sympathetic—even, she says half-jokingly, "madly in love" (*OC,* 6)—with Bigelow. And when she discovers he's a writer—admittedly of cheap detective thrillers—she confirms the paradox she immediately suspected (which is also suggested by his name): "This little guy's got a soul as big as all outdoors" (*OC,* 7).

Images reflected in the mirrors structure the story, a device that effectively reflects the story's central theme—the disparity between appearance and reality. The crazy mirrors reveal the story's inner truths. Convinced that Bigelow only needs a distorting mirror of his own to give him a true image of himself, Aimee orders a replica of the funhouse mirror delivered to his apartment. But before he receives it Ralph plays a cruel "joke," motivated largely by his envy of Aimee's admiration for the little "gink," replacing Bigelow's secret mirror with one that shrinks him even further. Seeing his grotesquely shrunken image in the new mirror, knowing his "secret" place has been violated and ridiculed, Bigelow races shrieking into the night. As Aimee departs to search for him she recoils from Ralph's reflection in the "blazing mirror." He turns to see his reflection: "A horrid, ugly little man, two feet high, with a pale, squashed face under an ancient straw hat, scowled back at him" (*OC*, 15). At last he has seen himself truly. He is "the dwarf." If Bigelow is spiritually as "big" as he is physically "low," Ralph is normal in appearance but spiritually grotesque.

"Skeleton" presents two grotesques: Harris, an apparently normal man who becomes alienated from his own bones; and M. Munigant, a gnomelike unlicensed medical practitioner specializing in such conditions, who contentedly munches on breadsticks during interviews and promises the only cure. In a collection of weird stories this is perhaps the most outlandish, yet Bradbury's treatment makes the bizarre premise both psychologically compelling and grimly humorous. Harris begins as a mere hypochondriac, but his obsession escalates with the curious but irresistible logic of paranoia. The more he learns about his bone structure the more horrified he becomes, until finally he has the ghastly revelation that a SKELETON lives inside him, that his head contains a SKULL: "this thing inside, this invader, this horror, was supporting his arms, legs, and head!" (*OC*, 69).

Mere alienation escalates to outright warfare, as Harris realizes his skeleton has tried to lure him to a desert death to deny M. Munigant the satisfaction of victory: "Vulture lunch off me, and there you'll lie, grinning. Grinning with victory" (*OC*, 77). When his flesh is back in control he returns to his mysterious savior who proceeds to— well—devour his adversary (exactly *how* is not entirely clear, but Bradbury's description evokes sensations rather like those of having impacted wisdom teeth removed under laughing gas). Harris's very normal wife, Clarisse, returns to what remains after the cure—her husband, looking like a jellyfish on the living room carpet, calling her name (*OC*, 80). Both absurd and oddly disturbing, "Skeleton"'s final image employs fantasy to dramatize the bizarre logic of the protagonist's alienation.

"The Jar" is a kind of parable about the peculiar attractions, the ambiguous meanings, of the grotesque. The story begins and ends whimsically by focusing on the central grotesque object—the "thing" in the jar—evoking its peculiarly potent suggestiveness: "It was one of those things they keep in a jar in the tent of a sideshow on the outskirts of a little, drowsy town. One of those pale things drifting in alcohol plasma, forever dreaming and circling, with its peeled dead eyes staring out at you and never seeing you. It went with the noise-lessness of late night, and only the crickets chirping, the frogs sob-bing off in the moist swampland" (*OC,* 81). In his one inspired moment, Charlie recognizes the thing's peculiar value, buys it, and takes it home to "the Hollow" where it attracts an awe-struck follow-ing—Charlie's first friends—who almost reverently contemplate its mysterious meanings, endlessly speculating about its origins.

But Charlie's malevolent and sarcastic wife Thedy investigates and destroys the mystery, revealing that the "thing" is only a papier-mâché and rubber illusion, designed to attract suckers. Thedy disap-pears—for good. Charlie's friends continue to stare at "the thing" and dream, wondering if perhaps it is different, even more poetically hor-rible, than before. Charlie finally had to create a grotesque reality to match the mysterious image in which they all believe. But the story ends as it begins, focusing on the mysterious ambiguity of the thing in the jar, emphasizing that its meaning does not derive from the thing itself but from the weird poetry it evokes in its audience. To adapt T. S. Eliot's and Coleridge's phraseology to an unusual context, the "thing" finally is an "objective correlative" of the otherwise inar-ticulate weird artist in Charlie's soul, who knows his ultimate respon-sibility is to suspend the disbelief of his audience, by whatever means are necessary.

Just as "There Was an Old Woman" is a whimsical variation on the theme of death, so "The Watchful Poker Chip of H. Matisse" is a whimsical variation on the theme of grotesque. Indeed, George Gar-vey is a most unusual grotesque, since his distinctive quality is being "a terrifyingly ordinary man" with a talent for "mummifying people instantly" (*OC,* 53) with his soporific conversation. But his life of un-relieved boredom is interrupted when a clique of avant-garde intellec-tuals become infatuated with his peculiar genius for invoking "monstrous ennui," for being a "delightfully mass-minded, keep-up-with-the-Joneses, machine-dominated chap leading a wishy-washy life of quiet desperation" (*OC,* 57). Actually, underneath his bland veneer he is, like Charlie, possessed of a genius of a subconscious, which knows what his audience wants. To his horror, everything he repre-sented becomes "in" as camp becomes fashionable, which threatens his artfully shepherded role as the colossal All-American Boob. But his subconscious adapts to even this frivolous shift of fashion. Gar-vey's final act of genius is to strike out against the prevailing taste for

Guy Lombardo and old radio shows by creating a new form of inspired tastelessness, thus regaining his snickering fans: he begins replacing his body parts with ornate art-objects, culminating in the poker chip painted by H. Matisse he wears in place of an eye. Bradbury's target in this uncharacteristic excursion into cultural satire is trendy intellectualism, which finds itself always one step behind the ingenious banality of George Garvey, as he moves from campy nostalgia to florid romantic decadence.

Monsters. *The October Country* represents an unusual array of "monsters," most of which would not be recognizable as such outside the contexts of the stories that present them: they include a normal-appearing infant, a crowd, a wind, and a female victim. The more obvious monsters—winged vampires and a psychic "witch"—turn out not to be monsters at all but members of the "Family," a closely knit, loving group with strong traditions. Bradbury's treatment of "monsters" illustrates his general approach to the conventions of weird fiction: he tends either to assimilate unusual materials into those conventions, or to present conventional motifs in unusual contexts, reversing traditional associations.

Bradbury's most conventional monster in this collection is the vampire in "The Man Upstairs," but here the highly domestic context in which the monster appears creates an unusual point of view and a wryly humorous but chilling effect. The story's gruesome but curiously antiseptic climax is set up by the opening image. Douglas, Bradbury's archetypal Green Town boy, is watching Grandma butcher chickens: "How carefully and expertly Grandmother would fondle the cold cut guts of the chicken and withdraw the marvels therein; the wet shining loops of meat-smelling intestine, the muscled lump of heart, the gizzard with the collection of seeds in it. . . . And then the ritual of taxidermy, stuffing the bird with watered, seasoned bread, and performing surgery with a swift, bright needle, stitch after pulled-tight stitch" (*OC,* 211).

The boy's fascinated but clinical point of view is next directed at Mr. Koberman, the cold and severe new boarder, whom Douglas instantly detests. Indeed, their relationship quickly becomes all-out war, as Douglas develops ingenious methods for tormenting his adversary during his daytime sleep—"beating a drum, bouncing golf balls, or just screaming for three minutes outside Mr. Koberman's door, and flushing the toilet seven times in succession" (*OC,* 216). Koberman, in turn, frames Douglas by breaking a colored glass window with his basketball. A conversation between the boy and his portly grandfather about how he *knows* we all have guts like chickens sets up the next critical clinical observation: when viewed through a shard of colored glass, Mr. Koberman—who works at night and cannot endure silver—is transparent, and the colored glass reveals he contains alien organs in strange geometrical shapes. Douglas finally performs an operation while Koberman is in his daylight trance, "staring at him with a hungry darkness" (*OC,* 221) as he emulates Grandmother's proficiency, first removing the alien parts, then stuffing the groaning carcass with his $6.50 collection of dimes. A curious example of how Bradbury at his best integrates a traditional horror theme with personal memories,[6] "The Man Upstairs" effectively fuses vampire folklore with tough-minded (there is nothing sentimental about the portrait of Douglas here) nostalgia for a time when children still learned about the "guts" of things in their own kitchens.

"The Crowd" and "The Wind" both extrapolate eerily from commonly observed phenomena. In "The Crowd" the "monster" is the group we have all seen gather so quickly to observe disasters. The story's premise is that this results from more than the lowest common denominator of human instinct, for the hero—survivor of an accident and the vulturous crowd it attracted—investigates old newspaper photos and discovers that the same faces always appear in the backgrounds to such accidents. But on his way to present the evidence to the police he has another accident, and he looks up dying to see their familiar faces, knowing he is doomed to join them. A similar motif appears in "The Wind," where the hero, who is sought out and pursued by a demonic wind he discovered in his world travels, finally is assimilated, together with countless other victims through the ages, into its eerie, conscious vortex of energy. Both of these stories are highly atmospheric and metaphorical, creating monstrous supernatural agents by vividly evoking the sinister overtones of commonplace but unsettling events—being trapped in crowds, or buffeted by winds—then presenting them in a fantastical, gothic context.

"Touched With Fire" and "The Small Assassin" present psychological monsters. The monster in "Touched With Fire" is "a murderee, a victim looking for a place to happen" (*OC,* 116–17). According to the theory developed by the two concerned protagonists, at the right temperature—exactly 92°, just hot enough to create raging rather than debilitating discomfort—such personality types inexorably induce murder. They try to warn her but almost succumb themselves to her genius for evoking murderous rage, managing to drag themselves away from committing carnage just as her wild-eyed husband turns the corner to home with a longshoreman's hook in his pocket. "The Small Assassin" also reverses the traditional role of the monster and the innocent victim, in a disturbing dramatization of parent abuse. The monster (modeled on Bradbury himself) is an apparently helpless infant with preternaturally "adult" consciousness, who conducts a murderous campaign against his mother. As she struggles hopelessly to convince her husband and her doctor she is not paranoid, Bradbury creates an eerie and painful atmosphere of horror out of an infant's cold stare and "the sound of small, moist, pinkly plastic lips" (*OC*, 132) in the night. This technique of defamiliarization, in which the gothic context evokes sinister overtones in what normally would be a soothing image of domestic tranquility, generates the haunting atmosphere in this reworking of the traditional theme of the demonic child (the father ultimately names the kid "Lucifer").

Bradbury's whimsical treatments of monsters depend upon the opposite effect—domesticizing the monstrous. Thus, in "Uncle Einar" (a figure based on one of Bradbury's favorite uncles) the peaceful bat-winged husband reluctantly agrees to serve simultaneously as a children's kite and as a clothesline, using the family laundry for his kite-tail as he hangs in the air attached by a string to the delighted children below. "Homecoming," a more poignant whimsical excursion, depicts a "Family" reunion from the viewpoint of the only "normal" child in an extended (through the centuries) family of vampires and monsters, all of whom try to help him accept his unnatural disabilities—mortality, fear of the dark, and a curious distaste for blood. A weird inversion of a Green Town drama about an unusual child's struggle for acceptance, "Homecoming"'s effectiveness derives from Bradbury's ability to evoke in an unusual context a child's excitement and apprehension about a big holiday celebration. As in so many of these stories, the basic premise provides an extraordinary perspective on the ordinary.

Though Bradbury's reputation has developed primarily from his accomplishments in science fiction, these early gothic stories are among his finest achievements. *The October Country* is perhaps his most underrated book, a collection that deserves to stand beside *The Martian Chronicles, Fahrenheit 451, Dandelion Wine, Something Wicked This Way Comes,* and Bradbury's other strongest short-story anthologies, *The*

Golden Apples of the Sun and *The Illustrated Man*. In these early weird stories, exploring the dark crannies and eerie attics of his childhood, he first learned to make poetry and drama of his personal experience. The best of these stories generate an authentically "weird" atmosphere through vivid imagery, musical cadences, bizarre but effective atmosphere, and—most unusual in the context of the genre magazines, perhaps—through wit.

When Bradbury did go on to explore Mars and the more sunny side of Green Town, his ability to "turn on the night" helped highlight new landscapes against shadows lingering from an earlier darkness. Indeed, one of his most astute science-fiction critics detected in one of these early tales a metaphor for what sometimes happened to Bradbury's art in later years, as the darkness began to dissipate: "Maybe Bradbury, like his own protagonist in 'Skeleton,' grew uneasy about the macabre forces in himself: or maybe success, that nemesis of American writers, was Bradbury's M. Munigant. Whatever the reason, the skeleton has vanished; what's left is recognizable but limp."[7] As Damon Knight suggests, the landscape of October Country lingers in the background of all Bradbury's best fiction, an ironic shading that gives his Martian parables their distinctive character, that provides a tonic bitter tang to the sweetness of dandelion wine.

The Halloween Tree

Though in the introduction to *The October Country* Bradbury characterized the weird story as "a type of story I have rarely done since 1946," he did return to the gothic form in two later novels, *Something Wicked This Way Comes* (1962) (which can be more fruitfully discussed in conjunction with *Dandelion Wine* [1957]), and *The Halloween Tree* (1972), an educational fantasy about the meanings of Halloween obviously intended primarily for a juvenile audience. Bradbury's "educational" intent is manifest throughout. Indeed, Carapace Clavicle Moundshroud (an engaging representative of Death), the boys' instructor, emphasizes his pedagogical role, even to the extent of describing their encounter with Osiris in an Egyptian pyramid as "Lesson Number One about Halloween."[8] But with no apologies for his didacticism, despite a sometimes overly breathless style, Bradbury succeeds in making his boys' educational odyssey into the "Unknown Country" of Death and the past fun—grim fun, to be sure, like Halloween itself. As all the boys agree at the end of their harrowing journey, Moundshroud succeeds in providing both a trick and a treat (*HT,* 173–74). Both because of its sumptuously ornate descriptions (illustrating, as Hazel Pierce suggests, Poe's art of the "arabesque"[9]), and because of its energetic pace, sweeping into and out of richly conceived mythical landscapes, *The Halloween Tree* effectively dramatizes Bradbury's rationale for his love of horror—that we need rich symbols, ceremonies, and art works to help us accept the intolerable reality of death.

Like so much of Bradbury's fiction, the novel is set in a version of Green Town—small-town heartland America—though the specific place and time are undefined. It is Halloween night, and the boys are dressed in their holiday finest: they include a skeleton, a witch, a gargoyle, a beggar, a mummy, a devil, and Death himself, wielding his scythe. Though they have no conception of the meanings of their outfits, they will by the night's end. But their natural leader, Pipkin, Bradbury's All-American Green Town boy, comes to the door pale and out of costume and tells them mysteriously to meet him at the "House," Green Town's one haunted mansion down by the ravine. There they encounter the Halloween Tree, one-hundred feet high and decorated with gargoyle-faced lighted pumpkins, all dancing eerily in the autumn wind. Their response to the tree formulates the questions the novel attempts to answer: "Like a Christman Tree only bigger and all those candles and pumpkins. What's it mean? What's it celebrate?" (*HT,* 30–31).

Out of a pile of autumn leaves emerges a skeletal hand, followed by a cavernous body that stretches, laughing, to the height of the tree itself. Their teacher, Moundshroud—protean in shape and form like everything except the boys in the night's dreamlike atmosphere[10]— returns to normal adult size, then confronts them with the mysteries they must explore to understand their own costumes and to save Pipkin, who cannot participate in the celebration of Death because he is in the hospital, where death is real, not symbolic. "Search and seek for lost Pipkin, and solve Halloween, all in one dark fell blow?" (*HT,* 44) he asks, and they all agree. Creating a kite in the shape of a pterodactyl from old circus posters plastered on a barn wall (an image that fuses Bradbury's delight in kites, circuses, and dinosaurs), grabbing on to each other's legs to form the kite's long motley tail, they sweep into the autumn wind and the "unknown country" where Moundshroud will serve as their guide.

Their quest immerses them in mythologies dealing with death, all originating, Moundshroud explains, in a mythical equation between Death and Night and Winter, which signify loss of Life and Light and Summer. And as they travel they discover the mythic origins of the costumes they wear: the mummy comes from the festivals of Osiris, Egyptian god of the dead; the Ape Man from the dim origins of autumn festivals in primeval fears of losing fire and the sun; Death from Samhain, the Celtic god of death, who harvests lives like grain; the witch, the beggar, the devil, and the gargoyle from older mythologies surviving into the era of Christianity and the Modern Age, outlawed and disowned but still surviving in the shadows; the skeleton from the Mexican festival *el día de muerte* (the day of the dead), in which they eat candy emblems of their own skulls and observe the unburied mummies of Guanajuato.

In each setting they encounter Pipkin trapped in the grasp of Death in a new cultural environment—interned as a mummy in Egypt, racing from Samhain's scythe in the body of a dog in Celtic Britain, carved into a gargoyle decoration in Notre Dame, last in line of the mummies in Guanajuato. Finally, Moundshroud binds them to a pact to save their friend: they must each give up a year from the end of their lives to restore him to health. Returning to the House in Green Town, Moundshroud underlines the moral of their lesson, then disappears at the chime of midnight. When they return home the boys discover Pipkin has recovered from an emergency appendectomy, and they trundle excitedly home as "the wind seized a thousand dark leaves and blew them away up over the sky and down over the earth toward the sun that would surely rise" (*HT*, 181).

The Halloween Tree is a quest story overtly designed to dramatize mythological history and to advance a theory asserting the fundamental importance of Halloween, horror stories, and fantasy in general. The boys themselves, caught up in the pageantry of the Mexican festival, draw part of the moral. Though Green Town still celebrates Halloween much of its meaning and spirit have been lost, and the loss is profound: "Up in Illinois, we've forgotten what it's all about. I mean the dead, up in our town, tonight, heck, they're forgotten. . . . Boy, that's lonely. That's really sad. But here—why, shucks. It's both happy and sad. It's all fireworks and skeleton toys down here" (*HT*, 147).

Through visceral experience of the meanings of the symbols and rituals from which their costumes originated, through direct exposure to the cultural contexts that created them, the boys now know that symbols of death and horror stories actually help humanize our relationship with the unknown. More appalling than any of the grisly and haunting images they encounter is the spiritual poverty of simply denying Death's presence. Not actually death itself but a symbol to represent strategies for emotionally coping with death, Moundshroud inspires both awe and affection. Representing the power of mythology in the figure of a teacher, he helps them face and penetrate the overwhelming mysteries of that "unknown country" from whose bourne no real traveler returns, but from which harrowed mythic travelers return in mythologies throughout history.

Certain of Moundshroud's lessons are also dramatized in Bradbury's science fiction. Implicit in Moundshroud's tutelage is a defense of "fantasy," no matter how grisly and shocking, against the tyranny of "realism," especially the insidious tyranny of reductionist realism posing as medical and psychological prescriptions for young minds. This defense of fantasy, especially of horror fantasy, is translated into science-fiction terms in *Fahrenheit 451* and several of the Martian stories. But Bradbury's ideas on the subject are expressed most directly, perhaps, in a *Playboy* essay entitled "Death Warmed Over" (1968), which might serve as a gloss of the basic argument of *The Halloween Tree.* "We have fallen into the hands of the scientists, the reality people, the data collectors," Bradbury laments, as he does battle with "the new scientific intellectual puritans [who] will deliver us from evil."[11]

Bradbury proposes two major arguments to support his defense of our symbols of evil, both dramatized in *The Halloween Tree.* One argument is aesthetic: these symbols are intrinsically powerful; they move our souls to awe and wonder. But the other derives from "practical hair-ball psychology"—for knowledge of death is a loathesome hairball in all our throats, and only through imaginative encounters with it do we digest what we can and purge ourselves of the rest. The mythical, fantastical tradition of horror inoculates us to endure contact with the reality and survive emotionally intact. "To fantasize is to remain sane," he maintains, contrasting the wondrous horror and release provided by stories of Dracula and the Wolf Man with the unrelieved horror of such modern realist films as *Our Man Flint,* where we see toilet paper pile up around the feet of the dying victim, where there is no imaginative release from the tyranny of gruesome reportage. "Instead of imagination, we are treated to fact, to pure raw data, which cannot be digested." Ultimately, Bradbury's defense of fantasy is an undoctrinal defense of the role of mythologies and religions in general: "Our religions, our tribal as well as personal myths, tried to find symbols then for the vacuum, the void. . . . We had to know. We had to lie, and accept the lie of labels and names, even while we knew we lied. . . . Thus we gave gifts of names to ward off the night."[12]

Thus, symbolic literature, the cultural equivalent of dreams in the individual psyche, inoculates us against horror, purges us of despair. But "Death Warmed Over" closes with a more visionary peroration about the power of "dreams," dramatized in another tradition, that of science fiction, which depicts mankind's metamorphosis in the new frontiers of space. Imagining a more psychically integrated culture of the future, Bradbury writes of dreams as prophetic icons that can lure us finally from the old "Garden" of earth to new pastures: "Then we shall call the ghosts home and the dead will return to teach us about death. . . . So cycle in cycle, fact circling dream and dream circling fact, Man, not the one thing but many, will continue his journey out of the Garden, on his way to becoming a thing he cannot now name, nor guess, but wish upon."[13] Curiously enough, preserving contact with our mythic past, our Ape Man dreams of Fire-Gods and Night-Demons, helps prepare us for our larger exodus into the void. Out of the boys' immersion in the "unknown country" of Death and the Past comes the hint of a new, as-yet-unexplored country beyond:

Q. Mr. Moundshroud, will we EVER stop being afraid of night and death?
And the thought returned:
When you reach the stars, boys, yes, and live there forever, all the fears will go, and Death himself will die. (HT, 178–79)

The old myths extrapolate from two basic equations: Light equals Life, and Darkness equals Death. But here and elsewhere Bradbury formulates the equation he sees implicit in the new myths of science fiction: Space equals Immortality. Like all messages from dreams and oracles, like all mythical statements, the literal meaning of this equation is not yet clear. Only a great new quest will reveal it. But to prepare ourselves, Bradbury maintains, we must embrace the old darkness, so that we finally can learn to leave it behind forever. The journey into the space wilderness, as he imagines it, is fearful and fraught with irony, but it is also our spiritual destiny. When we know intimately the landscape of October country, we may be ready at last to follow our new dreams to Mars.

Chapter Five

Entering the Space Frontier: Quests Mundane, Profane, and Divine

Bradbury's space-colonization fiction integrates two major myth systems to express the significance of mankind entering unearthly new environments: the biblical myths of the Garden and the Promised Land, and the American myth of the frontier. In fusing these myth systems Bradbury participates in an American literary tradition extending from contemporary science fiction back to initial responses to the New World of America. Since the first ambivalent Puritan accounts of their errand into the wilderness, American writing about frontier experience has evoked, explicitly or implicitly, these biblical analogies. And, given the strength of this tradition of frontier writing, it was only natural for Bradbury and other American science-fiction writers to dramatize the romance of space travel in terms of this central culture myth. Thus, American visions of the future often portray the frontier spirit revitalized by new challenges, in the fiction of scientifically oriented writers such as Robert Heinlein and Isaac Asimov as well as in Bradbury's science-fiction fables.[1]

Paradoxically, Bradbury's treatment of the science-fiction wilderness theme struck his initial audience as original and unsettling precisely because it is so deeply traditional. Essentially, Bradbury incorporates the dominant science-fiction theme of wilderness conquest into a central mythopoeic tradition of American frontier literature, extending from ironic American Renaissance writers such as Hawthorne, Melville, and Thoreau into the present. Because of his flamboyantly metaphorical style, Bradbury's fiction makes overt the frontier analogies implicit in other magazine fiction of the forties and fifties, but he also restores the potentially theological overtones and ironies of the wilderness symbol. If the New World of Mars is imaginatively linked to earlier visions of America as a New World, both images of the "New World" can also evoke biblical images of the

Garden and the Promised Land. Bradbury's characteristic irony illustrates the ambiguous implications of mankind's quest into these new
"New Worlds."

Overtly integrating the prevailing science-fiction myth with this
central tradition of mythopoeic American writing—a tradition at once
visionary and highly ironic—Bradbury's space-colonization fiction
dramatizes both the spiritual and the tragic dimensions of the theme,
placing the drama of the survival quest within the larger context of
a struggle to fulfill essentially religious aspirations. Fundamentally,
Bradbury utilizes the ironic potential in the biblical origins of the
frontier myth to warn about the tragic potential of our frontier heritage, as well as to evoke from it a stirring appeal to fulfill a manifest
destiny among the stars. Though Bradbury has expressed this underlying mythos in nonfiction writing throughout his career,[2] the first
critic to articulate the full range of his meaning was Willis McNelly,
who in 1969 perceived the central importance of the analogy between
the myth of wilderness conquest and the myth of space colonization,
and who also emphasized the spiritual dimension of Bradbury's treatment of the theme:

> For Bradbury, the final, inexhaustible wilderness is the wilderness of
> space. In that wilderness, man will find himself, renew himself, and there,
> as atoms of God, he will live forever. Ultimately, then, the conquest of space
> becomes a religious quest. . . . Ultimately the religious theme is the end
> product of Bradbury's vision of man, implicit in man's nature.[3]

Because of the ironic power of this wilderness fiction, because his
irony played against the prevailing traditions of magazine fiction in
the forties and fifties, Bradbury's space-colonization fiction has often
been misinterpreted. A visionary who believes the human race will
conquer death through spiritual rebirth in unearthly new frontiers, he
has been misconstrued as a pessimist who despairs of the future. And
indeed, his best fiction is filled with warnings, depicting the danger
of reenacting old tragedies through ignoring the dark side of history
and of human nature. If the science-fiction myth invites us back into
the Garden, we must reenter with knowledge gained from the old
story. For we will again encounter the serpent, in the form of the
"wilderness in man himself": "Man's other half, yes the hairy mammoth, the sabre-tooth, the blind spider fiddling in the venomous
dark, dreaming mushroom-cloud dreams."[4]

Bradbury's ambivalent wilderness imagery, evoking dreams of Paradise regained as well as of the Great Loneliness, is mirrored in his portrayal of human nature itself, which can be both the sensory consciousness of God and the spirit of the "dark brute"[5] within, wreaking destruction with increasingly lethal machines. Though his visions of our future in space are charged with irony, their ambiguous implications are finally resolved through the theme of metamorphosis. For ultimately Bradbury's space-colonization fiction suggests that we will learn from our past and meet the challenges of the new frontier. Just as settlers from the Old World painfully—with tragic consequences for the natives—formed a new civilization in America, so too the struggle to make this "final, inexhaustible wilderness" home will ultimately transform earthbound man into a being at home in its celestial dwelling places.

The Lure of the Space Frontier

Bradbury's reactions to a scene in John Steinbeck's *The Red Pony* illustrate the continuity between myths of the Old West and those about the space frontier (which Bradbury helped shape). In one of Steinbeck's most moving scenes in "The Leader of the People," last story in the cycle, an old man, once a wagon-train leader, sadly explains to his grandson Jody that the spirit of "westering" that impelled him and his people across the continent has died out. There on the California coast, where the grandfather's westward quest was halted by the sea, the boy feels the sadness of the old man's vision as he reminisces about a journey "as big as God." At night Jody dreams of the heroic past, so unlike the seemingly mundane present in which he lives. Apparently unnoticed by his grandfather, however, the boy suggests that perhaps, somehow, there might be challenges as great in his own lifetime.

Steinbeck's stance in *The Red Pony* is that of the modern western, focusing on the bittersweet memories of the grandfather, who has lived beyond his time to see the westward quest trivialized and forgotten as he interminably attempts to express what made it all so grand. But Bradbury, highly moved by the scene, saw the unrealized dramatic possibilities in Jody and his ranchhand friend Billy Buck, visualizing a new kind of frontier story in which they might embody the spirit of "westering" just as the old wagon train leader did before them: "From now on there is no East and West, only up. Because the

West is the westering thing, which was written of in *The Red Pony*
by Steinbeck, of course, so beautifully—Billy Buck standing at the
shore of the Pacific with nowhere to go. Except when I read that
when I was young I said, 'Hey, Billy, I got news for you. We've got
a frontier and we're gonna take it!' A lot of things were influenced by
my encounter with Billy Buck and Steinbeck that year. He helped
shape my thinking in *The Martian Chronicles*."[6]

Indeed, transported into the not-too-distant future, Steinbeck's
yearning young boy, Jody, might well be the hero of "King of the
Grey Spaces," which Bradbury feels was his breakthrough story in science fiction, the story in which he first defined his distinctive approach to the subject of space. "When I made the turn from
becoming an imitative writer to becoming a truly creative writer . . .
I began to do stories about myself and about the kind of boy I would
be if I lived in the future. I wrote stories like 'King of the Grey
Spaces,' which is no more than the story of a group of boys who want
to be astronauts."[7] A quiet drama about adolescent boys of the future
dreaming of going to the stars, the story's chief effect is to communicate the lure of the space frontier.[8]

Though the story captures through a boy's perspective the thrill of
entering the space frontier, it also emphasizes the personal sacrifice
such pioneering requires. When he prepares for the frontier, the hero
must relinquish his role on earth, his boyhood. The boys and their
"gang" spend their free time hanging around the rocket base, con-
versing in space age lingo, and watching rocket launches. They all
dream of being selected for astronaut training school, which selec-
tively enlists only the brightest and most fit. When the narrator is
selected his mother tells him she will adopt his best friend Ralph to
take his place, news which delights the hero yet also dramatizes the
poignant underside of his success, that by fulfilling his dream of space
he gives up the comfort and security of his earthbound life. This effect is foreshadowed by the attitude of his teacher who, knowing he
will be one of the "chosen," watches him taking an examination with
"envy and admiration and pity all in one," expressing the ambiguous
implications of the honor.

But if there is some sadness in the hero's success, the story nevertheless affirms that the dream he pursues is ennobling and enthrall-
ing. Though his mother is sad to lose him to the Board, she also
speaks to him of his dead father, a chemist, who worked in an underground laboratory where "he never saw the stars." Thus, by pursuing

the quest into space the hero not only fulfills his father's deepest dreams, he also sacrifices his personal life for all humanity to fulfill the spiritual potential of the species. The underlying analogy that informs the story is religious, as the boy's intense last talk with his mother makes clear: "We held to each other and whispered and talked and she said many things, how good this was going to be for us, but especially for me, how fine, what an honor it was, like the old days when men fasted and took vows and joined churches and stopped up their tongues and were silent and prayed to be worthy and to live well as monks and priests of many churches in far places. . . . This was a greater priesthood, in a way, she said . . . and I was to be some small part of it. . . . I would belong to all the worlds" (*RR,* 11).

"The Rocket Man" dramatizes the lure of the space frontier more painfully from a boy's perspective. The key roles in the earlier family drama are reversed: now the astronaut hero is the father; the point-of-view character, again, is a sensitive boy; and the mother, rather than a spokesman for the values of the new frontier, is cast in the more traditional role of helplessly opposing her husband's wanderlust, a role that the boy, with some reluctance, helps her play. Suspended in the middle of his parents' tragic marriage, the boy feels the emotional claims of both—of his mother and his father, of the home and of far places, of earth and of space. Like his mother, he longs for his father to remain home, and he fears for his father's life. But he also shares his father's overwhelming attraction to the mysteries of space; he is receptive to an enchanted aura about objects which have traveled to distant worlds: "And from the opened case spilled his black uniform, like a black nebula, stars glittering here or there, distantly, in the material. I kneaded the dark stuff in my warm hands; I smelled the planet Mars, an iron smell, and the planet Venus, a green ivy smell, and the planet Mercury, a scene of sulphur and fire, and I could smell the milky moon and the hardness of the stars."[9]

Because his attraction to the space frontier is irreconcilable with his life as an earthbound family man, the rocket man's powerful loves are a source of tragedy. Like many frontier heroes before him, he is caught between two worlds, unable to reconcile their opposing claims. "Don't ever be a rocket man," he warns his son, suspecting the boy's passion for space. "Because when you're out there you want to be here, and when you're here you want to be out there" (*IM,* 71). Trying to maintain a foothold in two opposing worlds, he is at home in neither.

Bradbury uses light imagery to express the emotional conflicts of "The Rocket Man." Within the terms of the story light is celestial and otherworldly, exercising an influence that the mother opposes with the absorbent warmth of the earth. A sympathetically portrayed though helplessly manipulative character, she cannot abide the sky. She especially fears starlight because she knows it casts a spell on her husband and son, luring them away from her. Because of the danger of her husband's job, she also perceives the night sky as a potential graveyard, so when he is gone she barricades herself behind heavy green shutters to shut out the starlight. But the news of his death establishes the final irony. He died in the sun itself, not among the stars, so she and the boy become burrowing night creatures: "The only days we ever went out to walk were the days when it was raining and there was no sun" (*IM*, 74). Initially battling the lure of starlight, the mother finally must retreat even from the light of day.

In "The Rocket Man" light represents the overwhelming power of the myth of space, a myth whose origins are ultimately religious but which fuses a religious "sense of wonder" with an evolutionary perspective on man's destiny. "The End of the Beginning," another quiet Green Town drama in which two older parents contemplate the significance of their astronaut son leaving earth, dramatizes this sweeping evolutionary perspective. As in many of these essentially philosophical space age tales, the protagonist's reverie about the meaning of space travel provides the story's climax. The theological overtones of the quest are evoked for him by words from the old spiritual, "A wheel in a wheel. Way in the middle of the air."[10] But he also integrates his sense that the trip is essentially a holy mission with an evolutionary interpretation of its meaning. The step into space ushers in an awesome new era, not merely from a human perspective but from a cosmic perspective as well, a perspective from which all previous human history appears as merely the final stage of life's bondage to earth. Indeed, when the father thinks of manifest destiny here he identifies mankind struggling to enter space with the first seaborne life to grope onto land:

All I know is its really the end of the beginning. The Stone Age, Bronze Age, Iron Age: from now on we'll lump all those together under one big name for when we walked on Earth and heard the birds at morning and cried with envy. Maybe we'll call it the Earth Age, or maybe the Age of Gravity. Millions of years we fought gravity. When we were amoebas and fish we struggled to get out of the sea without gravity crushing us. Once safe on the shore we fought to stand upright without breaking our new invention, the spine. . . . A billion years Gravity kept us home, mocked us with wind and clouds, cabbage moths and locusts. That's what's so god-awful big about tonight . . . it's the end of old man Gravity and the age we'll remember him by, once and for all. (*MM*, 23)

The story ends by counterpoising two images—the son's rocket lights a new spot in the sky, while the father philosophically mows his lawn, caught up in the magical whirr of rotating blades and falling grass as he relishes the moment, feeling like "all mankind bathing at last in the fresh water of the fountain of youth" (*MM*, 26). As this final New World image suggests, man enters the space frontier to be reborn, ultimately to be transformed by his new environment.

If Bradbury identifies man entering space with life moving from sea to land, he also dramatizes this transition through comparison to specifically American frontier experience, frequently evoking an analogy which is made manifest in an early story entitled "The Wilderness," a story that is essentially a poetic reverie about the analogy itself.[11] The plot is so simple it merely provides a vehicle with which to contemplate this central comparison between the Old West and space: a woman on Earth waits for her lover's call from outer space and tells him she has decided to homestead with him in his new home. Most of the story consists of the woman's thoughts before and after the call, stream-of-consciousness reflections that associate the challenges posed by the new frontier with heroic myths about the frontier past.

The story's central theme is manifest in the protagonist's contemplation of the setting. The phone call takes place at a rocket base in Independence, Missouri, 2003, which establishes the initial analogy to the wagon-train era of American development. "Long, long ago, 1849" the setting was oddly similar, filled with apprehensive but hopeful settlers waiting to depart with "their wagons, their indiscriminate destinies, and their dreams" (*GA*, 23). Later, she generalizes this frontier metaphor to encompass all of American history, from the initial discovery of the New World to her own destiny, emphasizing at the same time the continuity of the traditional woman's role in this mythology (a role that a new generation of writers has altered significantly)—reluctantly following her man as he pursues his dreams into the wilderness: " '1492? 1612?' Lenora sighed and the

wind in the trees sighed with her, moving away. 'It's always Colum-
bus Day or Plymouth Rock Day, and I'll be damned if I know what
one woman can do about it' " (GA, 29). And her final reflections as
she falls asleep generalize the American frontier experience to an essentially cosmic perspective: "On the rim of the precipice, on the
edge of the cliff of stars. In their time the smell of the buffalo, and
in our time the smell of the Rocket," she reflects. "This was as it had
been and would forever continue to be" (GA, 31).

A poetic revery about the relationship between our frontier heritage
and our space age future, "The Wilderness" anticipates a more book-
ish kind of story Bradbury developed in later years, in which he transports the spirits of his favorite authors out into the space frontier to
witness the wonders of the new wilderness and to articulate its significance. Thus, the spirit of George Bernard Shaw speaks through a
robot on board a rocket ship in "G.B.S., Mark V," and in "Forever
and the Earth"[12] a time machine transports Thomas Wolfe from his
deathbed to the future, where he composes an epic account of man's
entry into space. Because their protagonists so dramatically link the
future to the past, such stories emphasize both the thrill of entering
the unknown and the continuity of human experience.

"The Golden Apples of the Sun" develops the wilderness quest motif more actively. The kind of story that throughout Bradbury's career
has generated debate about where to separate science fiction from fantasy, "The Golden Apples of the Sun" combines a dense fabric of
mythological allusions with fanciful technology. A rocket descends to
the sun's surface to retrieve a "cup" (in a mechanical scoop) of the
sun's plasma, both for scientific study and simply to meet the challenge of entering the space frontier's living heart. To survive in this
environment the rocket is equipped with giant refrigeration units
which encase it in ice, an idea that appears to originate in boyhood
memories of watching icicles melt in spring sun (GA, 166). When
the auxiliary pump of the refrigeration unit breaks down the captain
and the crew, like frantic plumbers, fix the unit by hand in time to
ward off disaster.

But if the story's technology is essentially whimsical, it is rich in
mythology and literary allusions. The rocket itself has not one but
three mythological names—Capa de Oro, Prometheus, and Icarus—a device through which Bradbury identifies the quest into space with heroic myths of the past, as he also does in the tripartite name titling
a similarly conceived story, "Icarus Montgolfier Wright." Indeed, the

story is a bit self-conscious about its mythological and literary origins, opening with the captain explicating to his crew the numerous literary allusions invoked by their quest—from the reference to Yeats in the story's title, to Shakespeare's "Fear no more the heat of the day," to titles of twentieth-century novels that seem to echo the theme.

The mythological center of the story is made manifest in the captain's reflections as they complete their mission: the sun's plasma is "the flesh of God, the blood of the universe" (*GA*, 168). Like their mythological ancestors, though they now possess dazzling new technologies, they enter divine realms to possess new knowledge for their tribe. As in much of Bradbury's space-frontier fiction, man's quest for excitement and knowledge serves purposes articulated only by the inspired talkers who populate his tales. The lure of the frontier in his fiction is—to adopt the words of Steinbeck's wagon-train leader—"as big as God," inspiring a "westering" impulse which, like the American frontier experience itself, brings out the best and the worst in human nature.

"The Gardens of Space": Ironies, Visions, and Transformations

In 1965 Bradbury published a credo in *Playboy* (where it was complemented by an off-color cartoon). Articulating the mythos that informs his space-frontier fiction, "Remembrances of Things Future" begins by describing the future rushing upon us, its mysteries represented in symbols we must read with "prescience" to realize our destiny. Referring to "the rockets of earthmen writing fresh Columbian history upon tideless seas," Bradbury compares the New World of space with the New World of the Americas as they first appeared to European explorers—a comparison that informs much of his fiction, especially *The Martian Chronicles*. Only by utilizing sufficient vision, he argues, can we realize our unprecedented opportunity to fulfill the goals of "three searches": the "search for national purpose," the "search for peace," and the "search for a new image of God."[13]

As the range of motivations he alludes to suggests, Bradbury sees the "westering" impulse as a combination of various, sometimes conflicting motives, ranging from tribalism and materialism to an urge inherent in life to fulfill a spiritual destiny. Seeking larger profits, we wander into fresh pastures. And if the emphasis on the word "search"

suggests we are embarked on an epic quest, the emphasis on the
"search for a new image of God" emphasizes the continuity between
this fabulous future and fables of the past. Ultimately, the "westering" spirit that will take us to the stars utilizes our most advanced
technologies to pursue our most ancient dreams. For we enter the new
frontier seeking "wonders that will bloom for us in the gardens of
space." Ironically, by leaving the world of our birth, we seek to recover Eden, where man will be "back at the center of the universe,
where he once began, and from which he fell away at the beginning
of knowledge, and to which he must return."[14]

Though his essays unequivocally celebrate our entrance into the
gardens of space, Bradbury's fiction presents more disturbing and
complex images of the frontier process. Just as the biblical Garden is
a complex image representing the bliss of the unfallen, the ambivalent attractions of knowledge, and the origin of evil, so Bradbury's
fictional gardens are both alluring and destructive. Space itself has
ambivalent associations, for as it opens up new vistas of wonder and
beauty it also separates man from his roots. Thus, space appears both
as a natural cathedral of God and as a void where men's souls self-
destruct.

The unearthly environment of space brings out both the best and
the worst in the space pioneers who enter it, as is evident in "Kaleidoscope," in which the survivors of a rocket's collision with a meteor
are "thrown into space like a dozen wriggling silverfish" (*IM*, 19) to
die slowly as their life support systems wear down. Falling through
the void "as pebbles fall down wells" (*IM*, 20), they remain in radio
contact. In part, the story is a character study, revealing how different personality types cope with the knowledge of imminent death:
one goes mad; La Spere, the most contented in life, goes to his death
with spirited good will; Applegate and Hollis, after a vicious ex-
change, finally reconcile their differences, realizing that their mean-
ness in the end only reflects their frustrations in life; and Stone, filled
with wonder, drifts into an asteroid cloud, evoking the story's central
poetic aside, which captures both the beauty and the terror of space:

There were only the great diamonds and sapphires and emerald mists and
velvet inks of space, with God's voice mingling among the crystal fires.
There was a kind of wonder . . . in the thought of Stone going off in the
meteor swarm, out past Mars for years and coming in toward Earth every
five years, passing in and out of the planet's ken for the next million centu-

ries. Stone and the Myrmidone cluster eternal and unending, shifting and shaping like the kaleidoscope colors when you were a child and held the long tube to the sun and gave it a twirl. *(IM, 26)*

The story's title, "Kaleidoscope," expresses both this central image and another underlying theme of Bradbury's space-frontier stories, the interdependent relationship between inner and outer states, between the pioneer and his environment. Just as to some extent the beauty of a kaleidoscope is in the eye of the beholder, which finds form in random patterns, so attitudes toward the space frontier shape basic perceptions. One man's garden of delight is another's desert of desolation (a theme mirroring an earlier American debate about whether the area west of the Mississippi was a new Garden or the Great American Desert). For if there is a divine presence in space in Bradbury's fiction, it is a presence paradoxically dependent upon its observer, since to Bradbury humanity in its divine aspect *is* God witnessing His creation, and "without us God would be dead another billion years or forever."[15]

Bradbury frequently portrays "God"—sometimes referred to as the "Life Force," a concept he adopted from George Bernard Shaw—as an interaction between an intrinsically "dead" universe and a spiritual potential embodied in man's consciousness. Thus, when the astronauts in "Kaleidoscope" lose radio contact their voices die out "like the echoes of the words of God spoken and vibrating in the starred deep" *(IM, 26)*. Interacting with the celestial environment, the crew fragments to reveal man in all his aspects, profane and divine. As they drift into oblivion they express madness, pettiness, and vengefulness, but ultimately they also express spiritual delight and a kind of innocent reverence as well. Hollis, reflecting philosophically on his wasted, fearful life, returns to his origins where he appears as a "falling star" to a small boy on Earth.

"No Particular Night or Morning" dramatizes the frightening and destructive aspects of space pioneering. The story's theme, expressed in the title, is that space travel and the frontier process itself can encourage and exacerbate escapism. Hitchcock, the central character, seeks to retreat in space from the frustrations of his life—ultimately, to retreat from reality itself. As the story opens he has already developed a psychotic logic for denying his past, visualizing his past experiences as those of corpses who no longer exist, who have nothing to do with his present self. "You're cutting yourself off that way," ob-

serves a fellow astronaut, defining a psychological strategy of with-
drawal which culminates when Hitchcock launches from the rocket
into space itself, where his own retreat from identity is mirrored in
the void. The story develops a common motif of frontier fiction, that
the frontier process attracts not only the boldest and most enterpris-
ing, but the most desperate and unstable as well. Hitchcock is not
drawn to the frontier to build anew, but precisely to lose his past and
ultimately his self: "Space, thought Clemens. The space that Hitchcock loved so well. Space, with nothing on top, nothing on the bot-
tom, a lot of empty nothings in between, and Hitchcock falling in
the middle of nothing, on his way to no particular night and no particular morning. . . . " (IM, 114).

The divine aspect of space, however, is described in "The Gift," a
short vignette in which customs requires a couple and their young
boy, launching into space on Christmas Eve, to leave their meager
Christmas decorations behind. The father waits until midnight to
take the disconsolate boy to a cabin with a panoramic view, where the
boy looks entranced "out into space and the deep night at the burning
and burning of ten billion billion white and lovely candles" while
passengers sing "the old, the familiar carols" (MM, 140). If "No Particular Night or Morning" dramatizes the psychic dislocation created
by the frontier experience, "The Gift" communicates Bradbury's basic
faith that we can adapt our central rituals and symbols to help make
space our home, that we can rediscover old meanings in new metaphors: "I think the metaphors the Space Age has given us can trans-
cend the old metaphors. And we take Christ along with us, we take
Moses along, we take all the Old and New Testament, but we find
new ways of speaking from the midst of our technologies."[16]

Though space itself evokes both ironic and paradisiacal imagery in
Bradbury's fiction, the phrase "gardens in space" refers even more obviously to the "new worlds" discovered there. Mars, his most fully-
realized and frequently utilized setting, highlights both the diverse
motives of the settlers and the ambivalent promise of a new Garden.
But Bradbury's treatment of Venus emphasizes a different source of
frontier tragedy—the effects of a truly inhumane environment, whose
relentless rain destroys even the most hardy frontier spirits outside the
protection of artificial, earthlike havens. "The Long Rain" submerges
the reader in this Venusian atmosphere, accompanying survivors of a
rocket accident on a wilderness trek as they endure the "Chinese water

cure" exposure on Venus entails: "We're not made for water. You can't sleep, you can't breathe right, and you're crazy from being soggy" (*IM,* 54).

Bradbury's vivid imagery generates a nightmarish atmosphere. The men themselves have become "as white as mushrooms" (*IM,* 55); a jungle storm is "a monster supported upon a thousand electric blue legs" (*IM,* 56); a river "boiled out of the earth, suddenly, like a mortal wound" (*IM,* 61). Counterpoised against the hallucinatory horror of the jungle is the tantalizing dream of reaching a sun-dome, one of the artificial havens men have built to survive on this world. Indeed, the story's climax simply captures the ecstasy of dry air and sunlight after torturous immersion in the endless rain.

"All Summer in a Day" presents the Hell-world of Venus from children's point of view, evoking a more subtle and poignant sense of tragedy. In a frontier schoolroom on Venus children eagerly await the sun's appearance, an event approximately equivalent in frequency to an eclipse on Earth. Bradbury's description of the children identifies them with the riotous vegetation of the planet: "The children pressed to each other like so many roses, so many weeds, intermixed, peering out for a look at the hidden sun" (*MM,* 131). Starved for sunshine and open space, though they don't realize it, they romp in wild-eyed ecstasy in the sunlight, seeing clearly for the first time a landscape they cannot even recognize as alien to what they need: "It was the color of rubber and ash, this jungle, from the many years without sun. It was the color of stones and white cheeses and ink, and it was the color of the moon" (*MM,* 135).

But etched in against the general tragedy implicit in the children's short-lived ecstasy in the sun is the haunting figure of Margot, whose simple poem sketches her personal tragedy: "I think the sun is a flower / That blooms for just one hour" (*MM,* 132). A frail, sickly immigrant from Earth, she endures the hate of the other children because she remembers days of sunlight. Until the Venusian rains return, the children forget that they maliciously placed her in the closet when the great event began. When they return to the closet there is no sound inside. A haunting fable about the destructive side of human nature, "All Summer in a Day" reveals the snake from the Garden in the hearts of deprived children.

Science-fiction versions of the serpent appear in more obvious forms in other stories. In "The One Who Waits" *(LAM),* for instance, de-

structiveness is embodied (actually, disembodied) in the malevolent
consciousness of an alien, a psychic entity living in a Martian "Soul
Well" which possesses the bodies of a group of human visitors, destroys them one by one, then waits for new victims. "The City" presents another version of evil working in unexpected places. A rocket
crew exploring an abandoned city on a relatively unknown planet becomes an instrument for the city's revenge. Thousands of years earlier
the planet's inhabitants, betrayed and defeated in war, programmed
the city to redress the injury. With a bit of surgical alteration and
psychic programming, performed by the city's underground machinery, the crew is returned to earth carrying "golden bombs of
disease culture" (IM, 168) with which to infect the home planet, after
which the city, animated through the centuries exclusively by this
high-tech curse, enjoys "the luxury of dying" (IM, 169). "The Lost
City of Mars"[17] presents a more ambiguous version of this theme, in
which the live city is programmed to fulfill fantasies, rather than to
exact revenge. As does the carnival in Something Wicked This Way
Comes, the story's setting reveals the inner qualities of the characters
exposed to it, strengthening some and taking possession of others.

Many of Bradbury's space-colonization stories explore the ironic
possibilities in the biblical and frontier analogies to the "gardens in
space." But even in the tragic and ironic stories irony derives from
the contrast between grim realities and the ideal images Bradbury's
characters pursue. And in some stories the spiritual aspects of
the quest into space are overt rather than implied. "The Man"
treats the spiritual theme ironically, highlighting a paradox implicit
in the frontier quest—that it can easily become a frantic and self-de-
feating pursuit of "happiness," substituting possession of external
things for development of internal qualities. A somewhat comic version of Melville's Ahab, Captain Hart, initially a wheeling and dealing trader obsessed with defeating his competition, lights out in
breakneck pursuit of the Saviour, "the man," when he hastily concludes he just missed his latest visitation. His crew-member Martin,
the story's Ishmael-figure, visualizes the captain careening throughout
the galaxy, doomed to just miss the next coming at every landing.
As the captain departs, Martin and the local mayor return to the local
village where He has been waiting, of course, all along. Like Ahab,
Captain Hart does have moments of self-reflection, during which he
almost slows down long enough to perceive the disparity between his

obsessive mission and his true goals. His reflections become an ironic statement about the contradictory images that lure men into space:

"Why do we do it, Martin? This space travel, I mean. Always on the go. Always searching. Our insides always tight, never any rest."
"Maybe we're looking for peace and quiet. Certainly there's none on earth," said Martin.
"No, there's not, is there?" Captain Hart was thoughtful. "Not since Darwin, eh? Not since everything went by the board, everything we used to believe in, eh? Divine power and all that. And so you think maybe that's why we're going out to the stars, eh Martin? Looking for lost souls, is that it? Try to get away from our evil planet to a good one?"
"Perhaps, sir. Certainly we're looking for something." (*IM*, 43)

Ironically, Captain Hart's decision to pursue "the Man" rather than his own profit only intensifies his obsessive superficiality. He seeks for his "lost soul" everywhere except within himself. If he ever truly encountered the Man he would request "a little—peace and quiet" (*IM*, 52). But since he pursues spiritual enlightenment with the same driven avariciousness with which he pursued trading contracts, he never notices the contradiction between his methods and his ends. Nevertheless, his tragi-comic destiny illustrates the essentially spiritual origins of man's "search" in space: even the most mundane profiteers participate, however foolishly and self-destructively, in the quest for spiritual fulfillment.

Most of Bradbury's spiritual quest-figures are more humble and self-aware than Captain Hart. In its purest form—which simply generates a different system of ironies—Bradbury represents this spiritual quest through Catholic priests, who enter space eagerly seeking spiritual challenges and visitations. One of the most delightful early Mars stories, "The Fire Balloons," reveals "the Man's" presence in a new form, that of the blue globes that hover in the Martian hills. Because of his somewhat suspect "flexibility," the church selects Father Peregrine, possessed of an adventurous frontier spirit eager to adapt traditional orthodoxy to new environments, to lead a group of missionaries to the wild and wooly settlements on Mars. Conceiving of their quest as a search for new forms of sin in a new environment, Father Peregrine cannot resist the greatest challenge posed by his mission—determining if the curious "fire balloons" are indeed sentient beings possessed of souls, and designing an appropriate strategy for "saving" them if they are. When he determines that the curious beings are sentient, he proceeds, in a most enlightened and unorthodox spirit of missionary dedication, to adapt the church doctrine to the native culture. In a speech that represents Bradbury's own views on how traditional symbols can be adapted to new contexts, he justifies altering the central symbols of his faith: "We deal with symbols here. Christ is no less Christ, you must admit, in being represented by a circle or a square. For centuries the cross has symbolized his love and agony. So this circle will be the Martian Christ. This is how we will bring Him to Mars" (*IM*, 85).

But if Father Peregrine seeks to bring Christ to Mars, he finds instead that Mars restores to humans the living spiritual presence represented in Christian symbols. Father Peregrine's experience ironically parallels relationships between Christian missionaries and Native American cultures. And, whether or not Bradbury was consciously utilizing the parallel, Peregrine's substitution of the circle for the cross nicely resolves an historical conflict between the hierarchical models of Christianity (dividing the "saved" from the "fallen," "spirit" from "matter," etc.) and the "sacred hoop" that structures Native American ritual and belief.[18] But just as too few Christian missionaries, perhaps, realized they were "bringing religion" to profoundly spiritual cultures, so even Father Peregrine's flexible alterations of tradition ironically miss the point, as he is the first to perceive. For when the "old ones" finally come to his new ceremony and reveal their true nature he realizes his missionary impulse in this context is not merely inappropriate but fundamentally blasphemous. The old ones do not need new symbols to represent Christ since they, in fact, *are* Him, as even the very orthodox and rather dense Father Stone comes to recognize: "Father Peregrine, that globe there—. . . . It *is* Him, after all" (*IM*, 90). Having embarked on an adventurous mission to save souls, Father Peregrine returns to the frontier outpost strengthened in his true mission, knowing he has had a personal visitation from the spirit of Christ to assist in helping fallen humanity.

Other of Bradbury's overtly theological stories also dramatize conflicts inherent in adapting traditional symbols to the radically new contexts of the Space Age. "The Messiah" *(LAM)* presents another fervent Martian missionary whose dream of seeing "the Man" is satisfied more ambiguously. A telepathic Martian, trapped by the power of the missionary's fantasy, appears to him in his Easter devotion as the crucified Christ. Finally realizing he is fulfilling his spiritual quest by victimizing another sentient being, the priest ultimately releases the Martian after extracting a promise that he will represent Christ to him every year at Easter. Though the priest possesses admirable spiritual intensity, his "pact" parallels the ironic theme of *The Martian Chronicles,* in which settlers impose their own fantasies on their new environment, often with destructive consequences.

In "The Machineries of Joy," technically a realist story, Father Vittorini outrages his Irish peers both with his flamboyant Italian personality and with his enthusiasm for speculating about the impact of rockets on their faith. Presenting them to their dismay with Pope Pius XII's statement that "man has to make the effort to put himself in a new orientation with God and his universe," Vittorini turns an ongoing battle into a full-scale war, which ultimately is resolved when the Irish priests grudgingly accept both his colorful style and the modern age: settling down in front of a hitherto suspect television to watch the latest rocket blast-off, they contemplate whether these things are indeed God's new "machineries of joy." Pastor Sheldon, the most flexible of the Irish brethren, states the story's moral, both for spiritual leaders and for all mankind: "Why don't we climb on that rocket, father, and learn from it?"[19]

All of Bradbury's space fiction dramatizes in some form the conflicts and possibilities created by adapting to new environments. In its purest form this adaptation process becomes metamorphosis. "Chrysalis" presents a literal version of this theme, in which a man overexposed to radiation is transformed physically through "delayed hereditary mutation" (*SS,* 12) into "the next evolutionary structure of man" (*SS,* 13), which is biologically equipped to subsist in space. First published in *Amazing Stories* in 1946, "Chrysalis" is one of the few collected early stories whose melodramatic exposition illustrates Bradbury's early pulp style; but despite the awkward execution, the story does present a striking image of the metamorphosis theme implicit in much of Bradbury's more sophisticated fiction. Enclosed inside a hard shell Smith's body, like larval forms of insects in the chrysalis stage, transforms utterly, emerging finally as a being physically similar to humans but fundamentally altered. After escaping from the hospital the new man walks out under the desert sky, finishes a last cigarette which he grinds out "precisely under one heel" (*SS,* 26), then gracefully soars off into his new home in space.

This metamorphosis theme is most often simply an extreme version of the adaptation process in new frontiers. In "Dark They Were, and

Golden-Eyed" Mr. Bittering, alone among the Martian settlers, observes with horror that the frontier process has somehow reversed. Rather than adapting their environment to suit themselves, as they initially had every intention of doing, the settlers slowly transform into "Martians." Though they begin by naming their surroundings with their own names imported from Earth (the story was originally entitled "The Naming of Names"), they slowly revert to the old Martian names. Bickering points out indignantly that the peaches no longer look like peaches, but on one else cares. They all tan dark, their eyes turn golden, and they migrate to the hills. Finally accepting the transformation that the rest of the settlement has accepted peacefully, Bickering lies in a Martian canal contemplating the metamorphosis process, in lines that echo the song "Full Fathom Five Thy Father Lies" in Shakespeare's *The Tempest*. Just as the underwater body changes to something "rich and strange" in the Shakespearean song, so the settlers are changed in the "river" of the Martian atmosphere:

> If I lie here long enough, he thought, the water will work and eat away my flesh until the bones show like coral. Just my skeleton left. And then the water can build on that skeleton—green things, deep water things, yellow things. Change. Change. Change. Slow deep silent change. . . .
> He saw the sky submerged above him, the sun made Martian by atmosphere and time and place.
> Up there, a big river, he thought, a Martian river, all of us lying deep in it, in our pebble houses, in our summer boulder houses, like crayfish hidden, and the water washing away our old bodies and lengthening the bones—. (*MM*, 103)

When new settlers come from Earth they find only natives in the hills and the abandoned frontier town. Perplexed, they begin industriously planning to transform the environment, assigning new names to their surroundings, noticing occasionally that their concentration is unaccountably distracted. . . . But as they begin work on the planet, the planet is already exercising its subtle influence on them. Though they are not aware of it, the exploitative frontier psychology that brought them there is being transformed by the idyllic atmosphere of the Garden into which they have wandered.

Implicit in all the individual tragedies and revelations in Bradbury's space-colonization stories is a central drama about the settlers' relationship to the New World, a powerful theme derived from the central frontier metaphors of American writing: in space and Mars, as in American frontier mythology, conquering new frontiers wreaks tragedy, yet ultimately shapes a distinctively new and hardy culture. If the biblical myths of Eden and the Promised Land are evoked in this drama, so too is the world-view of conquered tribal cultures here on Earth—the concept of the New World not just as property but as Mother Earth, a living presence which alternately suffers, destroys, and shapes those who come to colonize.

Bradbury's most literal treatment of this "live planet" theme, "Here There Be Tygers," presents a planet that is a seductress, a conscious Garden who envelops explorers in her pastoral embrace. As in many of these stories, two characters represent the extremes of the frontier mentality, while a wise father-figure captain attempts to reconcile their opposing points of view: Chatterton, the developer, eagerly explains how men have to control planets or be controlled by them, an attitude which the captain describes as a prescription for "rape or ruin" (*RR*, 97). Chatterton gives the sexual metaphor a new twist when he explains that the planet's essence, that which he must dominate, is male, the feminine beauty only an alluring surface: "All hard underneath, all male iron, copper, uranium, black sod. Don't let cosmetics fool you" (*RR*, 98). Ultimately, the planet destroys Chatterton (who is devoured by tigers) and the rest of the crew, aware that they are being seduced by a loving embrace, decide to complete their mission, then return to settle down. But as they leave the planet erupts in volcanic fury, the fury of a woman scorned, and they realize they left the Garden of their own choice, and can never return. Only Driscoll, Chatterton's opposite, remains, whistling happily as he wanders among the fine wine streams and luxurious forests, blissfully at peace, restored to the Garden by the direct simplicity of his nature.

Though Bradbury's space-colonization fiction dramatizes tragedy and irony, it nevertheless projects powerful images of recovered Eden as well, which express his fervent conviction that, however problematic the process, mankind will in the end have the imagination and grace to be reborn in flesh and spirit in the "inexhaustible wilderness" of space. With George Bernard Shaw he visualizes humanity as the Godhead realizing itself, through the very intensity of memory and desire that drives us into new frontiers. We go "beyond Eden" to discover and create new gardens. Bradbury's metaphorical theology places faith in a new model of divinity: "God. Man. Machine. A strange, but certainly not an unholy trinity." But at the end of the search, ironically, we return to our fondest myths of our origins: "Tossed out of Eden, we now go to replant our Garden on God's own lawn."[20]

Chapter Six
The Martian Chronicles

Bradbury's best-known and most powerful treatment of the space frontier theme is *The Martian Chronicles*, the book that first established his reputation, whose overall design evokes in a unique way the ambiguous poetry in his vision of the frontier process. In many respects Bradbury's finest single achievement, *The Martian Chronicles* lyrically dramatizes relationships between his most potent images: Green Town (actually Green Bluff in this book), an idealized image of an Edenic American past; and Mars, representing the ambivalent promise of Edenic New Worlds in the space age future. As Eric Rabkin points out in "To Fairyland by Rocket: Bradbury's *The Martian Chronicles*," Bradbury's new frontier is deeply identified with lyricism itself, with fairyland images that refract back the heart's desires and secret fears of the pioneers. Fundamentally, Bradbury's subject here is the ambiguous promise of the American Dream, and the central symbols of his science-fiction fable represent the central conflicts that structure American mythology—the conflict between East and West (now Earth and Space), between the Old World and the New, between a barren present and both the lost Eden of memory (Green Town) and the new Eden shimmering in the almost accessible future (Mars):

As is well known, much of American literature can be viewed as a single myth in which much of human experience is organized into two dichotomous sets. In the East are civilization, old age, intellect, youth, the head, and cities; while in the West are the frontier, innocence, youth, emotion, the heart, and wilderness. In American myth people from the Old World journey to the New World in the hope of rejuvenation and the regaining of innocence, trying to return to a time before the Fall, to become what R. W. B. Lewis has called "The American Adam." Life on the frontier or in the wilderness is supposed to be redemptive; Natty Bumppo is superior to the East Coast stay-at-homes. As we see in the transatlantic novels of Hawthorne and James, all Americans are morally superior to the Old World Europeans. Suckling at what Fitzgerald called the "fresh, green breast of the New World" is supposed to make one innocent again—young and strong and sensitive. The wilderness experience, like the later melting pot, is supposed to convert Europeans into true Americans. But of course the myth has in many ways proved hollow: financial independence often leads to barbarism and wage slavery; the westward-rolling tides of "Americans" have wiped out the indigenous "Native Americans"; moral uprightness and religious freedom often petrify into righteousness and religious exclusivity. Finally, racism has blighted the land, from the landing of the first slave ship in 1619 until and including the present. These are the conditions Bradbury would have his fairyland book change.[1]

Reading *The Martian Chronicles* in this context helps to answer criticisms that have been directed at the book's style, theme, and structure. Indeed, because it is the most extended expression of Bradbury's metaphorical, ironic style, much of the controversy about the quality of Bradbury's science fiction has centered on debate about this particular book. Thus, while *The Martian Chronicles* is usually recognized as the most eloquent of Bradbury's "poetic" science fiction, it also provides the primary evidence that his science fiction is scientifically inaccurate, fundamentally opposed to "progress," and inconsistent. But most of the controversy about the book's inaccurate science is simply irrelevant when it is read as a metaphorical comment on the American Dream, rather than as a literal portrait of space colonization. And the charge of pessimism oversimplifies the book's intent, which, like much science fiction, seeks to prevent disaster rather than to predict it: "*The Martian Chronicles* and *Fahrenheit 451* come from the same period in my life, when I was warning people. I was *preventing* futures."[2] As Rabkin suggests, even as it ironically dramatizes the danger of repeating old tragedies, Bradbury's parable also celebrates the essential values represented in the American Dream.

The charge that the book as a whole lacks unity, that "*The Martian Chronicles* do not make a whole greater than the sum of the parts,"[3] raises interesting questions both about the book's origins and about its overall design. Many of the stories were written before the book itself was conceived, and some of the stories portray varying, even somewhat contradictory, images of both Mars and the Martians. Thus, the book has been portrayed as an anthology of disconnected stories set on Mars, rather than as a unified work of art. But Bradbury's own reflections about the book's origins indicate that he discovered a distinctive pattern in his Martian fiction, which he had not been consciously creating. In 1949 he took Norman Corwin's advice and went to New York to meet with publishers and editors. When

asked by Walter Bradbury (no relation), a Doubleday editor, whether
he had a novel in the works, Bradbury initially replied that he didn't.
Yet after considering the possibility that there might be a pattern in
the Martian stories he'd already written, he suddenly visualized the
design of the book. He returned to his room and immediately put
together the outline of *The Martian Chronicles,* discovering in the process that for years he had been creating key episodes in a kind of book
he had envisioned years earlier, after reading Sherwood Anderson's
Winesburg, Ohio:

> I think Kuttner told me about *Winesburg, Ohio,* and I read it and started
> making notes and I said to myself, "God, I'd love to write a book like that
> some day about Mars." I even made some notes. I think I called my book
> *Marsport, Mars* . . . I lined up a whole lot of characters, the way he did.
> And then I put the stuff away and forgot all about it. And I wrote my vari-
> ous Martian stories over a period of the next four or five years. Then I went
> to New York on the Greyhound bus and my editor there said, "We don't
> publish books of stories. Don't you have a novel? What about all those Mar-
> tian stories? Wouldn't they fit together in a pattern?" And I said, "I'll be
> damned. Yes, they would." So I went back to the YMCA and sat up until
> two in the morning, did an outline, took it to him the next day, and got a
> contract on the book by the time I left town. So that was all due to *Wines-
> burg, Ohio.*[4]

Like *Winesburg, Ohio, The Martian Chronicles* is structured by a common setting and theme. As Bradbury observes, the stories themselves
are "thematically quite close" and "the tone is the same all the way
through."[5] Moreover, as several critics have illustrated in detail,[6] an
underlying analogy to American frontier experience clearly structures
the book into three major sections. As the title implies, *The Martian
Chronicles* weaves together a tapestry of short pieces and vignettes to
chronicle the overriding drama of the pioneers' relationship to the
New World, depicting the beginning, development, and conclusion
of the frontier process on Mars. And the book's structure clearly illustrates these three stages of the process. Though such a schematic table
of contents might have violated the book's lyrical atmosphere, Bradbury's outline might well have labeled as follows these major divisions
in the action:

> I. Invasion and Exploration: "Rocket Summer" through "—And the
>   Moon be Still as Bright," 1–72.

Thus, if *The Martian Chronicles* is not in the strict sense a novel, it is, nevertheless (like *Winesburg, Ohio*) a unified book with a theme, what Forrest Ingram has called a "short story cycle": an old tragedy is enacted in the new Eden of Mars, culminating nevertheless in an image suggesting that a more integrated new culture may emerge from the destruction of the frontier process.[7] But the primary effect of the book is ironic, for through most of the book Bradbury's lyrical style dramatizes the self-destructive psychology of American frontier heritage, which destroys what it most loves in the process of "civilizing" it. Rather than depicting wilderness conquest as a triumphant affirmation of manifest destiny, as did most frontier science fiction of that time, *The Martian Chronicles* explicitly echoes the elegiac themes of Western fiction. Spender, the most renegade of Bradbury's frontiersmen (most of whom are simply good American boys), delivers one of the clearest statements of this theme early in the novel. It is an elegy of anticipation, foreshadowing an inevitable future projected from an American heritage of cultural imperialism:

It wouldn't be right, the first night on Mars, to make a loud noise, to introduce a strange silly bright thing like a stove. It would be a kind of imported blasphemy. There'd be time for that later; time to throw condensed-milk cans in the proud Martian canals; time for copies of the *New York Times* to blow and caper and rustle across the lone gray Martian sea bottoms; time for banana peels and picnic papers in the fluted, delicate ruins of the old Martian valley towns. Plenty of time for that.[8]

The contemporary details link this passage imaginatively to *The Ugly American* as much as to American frontier experience, as do Spender's bitter childhood reminiscences about traveling to Mexico with his family: "I'll always remember the way my father acted—loud and big. And my mother didn't like the people because they were dark and didn't wash enough. And my sister wouldn't talk to most of them" (*MC*, 64). But within the larger context of the book American cultural chauvinism is only an irritating contemporary manifestation of the arrogance and exploitative materialism exhibited throughout our frontier history. In Bradbury's hands the planetary colonization theme is a vehicle for ironic commentary on the American character, and the pioneers of *The Martian Chronicles* fall into three categories: they are either offensive and insensitive dudes, naive American boys, or true frontiersmen capable of appreciating the planet's alien environment and native culture. Though the ugly American analogy is employed extensively it is subsidiary to the frontier analogy, which provides the controlling motifs for the book.

Spender himself, the renegade astronaut, is a science-fantasy version of the "white Indian," the American frontiersman gone native. He is quickly transformed from an American to a Martian hostile by the influence of the Martian environment. " 'I'm the last Martian,' said Spender . . . taking out a gun" (*MC*, 58). Thus Bradbury re-enacts in a new setting the most frightening prospect the New World posed to the original Puritan settlers—the possibility that they might be transformed to "savages" by their new wilderness home. And when Spender seeks an ally he falls back on the frontier analogy for persuasion, attempting to lure a crew member of Indian heritage to join his resistance.

"How would you feel if you were a Martian and people came to your land and started tearing it up?"

"I know exactly how I'd feel," said Cheroke. "I've got some Cherokee blood in me. My grandfather told me a lot of things about Oklahoma territory. If there's a Martian around I'm all for him." (*MC*, 59)

Indeed, this interchange between Spender and Cheroke makes manifest the system of analogies that informs much of *The Martian Chronicles*. Mars is the New World, the new West; the Martians the Indian nations subdued by the coming of the white man; the settlers from Earth the pioneers who came to transform the Indian lands into America.

None of these analogies, however, works as a simple one-to-one correspondence. The vignettes and stories in *The Martian Chronicles* vary widely in tone and theme and are not always entirely consistent with each other. Thus, though Mars usually appears as a pastel desert planet, rather like Arizona lined with ancient canals, it appears from at least one story ("The Green Morning") that it is a lush equivalent of the Ohio River valley, where the soil is black loam waiting for the plow. Though the planet is most fundamentally identified with the New World of America, it has strong associations with legendary fairylands as well.[9] This is particularly true in the opening stories, which create an intense, decadently langorous fin de siècle atmosphere that conveys as much of Celtic twilight as of New World promise. "Up and down green wine canals, boats as delicate as bronze flowers drifted. In the long and endless dwellings that curved like tranquil snakes across the hills, lovers lay idly whispering in cool night beds. The last children ran in torchlit alleys" (*MC*, 14). The Martians of these early stories have the impish malevolence of fairyland folk rather than the gracious dignity attributed to them after their extinction. Even the visitors from Earth are slack-jawed American boys out to see the sights as often as they are industrious pioneers.

Mars in *The Martian Chronicles* is both fantasy and history, both fairyland and the New World. (It is not at all the planet that scientific observations have described, which has created confusion ever since *The Martian Chronicles* was first published about whether it is "science" fiction at all.) The New World analogy is invoked most explicitly in the short vignettes portraying stages in emigration from Earth, though it is implicit throughout the book. A passage from "The Settlers" suggests much about the nature of Bradbury's Mars. The immigrants came to Mars because "they felt like Pilgrims or did not feel like Pilgrims," and their motivations are those traditionally associated both with the immigrants who came to America and with Americans who chose to move to the frontier. "There was a reason for each man. They were leaving bad wives or bad jobs or bad farms; they were coming to find something or leave something or get something. . . . They were coming with small dreams or large dreams or none at all" (*MC*, 72). As this passage suggests, the concept of the New World is deeply identified with "dreams." Though Bradbury's conception of Mars appears to be inconsistent, its very ambivalence is a source of imaginative power. As both New World and fairyland, Bradbury's Mars ultimately represents the tantalizing destructiveness of the American Dream.

In "Night-Meeting" an elderly gas station attendant describes Mars as a kaleidoscope (*MC*, 79). The metaphor is especially significant because the old man who develops it is one of a few characters—chief of whom is Spender, the renegade—who are capable of appreciating the special qualities of Mars. His philosophy is that of the genuine frontiersman, who identifies with the New World against the Old: "If you can't take Mars for what she is, you might as well go back to Earth. . . . Don't ask it to be nothing else but what it is" (*MC*, 79).

But the description of Mars as a kaleidoscope suggests more than the pleasures of an exhilarating new environment. It suggests also the planet's shifting identity, like a crazy mirror that reflects back in distorted and exaggerated forms images projected on it by the invading American culture.

One of the most potent images in *The Martian Chronicles* is the town of Green Bluff, Illinois, encountered by the Third Martian Expedition. It is one of Bradbury's representations of the vanished American Dream, the small American town lost to history that preserves extended families intact and values domestic feeling and rural tranquility. It is, especially, the dream of an American boy, sentimentalized in the style of a Norman Rockwell painting, filled with benign parental figures, cold lemonade, and green lawns—all of which possess a remarkable attraction in Bradbury's fiction. But Mars is not really the American Dream come true, of course. It merely reflects back the invaders' deepest longings, disguising a reality that is alien, "some other shape, a Martian shape" (*MC,* 46). By disguising Martian reality behind the illusions they project of the American Dream, the Martians lure the Americans from their spaceship and succeed in destroying them. But the story's final image is a haunting and enigmatic coda to the massacre. Though there is no practical benefit to be gained by maintaining the illusion once the invaders are dead, the Martians proceed to conduct a mass funeral in small-town American style with "faces melting now from a familiar face to something else" (*MC,* 48). This image of Martians maintaining the nostalgic fantasies of the American invaders even as they bury them strikes a particular note of sinister poignance that is characteristic of Bradbury's Martian fable. The planet is both lethal and oddly receptive. Like the American Dream, which is the more tantalizing because it is not clearly defined, Mars appears to fulfill almost inarticulate longings—but the lure of the dream is often fatal.

One of the functions of Mars in *The Martian Chronicles*—as kaleidoscope, crazy mirror, New World, and distant shore—is to define the contradictory fantasies imposed upon it by the invading American culture. The lure of the frontier is many things to many different kinds of settlers, and the colonization process is an interaction between pioneer ambitions and the alien reality of Mars, whose true nature remains ultimately mysterious. The first explorers are true frontiersmen, identified with the best qualities of America's frontier heritage, who value the New World for itself. They approach the new frontier with dignity and unarticulated reverence, representing the aspiration for a free, unhampered life that is the most admirable heritage of the American past. They brave loneliness—the most frightening of conditions in Bradbury's fiction, which makes it the final test of personal mettle—because they welcome the challenge of the new and strange, and are not dependent upon the artificial comforts and emotional supports provided by civilization:

> Mars was a distant shore, and the men spread upon it in waves. Each wave different, and each wave stronger. The first wave carried with it men accustomed to spaces and coldness and being alone, the coyote and cattlemen, with no fat on them, with faces the years had worn the flesh off, with eyes like nailheads, and hands like the material of old gloves, ready to touch anything. Mars could do nothing to them, for they were bred to plains and prairies as open as the Martian fields. They came and made things a little less empty, so that others would find courage to follow. (*MC*, 87)

This image of colonization as a series of waves, "each wave different, and each wave stronger," emphasizes the irony traditionally associated with the enterprise of frontiersmen. They go to the frontier to escape the constraints and indignities of life in civilization. But their very self-sufficiency and distaste for the culture left behind blaze the trail for settlers like Sam Parkhill, the hot dog vendor of "The Off-Season," who descend upon the New World like locusts to strip it for their own advantage. And behind the plunderers comes the final invasion by the official representatives of culture whom Bradbury refers to derisively as the "sophisticates."

> But after everything was pinned down and neat and in its place, when everything was safe and certain, when the towns were well enough fixed and loneliness was at a minimum, then the "sophisticates" came in from Earth. They came on parties and vacations, on little shopping trips for trinkets and photographs and "atmosphere" . . . they came with stars and badges and rules and regulations, bringing some of the red tape that had crawled across Earth like an alien weed. . . . They began to plan people's lives and libraries; they began to instruct and push about the very people who had come to Mars to get away from being instructed and ruled and pushed about. (*MC*, 103)

This final inundation with idle tourists and bureaucrats threatens the frontier spirit itself. "Usher II" identifies the frontier in this final stage of colonization with fantasy, freedom of the imagination, and

depicts the Martian frontiersman's macabre last-ditch resistance to
cultural regimentation imported from Earth. The frontier is finally a
province of the psyche, what is left of the dreams associated with the
New World. But the dreams are products of the invaders. Mars itself remains an
inscrutable and alien environment that colonization never truly transforms. The invaders from Earth appear as frantic insects, fervent to
re-establish their familiar environment in a strange new setting:

The rockets came like locusts, swarming and settling in blooms of rosy
smoke. And from the rockets ran men with hammers in their hands to beat
the strange world into a shape that was familiar to the eye, to bludgeon away
all the strangeness. . . . And when the carpenters had hurried on, the
women came in with flowerpots and chintz and pans and set up a kitchen
clamor to cover the silence that Mars made waiting outside the door and the
shaded window. (*MC*, 78)

The comparison to swarming insects suggests frantic avariciousness,
but it also suggests ultimate ineffectuality. The Earthmen leave in the
end, and the planet Mars returns to its primal emptiness, a graveyard
of imported hopes and dreams, containing the ruins of two extinct
cultures, Martian and American.

Like much Western fiction, *The Martian Chronicles* is ultimately
about the relationship of alien intruders to the land. Just as the Indian in American fiction is deeply identified with the American wilderness, so the ancient Martian culture in *The Martian Chronicles* is
identified with the alien reality of Mars. The vignette entitled "The
Naming of Names" describes the contrast between newly coined
American names for Martian places and the "old Martian names," and
the contrast parallels that between names given by white settlers in
America and those surviving from the Indian languages. "The old
Martian names were names of water and air and hills. They were the
names of snows that emptied south in stone canals to fill the empty
seas. And the names of sealed and buried sorcerers and towers and
obelisks" (*MC*, 102). The names given by the American settlers, by
contrast, are "the mechanical names and metal names from Earth"
(*MC*, 103). Names here are an index of cultural attitudes. They express differences in attitude that parallel the extended historical conflict between Indian tribes and encroaching white settlers about the
meaning of "ownership" when applied to the land.

To the Martians, as to the Indian tribes, the land is sacred and magical. Names pay tribute to the spirit of place. To the American invaders, however, land is property. This conflict is the source of the poignant humor of the misunderstanding depicted in "The Off-Season," where ghostly, whimsical Martians appear to Sam Parkhill to give him the "deed" to land that has become, from his hot dog vendor's point of view, worthless. American names reflect basically exploitative attitudes. They are either transported directly from America to disguise the alien reality of Mars, or they label places on the basis of the natural resources they provide, their potential for profit: "IRON TOWN, STEEL TOWN, ALUMINUM CITY, ELECTRIC VILLAGE, CORN TOWN, GRAIN VILLA, DETROIT II" (*MC*, 103). To the settlers Mars is "haunted" (*MC*, 56) by remnants of the ancient Martian culture and by the spirit of the planet itself, just as the American imagination is haunted by memories of decimated Indian cultures and by the images of the virgin land that has been transformed by colonization and industrialization. Thus, Bradbury's Martian fiction reactivates in a futuristic setting the ghosts that haunt the American past.

The Martian Chronicles concludes by foreshadowing a version of the myth of the American as Adam, the new man formed by the influence of the New World (a major motif of nineteenth-century American literature, discussed in R. W. B. Lewis's *The American Adam*). Only here the American myth is transposed into the future, so that the new man is the American as Martian. Thus, the novel's final image is of American children gazing at their reflections in the waters of a Martian canal, absorbing the fact that they themselves are the Martians of the future. They are irrevocably cut off from their origins in the Old World that has been consumed in its own corruption, "strangled itself with its own hands" (*MC*, 180). The drama of colonization in *The Martian Chronicles* begins with first contact and ends by depicting the American family as a nucleus out of which a new Martian culture can develop, a culture that combines the wisdom of the decadent old Martian civilization with the vigor of the American pioneering spirit. But the ending implies that to become truly Martian the American pioneers must become children of nature again, susceptible to the shaping influences of their New World, whose nature remains as mysterious at the close of the book as it is in the beginning.

Though *The Martian Chronicles* ends with a new beginning, most of the novel is preoccupied with the tantalizing deceptiveness of the

New World image to Americans drawn to it by the lure of the frontier. Bradbury's tales of Mars invoke two contradictory strands in the mythology that shapes conceptions of American history. In its final, ineffable image the book invokes the history of refugees from Europe who were transformed into a new people by their new environment. In its more ironic aspects the novel describes the process by which ruthless agents of "progress" destroyed a native culture, only to transform the rich promise of the New World into the machinery of a superficial and parochial culture. The ambivalence about the implications of American history that is reflected in American frontier mythology is a part of the emotional ambivalence of *The Martian Chronicles*. The colonization process is both imperialistic conquest and metamorphosis, both a ravaging of the land and spiritual union with it.

The New World archetype refers both to American history and to characteristically American aspirations, both to the past and to desires projected into the future. The historical frontier was the original land of promise on which American dreams were projected. In Bradbury's image of Mars the promise of the old frontier is fused with the deepest desires and hopes of immigrants from a future in which the promise of America itself has gone sour. This identification of Mars with the allure of the American Dream is expressed hauntingly in "The Martian," where a last Martian survivor is hounded to death by a horde of American settlers all pursuing the image of the person they cherish most—an especially evocative image in a novel whose primary theme is the frantic quest to make dreams come true in a world whose true wonder is apprehended by only a few. The Martian originally appears as "Tom," an elderly couple's barefoot boy returned to life, like the spirit of Tom Sawyer resurrected from a more innocent past. But the Martian, like Mars itself, becomes all things to all its pursuers:

All down the way the pursued and the pursuing, the dream and the dreamers, the quarry and the hounds. All down the way the sudden revealment, the flash of familiar eyes, the cry of an old, old name, the remembrance of other times, the crowd multiplying. Everyone leaping forward as, like an image reflected from ten thousand mirrors, ten thousand eyes, the running dream came and went, a different face to those ahead, those behind, those yet to be met, those unseen. (*MC*, 129)

This image of Americans pursuing the images they project on to Mars with avaricious desperation expresses much of the theme and emotional tone of *The Martian Chronicles*. It represents both the most appealing and the most destructive elements of the American character as Bradbury interprets it. There is the poignance of longing and aspiration, and the ruthlessness with which the quest is pursued—for wealth and power, for love, for an unreal innocence, for final possession of the dream. Mars in *The Martian Chronicles* evokes the sense of wonder evoked originally by the New World of America. But the human drama enacted against the backdrop of the planet's enigmatic presence reflects an ironic awareness of how that wonder has been dissipated. Because Bradbury's Mars is so thoroughly a product of fantasies imposed upon it, the planet itself never has a clearly defined identity. Settlers identify the New World so deeply with their dreams that Mars remains to the end a dreamland of American aspirations and anxieties. Yet though the physical environment of Mars changes from story to story the nature of the planet itself, with all the ambivalence and mystery that surrounds it, is the central subject of the book. The chronicles are unified by the planet's dreamlike aura, the special atmosphere blending magical promise and disorienting malevolence that envelops American invaders.

Yet if the first wave of colonists never truly know the new land, the conclusion suggests that ultimately the frontier process will form new "Martians" who can learn from and thus escape from the destructive patterns of the past, who can truly adapt to their new environment rather than merely impose old fantasies upon it. Since *The Martian Chronicles* dramatizes the relationship between ancient Edenic stories and the frontier values embodied in the American Dream, Bradbury's own reflections in 1980 on the ambivalent meanings of American frontier history also state the underlying message of his most famous early book of warning: "I believe in what we Americans have done to this country, with all the rape that went with it. I mean I don't approve of the rape, but it's there, there's nothing I can do about it. You try to correct the things that are worst about it, and you try to make recompense to the Indians for what was done to them. . . . But the mistake that was made during Spender's time will not be repeated. The literary event I described . . . won't happen again on other worlds. We've shown we can think about these things and plan and be practical and romantic at the same time. . . . You don't have to give in to the wilderness, and you don't have to kill it. You can work with it."[10]

Chapter Seven
Images of the Future: Technology and the Frankenstein Myth

Though Bradbury has written passionately of space exploration throughout his career, he has also produced a large body of science fiction focusing on technological and social issues. Because he associates space travel with the American frontier myth, his space-travel fiction, however ironic, tends ultimately to celebrate our destiny in the cosmos, which he identifies with immortality. His images of earthbound futures tend to be more unrelievedly grim. Partially because Bradbury's implicit mythology identifies earthbound futures with death, his science-fiction stories set on earth tend to be warnings, projecting futures in which unresolved contemporary problems have become monstrous in scope. Yet some of the later stories especially celebrate the potential benefits of technology and progress. The title of Marvin E. Mengeling's excellent essay, "The Machineries of Joy and Despair: Bradbury's Attitude toward Science and Technology,"[1] accurately describes the range of possibilities projected in these fictions, which metaphorically express Bradbury's deepest loves and fears.

Bradbury himself has never despaired that we are doomed to inherit his "machineries of despair," for he has always regarded such warnings as part of science fiction's healthy functions—to dramatize current problems with crazy mirrors, designed to help us avoid the potential dangers they reflect. Indeed, in *Fahrenheit 451* the most ominous threat of the future is our tendency fatuously to ignore problems. Thus, Bradbury's reputation as a "technophobe," blindly opposed to technology and progress, was never deserved, even during the period when he wrote his bleakest fiction. And his science fiction has changed in emphasis over the years, increasingly adopting a tone of celebration rather than of warning.

In a general sense, Bradbury's early shift in attitudes about the fruits of technology parallels the disillusionment of many in his generation. As an adolescent, he was an enthusiastic member of Technocracy, Inc., an organization devoted to the Wellsian faith that science and social engineering could create utopia. His disillusionment at discovering that Technocracy, Inc. was linked to fascism only anticipated the impact of the Second World War and the Bomb, experiences that gave the Frankenstein myth new meaning, whose impact inspired some of Bradbury's most powerful science-fiction imagery in the forties and fifties. Yet by the sixties he was becoming predominantly celebratory in tone, both about the impact of technology and about the future. As Gary K. Wolfe observes, Bradbury's relationship to the science-fiction community is especially ironic, since he adopted this celebratory style just when his earlier vein of irony and stylistic experimentation became fashionable:

> Bradbury built an enormous reputation virtually on style alone—and then, when the rest of the writers in the genre began to discover the uses of stylistic experimentation, turned ever more toward self-imitation and the recapitulation of earlier themes. When science fiction seemed almost exclusively a literature of technophiles, Bradbury became a lone symbol of the danger of technology, even to the point of refusing to drive an automobile or fly in an airplane. But when science fiction came increasingly to adopt an ambivalent attitude toward unchecked technological progress, Bradbury became an international spokesman for the virtues of space-flight and technological achievement.[2]

The final irony, perhaps, is that Bradbury's early ironic fiction seems to have made greater imaginative impact than his later celebrations. Though he has continued to express his enthusiasm for the future in numerous formats, most notably in his three volumes of poetry, his early "warning" fiction expressing his distaste for the most ominous aspects of mid-century American culture still is central to his literary reputation. His most sustained work in this vein, *Fahrenheit 451,* provides an earthbound nightmare alternative to the ironic space romance of *The Martian Chronicles.* If mankind does not fulfill its destiny in space, Bradbury's mythos suggests, the best we can hope for is to survive the coming apocalypse with some of our cultural heritage intact.

Though Bradbury's science fiction projects both positive and negative images of the future, his ironic, nightmarish stories from the forties and fifties have had the greatest impact. J. B. Priestley observed in 1953 that Bradbury, representing the best of science fiction by being "genuinely imaginative and having some literary merit," was concerned "not with gadgets but with men's feelings." But the feelings he found most powerfully expressed were overwhelmingly fearful, evoking images of new versions of hell:

> They [Bradbury's "dreams"] are very sinister. When they impinge themselves on us they fill us with a sense of desolation and horror. Compared with these glimpses of the future, most of the old hells seem companionable and cozy. This is a world, we feel, to get out of as soon as we can. An excellent covering title for these tales of tomorrow would be *Better Dead*. The price our descendants pay for our present idiocies is terrible. After us—not the deluge, but the universal nightmare.[3]

The description does not apply to the full range of Bradbury's science fiction, and much of this desolate imagery is more satirical than genuinely fearful in tone. But Priestley's description expresses the impact on his audience of Bradbury's darkest glimpses of possible futures. Some of the shock of his futuristic nightmares comes from his skill at defamiliarizing the commonplace, so that the future shows us familiar things transposed into sinister new forms. As Priestley observes, the future becomes a haunting extension of the present: "One of Mr. Bradbury's favorite devices, not without its symbolism, is the sudden transformation of the familiar and friendly into something appalling and menacing, so that just when you think all is well you are trapped."[4] But Bradbury also reverses this technique, domesticizing what at first seems alien and threatening. And many of his most nightmarish themes have evoked positive visions as well, so that his celebratory stories often provide an optimistic counterpoint to his warning fictions.

Bradbury best explains the origins of many of his warning stories in an essay entitled "The Joy of Writing," in which he proclaims that strong writing comes from strong passions, whether they be love or hate, awe or anger. Drawing upon his own experience, he recommends to aspiring writers that they examine their strongest emotional reactions, even those that might appear as petty prejudice, to mine material for fiction: "How long has it been since you wrote a story where your real love or real hatred somehow got onto the paper? When was the last time you dared release a cherished prejudice so it slammed the page like a lightning bolt?"[5] To illustrate how this applies to his own writing, he uses two stories as illustrations: he wrote "Sun and Shadow," a realist story in which an elderly Puerto Rican man ruins a photographer's day by dropping his drawers in the background of his pictures, to express his exasperation at the phony "native" backgrounds employed in *Harper's Bazaar* fashion photography; and he wrote "The Pedestrian," a science-fiction story set in a repressive future anticipating that of *Fahrenheit 451,* to express his anger at being questioned by police on evening strolls:

> When was the last time you were stopped by the police in your neighborhood because you like to walk, and perhaps think, at night? It happened to me just often enough that, irritated, I wrote "The Pedestrian," a story of a time, fifty years from now, when a man is arrested and taken off for clinical study because he insists on looking at untelevised reality, and breathing un-air-conditioned air.[6]

The essay illustrates how science fiction, like realism, can comment on contemporary problems. And it also emphasizes Bradbury's essentially satirical intent. Clearly, "The Pedestrian" and warning fictions like it are intended not as gloomy prophecies but as metaphors expressing Bradbury's emotional reactions to patterns in contemporary life. The "joy" of such writing derives from ridiculing absurdity, and the apparently predictive science-fiction medium simply provides the satirist a crazy mirror in which to reflect current folly in exaggerated forms. As Bradbury suggests, much science fiction is at once satirical and extrapolative, commenting both on contemporary life and on speculative futures. Like "The Pedestrian," this tradition of science fiction comments ironically on the present by projecting familiar technological or social irritations into futures where they, like Frankenstein's monster, loom large and haunt those individuals or societies who created them.

Though Bradbury is essentially enthusiastic about the benefits of technology, he has always cherished certain fundamental prejudices about specific types of machinery—particularly automobiles and television—he sees as either intrinsically or potentially destructive. Observing his own advice in "The Joy of Writing," he has mined these prejudices in his science fiction, which abounds with images on technological artifacts become monstrous. The irony underlying all these stories is that which informs Mary Shelley's gothic romance, *Fran-*

kenstein (which, if not the world's first science-fiction novel, as Brian Aldiss maintains, certainly has provided science fiction one of its major themes): like the naive scientist Frankenstein, we may create technological wonders with the best of intentions, but our most ingenious artifacts of "progress" can destroy us if we don't comprehend their powers and limitations. Adapting this ironic theme to express his anger and irritation, Bradbury has projected futures in which Frankenstein's monster looms in artifacts as apparently innocent as telephones and television sets, as well as in such obviously ominous developments as totalitarianism and the Bomb.

"The Veldt," perhaps Bradbury's short-story masterpiece on this theme, provides a haunting, complex image of ultimately self-destructive overdependence on technological comforts. The title itself eloquently expresses this theme, since the "veldt" refers to the savage center of an immaculate high-tech home of the future—the "nursery," where a technological toy designed to enhance children's playful fantasies instead destroys its owners. Rather than charming fairylands, the children create the veldt, where bloodthirsty lions consume their parents. Bradbury adapts the Frankenstein myth with subtle and chilling effect, since the monsters in the machine really emanate from the hearts of two normal-appearing children, George and Lydia Hadley, who love their fabulous nursery more than their doting parents. Ultimately, the new toy becomes the instrument of their inner rage.

By creating the "monster" in the heart of an apparently normal American family, Bradbury brings the Frankenstein myth home in the most literal sense, while creating a complex image of the potential dangers posed by television, an entertainment medium whose impact was first being felt as he wrote the story (published in 1950). But the story does not merely satirize a technology Bradbury mistrusts (as do some Bradbury stories of this type). For the story focuses not on the machine itself, but on the disturbing psychology of the family that has unwittingly enslaved itself to it. As in much of Bradbury's most haunting fiction, we begin among familiar things, only to find ourselves ultimately trapped by a menace all the more horrifying for being disguised by comfortable appearances.

Though Bradbury's extrapolation from television has satiric overtones, "The Veldt" is tragic rather than comic in tone. With its marvelously intricate video and olfactory technology, capable of instantaneously transforming fantasy into reality, the nursery is only the central symbol of an environment in which humanity has become addicted to the services of machines. The parents realize haplessly that the children's pathologically dependent relationship to the artificial world of the nursery only carries to an extreme the entire family's relationship to their home: "I feel I don't belong here. The house is wife and mother now and nursemaid" (*IM*, 10). And when their friend the psychologist analyzes the implications of the veldt the children have created, his interpretation focuses on the heart of darkness in the home, the children's underlying motivation for wishing to murder their parents:

"You've let this room and this house replace you and your wife in your children's affections. This room is their father and mother, far more important in their lives than their real parents. And now you come along and want to shut it off. No wonder there's hatred here. You can feel it coming out of the sky. Feel that sun. George, you'll have to change your life. Like too many others, you've built it around creature comforts." (*IM*, 16)

Ultimately, "The Veldt" warns not about the danger of technology itself, but about the consequences of substituting technological marvels for basic human needs. The technological "monster" is only a sensitive piece of machinery, after all, which enhances the latently murderous dynamics of spoiled children and overly solicitous parents. The machine simply literalizes the underlying emotions of the family, creating real jungles and lions to express the murderous rage disguised behind the children's forced politeness and impatience. Though they apparently murder to preserve their beloved machine after the father decides to shut it down, their deeper motivation stems from parental deprivation: they identify so fiercely with the nursery because the parents substituted it for themselves. In "spoiling" their children, the parents have actually deprived them of necessary human contact—just as the parents, in turn, realize they secretly hate the efficient modern home that satisfies their every desire, yet leaves them feeling depersonalized and useless.

Some of Bradbury's warning stories about machines are more satirical than tragic. The hero of "The Murderer" has declared war against all machines that make noise. In his world, this places him in opposition to the very fabric of reality, since life is filled with the ever-present clatter of radios, talking wristwatches, and sappily conversational homes. The "murderer" himself states the story's theme in an interview with a psychiatrist, explaining the origins of his obsession with murdering machines. Obviously a whimsically conceived spokesman for a forthcoming revolutionary movement, he expresses Bradbury's irritation with developments already evident in mid-century:

"I'm the vanguard of the small public which is tired of noise and being taken advantage of and pulled around and yelled at, every moment music, every moment in touch with some voice somewhere, do this, do that, quick, quick, now here, now there. You'll see. The revolt begins. My name will go down in history." (GA, 61)

However, even this self-martyred "murderer" qualifies his indict-ment by observing that the hellish din he battles against results from a good idea carried too far: "It was all so enchanting at first. The very *idea* of these things, the practical uses, was wonderful' " (GA, 61–62). And the story's satire is more zany than grim, an effect created both by the murderer's exaggerated revolutionary rhetoric and by the descriptions of the psychiatrist's environment that open and close the story. A man cheerfully adapted to the social norm of his time, the psychiatrist wades through incoherent tides of music and noise doing his daily routine: "The drawer buzzed. Music blew in through the open door. The psychiatrist, humming quietly, fitted the new wrist radio to his wrist, flipped the intercom, talked a moment, picked up one telephone, talked . . . picked up another . . . picked up the third . . . talked calmly and quietly, his face cool and serene, in the middle of the music and lights flashing. . . . " (GA, 62–63). Through the psychiatrist's point of view, Bradbury establishes an at-mosphere of addled superficiality which, like that of Aldous Huxley's *Brave New World*, would drive us, as well as the outlaw hero, insane.

"Almost the End of the World" also satirizes our domination by noisy machines, focusing especially on the addictive effect of televi-sion. Willy and Samuel, two desert rats on one of their infrequent excursions into town, notice that Rock Junction, Arizona, has been gaudily transformed. The entire town has been freshly painted in out-landish, bold colors. The local barber explains the peculiar effect of "the great Oblivion" (MJ, 77), caused by a sudden increase of solar flare activity, which has effectively destroyed both radio and television communication. The barber whimsically describes the apocalyptic ef-fect of watching the televisions die, the entire town's shock at con-fronting a sudden emptiness at the center of their lives: "It was like a good friend who talks to you in your front room and suddenly shuts up and lies there, pale, and you know he's dead and you begin to turn cold yourself" (*MJ, 75*).

As the barber's exaggerated personification makes clear, Bradbury has transformed the tragic theme of "The Veldt" into broad satire about media addiction. At a loss about what to do with new-found time, the entire town finally explodes into action, cleaning and painting everything in sight. The story ends with Willy and Samuel, freshly barbered, eagerly driving their freshly painted car to Chicago to see what an entire freshly painted city looks like. As the title suggests, the story's humor derives from using apocalyptic rhetoric to describe the effect of deprivation on television addicts, a theme which Bradbury treats savagely and poignantly in *Fahrenheit 451*.

Two of Bradbury's robot stories treat the Frankenstein theme in a more macabre satirical manner. "Marionettes, Inc." (*IM*) deftly dramatizes the underlying appeal of robots as surrogates for the self, then reveals the latent threat they imply. Braling, whose marriage has been notoriously unhappy, introduces his friend Smith to Braling Two, his robot surrogate self, who entertains his shrewish wife while he vacations. Smith, whose wife literally loves him to distraction, eagerly takes the address of the illegal robot company, only to discover when he returns home that his loving wife is actually a robot. Meanwhile, Braling Two informs Braling that he has fallen in love with his wife. Placing his master in his robot box in the cellar (now a coffin—shades of Poe's "The Cask of Amontillado") Braling Two returns to his loving wife, a surrogate husband more genuine than the original. A tautly constructed satirical chiller, "Marionettes, Inc." creates eerie domestic comedy out of the identity problems of men and machines.

"Punishment Without a Crime" (*LAM*) develops a similar theme in a less humorous tone. Here robots serve as surrogate murder victims. George Hill, obsessed with the emotional wounds left by a wife who betrayed him for a lover, finally checks into Marionettes, Inc. for the illegal satisfaction of murdering a robot replica of his ex-wife. But immediately afterwards the police arrest him and try him for murder under a new law, which makes murder of robot surrogates equivalent to murder of humans. He finally accepts the apparent logic of the sentence and awaits execution with some peace of mind, until his wife arrives to visit him in his cell. Only when he sees her leaving with her lover does he suddenly become frantic at the absurdity of his sentence: realizing he will die for murdering a woman who continues to live happily with her new lover, he screams in anguished frustration as they drive away. A victim not of the machine itself but of legal absurdities created by its impact, he, like Braling, discovers that the apparent convenience of surrogate humans leads to his own destruction.

Several of Bradbury's warning stories about technology are essentially fables set in a mythic past rather than the future. "Perhaps we are Going Away" (*MJ*) presents the white man's arrival in the New World through the eyes of a native grandfather and his grandson, Ho-Awi. Drawn to the shore by eerie premonitions such as birds flying south in summer beneath the "god-filled, cloud-filled sky" (*MJ*, 80), they finally glimpse the alien beings, "men with faces like white-hot coals" clothed in "turtle-cases" (*MJ*, 83) of armor. Intuitively they realize the world they know will never be the same. In "The Flying Machine" (*GA*) an enigmatic Chinese emperor executes a man who invented a flying machine, explaining that in its inventor's hands the machine is indeed a marvelous toy, but that in evil hands it could lead to incalculable destruction: "Who is to say that such a man, in just such an apparatus of paper and reed, might not fly in the sky and drop huge stones upon the Great Wall of China?" (*GA*, 54). "The Dragon" (*MM*) presents valiant knights on a strange moor where time seems suspended (as in Bradbury's Martian story, "Night Meeting"), preparing for a doomed battle against a mysterious "fire-dragon." As the leader rides to his death the point of view shifts to that of a railroad train's operators, all of whom saw the knight charge head-on into the engine from the darkness. The knight hopelessly battling the machine represents Bradbury's theme in all these fables, which symbolically dramatize the overwhelming impact of technology.

The chief postwar symbol of technology gone awry was, of course, the Bomb, and like most science-fiction writers of the time, Bradbury wove the new Doomsday Machine into apocalyptic fiction. The mushroom cloud appears near the conclusions of both of his science-fiction novels, *The Martian Chronicles* and *Fahrenheit 451*, and it is also a recurring theme in his short stories, in which he characteristically dramatizes its impact from a domestic point of view. "The Last Night of the World" (*IM*) presents the theme in an eerily matter-of-fact tone. A husband talks to his wife about a dream of premonition all the adults they know share. They all know that this is the last night, that the bombers are on their way, that there's nothing to do but wait. She gets up to turn off a faucet she left running and they both laugh quietly at the sudden absurdity of the habit, as they say their last "good night" (*IM*, 94). In "Embroidery" a group of women embroider a quilt as they wait for the end at 5:00. One can't decide whether to shell peas. One pulls out the pattern of a pretty landscape. When the blast impact arrives they are all working frantically, trying not to see anything but the quilt, as Bradbury adapts the embroidery image to describe one of the women being unravelled by fire: "It was plucking at the white embroidery of her flesh, the pink thread of her cheeks, and at last it found her heart, a soft red rose sewn with fire, and it burned the fresh, embroidered petals away, one by delicate one. . . ." (*GA*, 76).

"The Garbage Collector" and "The Highway" register the Bomb's impact indirectly, presenting foreground vignettes in which the mushroom cloud remains in an ominous background. The protagonist of "The Garbage Collector" tells his wife he's thinking of quitting his job. Civil defense authorities have installed new radios in the garbage trucks to help coordinate collection and disposal of corpses if war breaks out. Accepting this doomsday scenario as part of normal life appalls him. "I'm afraid if I think it over, about my truck and my new work, I'll get used to it. And, oh Christ, it just doesn't seem right a man, a human being, should ever get used to an idea like that" (*GA*, 148). Their children come bursting through the door as he reflects, "just in time" his wife sighs with relief, obviously hoping he will adjust reasonably to the MAD (Mutual Assured Destruction) new reality of postwar life.

In "The Highway," another vignette in which a quiet surface highlights an ominous background, Hernando, a Mexican peasant farmer, watches American cars streaming north on the freeway. An overheated car pulls up. The frantic American driver asks for water for the radiator, informing Hernando that the "end of the world" has arrived (as in *The Martian Chronicles*, Americans rush to be "home" during apocalypse, rather than to avoid it). After the afternoon rain Hernando looks at the surrounding jungle and his plowed field and muses, "What do they mean, 'the world'?" (*IM*, 42). As in "There Will Come Soft Rains" (*MC*) Bradbury presents the "end of the world" from the detached perspective of the surviving natural order. Ironically, in our own era of overwhelming nuclear arsenals and nuclear winter scenarios, even this chilling version of the Frankenstein myth may seem overly optimistic: we have finally created "monsters" that can destroy not only ourselves but Hernando and soft rains as well.

These warning fictions speak for themselves, and writers are rightfully judged not merely by their own sense of what their message is, but by the imaginative impact of their creations. Nevertheless, Bradbury's own statements about his intentions place his "new maps of hell"[7] in an interesting, ultimately reassuring, perspective. For instance, though his fiction effectively registers the Bomb's overwhelming impact on postwar consciousness, he has concluded that the nightmares it creates are profoundly beneficial to us all: "You look at these things over a period of thirty years and then you see that the hydrogen bomb has . . . prevented major wars, and that's great. Anything that titanic has got to be good, because it's so frightening we don't *dare* have major wars anymore. So I'm optimistic. . . . The generations after us will have little wars, but nothing like World War I or II ever again."[8]

To Bradbury, science fiction's very ability to disturb, to activate the imagination by visualizing the worst, provides our best hope for the future. Just as horror films inoculate us against that potentially debilitating disease of consciousness, obsession with mortality, so science-fiction warnings provide us the symbolic tools we need to control the machines. As Bradbury explains, science-fiction stories "are a convenient shorthand symbolic way to write of our huge problems. Smog, freeways, cars, atom bombs, most of mankind's trouble these days comes from an abundance of machinery and an undersupply of imagination applied to that machinery. S-f supplies the imagination whereby to judge, suggest alternatives, and provide seedbeds for future improvements."[9]

Chapter Eight
Fahrenheit 451

If *The Martian Chronicles* (1950) established Bradbury's mainstream reputation as America's foremost science-fiction writer, publication of *Fahrenheit 451* three years later (1953) confirmed the promise of the earlier book. Indeed, these two science-fiction novels from the early fifties seem destined to survive as Bradbury's best-known and most influential creations, the most sustained expressions of his essentially lyrical treatment of science-fiction conventions. *The Martian Chronicles* presents the pioneering space romance in a distinctive tone of poignant irony and elegy; *Fahrenheit 451* counterpoises this ironic otherworldly drama with a searing vision of earthbound entrapment, evoking a painfully ambivalent poetry of incineration and illumination from the conventions of antiutopian fiction. Whereas *The Martian Chronicles* portrays entrapment in memory, the difficulty of accepting and adapting to an alien environment, *Fahreinheit 451* dramatizes entrapment in a sterile and poisonous culture cut off from its cultural heritage and imaginative life, vigilantly preserving a barren present without past or future. Though *Fahrenheit 451* has been accused of vagueness and sentimentality, it remains one of the most eloquent science-fiction satires, a vivid warning about mistaking, in Orville Prescott's phrase, "mindless happiness and slavish social conformity"[1] for "progress."

Fahrenheit 451 fuses traditional themes of antiutopian fiction to focus satirically on the oppressive effect of a reductionist philosophy of "realism" translated into social policy. A very American satire, written in response to the cold war atmosphere after World War II, the novel's sarcasm is directed not at specific government institutions but at antiintellectualism and cramped materialism posing as social philosophy, justifying book burning in the service of a degraded democratic ideal. *Fahrenheit 451* depicts a world in which the American Dream has turned nightmare because it has been superficially understood. For all his burning eloquence Captain Beatty represents Bradbury's satirical target, not Big Brother but the potentially tyrannical small-mindedness of the common man, perverting the most basic community institutions to enforce conformity. The underground scholar Faber warns Montag that the captain's rhetoric, like the seductive brilliance of fire, destroys the foundations of true freedom in its leveling blaze: "Remember that the Captain belongs to the most dangerous enemy to truth and freedom, the solid unmoving cattle of the majority. Oh, the terrible tyranny of the majority."[2]

Given this satirical target—the debased Americanism of McCarthyism—the ironically reversed role of the "firemen" serves admirably as Bradbury's central metaphor, since it represents both the charismatic seductiveness of demagoguery and a perversion of the community values of Green Town, Bradbury's symbol of the American tradition at its best. Indeed, the power of *Fahrenheit 451*'s imagery derives from this ironic inversion of values in an institution that once evoked Bradbury's boyish awe and respect. Writing of the personal memories that inform the novel, he recalls how like many boys he idolized local firemen prepared to battle the "bright monster" of fire:

And I did pass the firehouse often, coming and going to the library, nights and days, in Illinois, as a boy, and I find among my notes many pages written to describe the red trucks and coiled hoses and clump-footed firemen, and I recall that night when I heard a scream from a part of my grandmother's house and ran to a room and threw open a door to look in and cry out myself.

For there, climbing the wall, was a bright monster. It grew before my eyes. It made a great roaring sound and seemed fantastically alive as it ate of the wallpaper and devoured the ceiling.[3]

In his memory, the firehouse is the protector of library and home. And this heroic image of the community firehouse, the curiously thrilling terror of fire, inspire the angry lyricism of Bradbury's vision of the American Dream gone awry: for in this appalling future the community firehouse has become the impersonal agent of fire itself, destroying rather than preserving the community institutions Bradbury cherishes above all others—family life, schools, and, most fundamentally of all, perhaps, the local library. As Donald Watt demonstrates in "Burning Bright: *Fahrenheit 451* as Symbolic Dystopia,"[4] ambivalent associations with fire, both destroyer and center of hearth and home, fundamentally structure the novel. But the ambivalence evoked by fire metaphorically represents the ambivalent implications of American democracy, the possibility that the communal spirit of Green Town could become an American form of totalitarianism, a "tyranny of the majority" as fearful as the tyranny of Big Brother, founded on shallow misunderstanding of rationality, science, and the nature of "happiness."

Yet if *Fahrenheit 451* gains power and specificity from its American frame of reference, the satire also applies to patterns that can recur in all societies, whenever reductionist philosophies result in the sacrifice of individuals and free play of imagination for the common good. Bradbury's satire is directed not at American ideals but at simplistic perversions of them, as well as at the American innocence that assumes totalitarianism can't happen here. However, horror at Hitler inspired the book's original conception, that to burn books is to burn people: "When Hitler burned a book I felt it as keenly, please forgive me, as burning a human, for in the long sum of history they are one and the same flesh."[5] And though Hitler is defeated, and McCarthy's era finished, they will always have successors who will keep the firemen at work: "For while Senator McCarthy has been long dead, the Red Guard in China comes alive and idols are smashed and books are thrown to the furnace all over again. So it will go, one generation printing, another generation burning, yet another remembering what is good to remember so as to print again."[6] Ultimately, *Fahrenheit 451* warns that tyranny and thought control always come under the guise of fulfilling ideals, whether they be those of Fascism, Communism, or the American Dream. Yet the cyclical pattern Bradbury describes also suggests the positive implications of one of the book's central symbols, the Phoenix: for, like the Phoenix, mankind always arises from ashes to rediscover and refashion a desecrated cultural heritage.

Though *Fahrenheit 451* has been compared frequently to Orwell's *Nineteen Eighty-four*—an obviously influential model—it actually combines the oppressive atmosphere of Orwell's police state with a cultural milieu derived from the other major model in the science-fiction antiutopian tradition, Huxley's *Brave New World*. Indeed, the novel's affinities with *Brave New World* are profound, since they establish the basic thrust of Bradbury's satire, which is not directed at authoritarianism but at a more characteristically American problem, a reductionist, materialist image of human nature and human culture reinforced through mass entertainment media. Though the novel's basic mechanics of thought control derive from Orwell, Bradbury's satirical vision does not focus primarily on government itself but on the potentially poisonous superficiality of mass culture, on whose behalf the firemen work. As in Huxley's satire (itself profoundly influenced by American culture in the twenties), the power of totalitarianism in *Fahrenheit 451* derives primarily from pleasure rather than pain, from addiction to mindless sensation rather than from fear of government oppression. The firemen work for the "people," not for an established hierarchy. Indeed, compared to Big Brother the firemen are haphazard and mild agents of repression.

Next to Orwell's vision of totalitarianism, Bradbury's appears vaguely defined, both ideologically and politically. Montag's entrapment generates nothing like the weight of despair that crushes Winston Smith's spirit. Yet understanding the American context in which Bradbury writes clarifies the logic of this political vagueness, since his major satirical target is the leveling impulse of mass culture, rather than the rigidity of ideology. As Kingsley Amis suggests, Bradbury's style is very different from Orwell's, working through key symbols rather than through elaborately imagined detail. Yet the final effect is similarly impressive: "The book [*Fahrenheit 451*] emerges quite creditably from a comparison with *Nineteen Eighty-four* as inferior in power, but superior in conciseness and objectivity."[7]

As is true of all Bradbury's best science fiction, *Fahrenheit 451* dramatizes its central extrapolations with lyrical intensity, creating an atmosphere of entrapment that originates in the mind-numbing addictiveness of mass culture as much as from the firemen themselves. The novel's most powerful scenes are not the sometimes tedious expositions in dialogue, but descriptive passages, asides, which capture the inarticulate spiritual desolation disguised by the busy, upbeat appearances of this world. As they burn, books and magazines appear as "slaughtered birds" drenched with kerosene, expiring with a dying fall: "A book lit, almost obediently, like a white pigeon, in his hands, wings fluttering" (34). Montag sees himself in the mirror as "a minstrel man, burnt-corked" smiling a smile that "never ever went away, as long as he remembered" (3–4). The single most powerful scene evoking this atmosphere of glazed entrapment, perhaps, is the description of Mildred dying of an overdose of sleeping pills in their bedroom, a "cold marbled . . . mausoleum after the moon has set" (10). She is at her most appealing in this icy trance, like a princess cast under deathly enchantment by incantations from her "Seashell ear thimbles" and the hypnotic ritual activity of her television "walls," imaging forth in her "moonstone" eyes a despair she can never consciously acknowledge: "Two moonstones looked up at him in the light of his small hand-held fire; two pale moonstones buried in a creek of clear water over which the life of the world ran, not touching them" (12).

This icy alienation is the inner reality preserved by the fierce blaze of the firemen, a sterile desert of "happiness" within the widening circle of flames. Mildred's waking self, hungry only for distracting sensations, has irrevocably disassociated itself from her interior life, a subliminal meaning Truffaut artfully visualized by casting the same actress as both Mildred and Clarisse. Montag himself has never been able to distance himself so utterly from his inner self, that "subconscious idiot that ran babbling at times" (10) inside his skull. It is this irrepressible inner self that projects his culture's hidden despair into cosmic imagery of alienation, imagining their noisy machines might leave them snowbound in stardust: "He felt that the stars had been pulverized by the sound of the black jets and that in the morning the earth would be covered with their dust like a strange snow. That was his idiot thought as he stood shivering in the dark, and let his lips go on and on, moving and moving" (13).

Structurally, *Fahrenheit 451* moves from these early images of entrapment and alienation ("Part One: The Hearth and the Salamander"), through Montag's acknowledgement of and integration with the voice of his inner self (which becomes for a while the literal voice of Faber in "Part Two: The Sieve and the Sand"), to the final journey downriver to refuge in the wilderness ("Part Three: Burning Bright"). There those who have preserved their own inner life and man's cultural heritage quietly observe the final apotheosis of the culture that drove them out, as it finally consumes itself in flames. Thus, as the novel develops, the ambiguous connotations of Bradbury's central symbols express the emotional impact of his theme, the process of death and rebirth for Montag and the interior values he represents.

As the title suggests, fire provides the central metaphors for *Fahrenheit 451*. It opens and closes with contrasting images of fire and light, and the shifts in their symbolic associations illustrate how the novel's theme develops. In the opening description Montag revels in flame, like the mythical salamander, a blackened emblem of his culture's exhilaration in sensationalism and destruction: "It was a pleasure to burn. . . . While the books went up in sparkling whirls and blew away on a wind turned dark with burning" (3). This fire is associated with darkness rather than light. But by the book's conclusion Montag has learned of the other fire of the "hearth," which warms and lights both "home" and "heart." Watching an old woman martyr herself in a pyre of her own books ignites a blaze of illumination inside him he cannot extinguish: "This fire'll last me the rest of my life" (47). When he stumbles upon his first campfire in the wilderness, he finally comprehends fire's natural role in the "hearth," and he draws the moral himself: "It was not burning, it was warming" (130).

In the campfire's glow Montag finally experiences the warmth of genuine human community, the slow lilt of relaxed conversation that in other contexts Bradbury identifies with talk at dusk on Green Town porches: "The voices talked of everything, there was nothing they could not talk about, he knew, from the very cadence and motion and continued stir of curiosity and wonder in them" (130). And after the cities are scorched in the salamander's final revelry, the glow of the morning campfire blends into the light of a new day, as fire and light once again assume their roles in the natural cycle: "They finished eating and put out the fire. The day was brightening all about them as if a pink lamp had been given more wick. In the trees, the birds that had flown away quickly now came back and settled down" (147).[8] Thus, the phoenix spirit of mankind regenerates new life from ashes, as Montag walks in the wilderness and savors the prophetic lines from Revelation: "*And the leaves of the tree were for the healing of the nations*" (147).

Like all of Bradbury's best fiction, *Fahrenheit 451* creates its best effects through vivid style. Yet it is also unique among his major writings for the sustained tautness of the narrative. Two of his other book-length fictions, *The Martian Chronicles* and *Dandelion Wine,* are not so much novels as patterned collages of vignettes and short stories. And his other major novels, *Something Wicked This Way Comes* and *Death Is a Lonely Business,* are baggy monsters by comparison, in which the lyrical asides threaten to subvert the central narratives. But in *Fahrenheit 451* Bradbury achieved his central artistic objective, to rewrite the original novella, "The Fireman," with the sustained intensity of his best short fiction: "I wanted to write a short novel and have it as 'truthful' as my stories. A novel, that is, with a skin around it and its own essence and being sacked up inside."[9] This results, as Kingsley Amis describes it, in a "fast and scaring narrative"[10] that successfully utilizes Bradbury's lyrical gifts to musically develop its disturbing theme.

An illustration of the fact that science fiction can comment eloquently on social problems, a story that translated effectively into Francois Truffaut's film, *Fahrenheit 451* deserves its reputation as one of the best American books of the postwar era. Willis McNelly calls it "in every way a magnificent achievement, perhaps his best book,"[11] and Mark Hillegas described it in the mid-sixties as "the archetypal anti-utopia of the new era in which we live."[12] Fueled by Bradbury's lifelong passion for books and libraries, by his indignation at seeing American ideals defiled, *Fahrenheit 451* succeeds in warning of fire's seductive appeal while also affirming the power of man's phoenix-nature—the capacity to be warmed with inner illumination in desperate circumstances, to endure and rebuild new hearths in the ashes of history.

Chapter Nine

Autobiographical Fantasy in Green Town: *Dandelion Wine* and *Something Wicked This Way Comes*

To describe Bradbury's work in terms of distinct periods would over-simplify and distort his career. From the beginning he has written consistently in a variety of genres and published in a diverse array of markets, ranging from genre magazines specializing in science fiction, fantasy, and weird fiction to slick magazines publishing essays and predominantly realist fiction. Nevertheless, Bradbury has shifted his emphasis over the years. His reputation as a science-fiction and fantasy writer essentially derives from his work in the forties and early fifties, culminating in his two science-fiction novels, *The Martian Chronicles* (1950) and *Fahrenheit 451* (1953). But in the fifties he began exploring a new vein of essentially autobiographical fantasy (or fantastical autobiography), transforming his boyhood experience into symbolic vignettes about growing up in America. Two later major novels, *Dandelion Wine* (1957) and *Something Wicked This Way Comes* (1962), explore this new fictional landscape, which produced much of his best writing in the fifties and early sixties, when he discovered the poetry of small town life in Green Town, his fictional re-creation of his own home town of Waukegan, Illinois.

These two Green Town novels differ considerably in style and theme, yet they also complement each other thematically. *Dandelion Wine* employs fantastical vignettes to record a twelve-year-old boy's initiation into the mysteries of life and death; *Something Wicked This Way Comes* replaces this younger protagonist with two older "best friends" representing opposite qualities—Will and Jim, one light and one dark, each about to turn fourteen on Halloween night—who play the central role in an allegorical gothic fantasy about a difficult transition into adolescence. Though both the central characters and the genre change, *Something Wicked This Way Comes* completes the initiation process begun in *Dandelion Wine,* resolving a drama about growing up which is symbolically represented by the shift in seasons—from summer to autumn, from pastoral boyhood to the excitement and terror of leaving childhood behind at the carnival. Back in 1961, when he was finishing *Something Wicked This Way Comes* as well as planning an as-yet-uncompleted third Green Town novel to be entitled *Farewell Summer,* Bradbury described the underlying maturation pattern structuring his Green Town stories:

> *Dandelion Wine* is a rather gentle leading-up to a little more complex novel, which the second one [*Farewell Summer*] will be. It's about the real testing of a boy at the end of the summer when too much knowledge has been gained too quickly.
>
> . . . .
>
> I've done a third book [*Something Wicked This Way Comes*] about the same town and almost the same boys. You might say it carries these same people forward with an even bigger jump into fantasy, into allegory.[1]

And twenty years later, describing how the still-unpublished *Farewell Summer* would thematically link the earlier books, Bradbury emphasized the underlying seasonal metaphor connecting his Green Town stories:

> Somewhere along the line I have a feeling everything is going to fuse. *Dandelion Wine* starts with the first day of summer and ends with the last day of summer. *Farewell Summer* is in a one-or-two-week period at the end of summer when summer comes back for a moment, and there's the sort of thing they refer to as a "farewell summer," a false summer. And at the end of it I've introduced the characters of Will and his friend [Jim]. You can hear calliope music in the distance.[2]

As is evident from these comments, the basic structure of the Green Town myth is intact even if *Farewell Summer* never appears in print. The calliope music that opens *Something Wicked This Way Comes* ushers in the final stage of Bradbury's drama about growing up with the country, for the carnival's arrival foreshadows the end to innocence which resolves so many American stories. And if the Green Town saga interprets Bradbury's own transition from childhood in symbolic terms, it also incorporates his personal experience into a larger mythical pattern.

Bradbury's alterations of the actual facts of his life illustrate how these Green Town initiation dramas are on one level symbolic of American experience in general, which is the source of their emotional resonance and broad appeal. In 1928 Ray Bradbury was eight years old in Waukegan, Illinois. But in 1928 his mythicized persona, Doug Spaulding, is twelve years old in Green Town, an alteration that subliminally links the protagonist's first initiations into maturity to the crash that awaits the country itself, when the prosperous and apparently secure twenties precipitated the Great Depression that followed. Green Town itself represents a precarious American cultural ideal of lost innocence, just as Bradbury's Green Town boys represent the values of youth that must adapt to meet the challenges of adulthood, to survive the inevitable encounter with the ancient carnival of evil.

Dandelion Wine

Like *Fahrenheit 451*, *Dandelion Wine* presents its central metaphor in its title. Just as the yearly winemaking ritual stores the essence of summer dandelions for winter pleasure, so the book itself preserves Bradbury's most intense memories of a midwest boyhood in the twenties to be savored in these less innocent times, following the Depression, the War, and the Bomb. If *Fahrenheit 451* is Bradbury's vision of pursuit of the American Dream turned smug and intolerant, *Dandelion Wine* preserves images and rituals from an era when the Dream was intact, in however incomplete and imperfect a form. Obviously, this kind of writing risks descending into easy nostalgia and sentimentality, a risk Bradbury's lyrical style always takes in any case, sometimes resulting in a vintage too sugary for mature tastes. And by its nature, dandelion wine is less suited for dinner than for sipping in late evening next to a comfortable fire. Yet Bradbury's wine in this book succeeds in balancing sweetness with the robust flavors of real green lawns, tinged with a savory aftertaste suggestive of stray wild blossoms from a nearby ravine. As Robert O. Bowen observed in the *Saturday Review*, Bradbury's Norman Rockwell images capture genuine vitality, and they are etched against dark and brooding backgrounds, invested with the grace of irony and humor:

There is Beating the Rugs, The Last Trolley Ride, and richest of all, Bottling the Dandelion Wine. Sentimental perhaps. More likely these are the valid product of a poetic imagination, for the book contains both the sadness of death and the joy of life. No other writer since Mark Twain has caught the vitality and innocence of small-town American youth with as fine and mature a perception as Ray Bradbury's.[3]

Bowen's description highlights the polarities that structure *Dandelion Wine*: the "sadness of death" dramatizing the "joy of life," the often dangerous and irreverent "vitality" that accompanies youthful "innocence." But the emphasis on ceremonies points to Bradbury's central subject. For in this summer of 1928 such polarities are still harmoniously connected, and Green Town represents a vanishing ideal precisely because its ceremonies still recognize such polarities and hold them in balance. The particular magic of this summer derives largely from Doug's new awareness that everything around him is significant, that apparently minor events can embody the deepest rhythms of communal and personal life. His initiation into the mysterious powers of his own consciousness also attunes him to the latent power of the community rituals that surround him.

Doug's new power of vision as Green Town's youthful seer parallels his visionary experience while picking fox grapes that opens the book (originally titled "Illuminations," 4–11),[4] an experience that changes nothing physically yet profoundly alters his experience through a transformation of consciousness. Afterwards, he no longer lives blindly, but with enhanced awareness of vitality within and around him: "I want to feel all there is to feel, he thought. . . . I mustn't forget, I'm alive, I know I'm alive, I mustn't forget it tonight or tomorrow or the day after that" (11). In the weeks that follow, Doug's new awareness reveals the inner life of the community in which he lives. Eagerly recording the patterns that structure their lives, like an inspired fledgling anthropologist, he observes the pulse of vitality in Green Town ceremonies, the organic rhythms of the book's most impressive "Happiness Machine":

> *Thinking* about it [rituals], *noticing* it, is new. You do things and don't watch. Then all of a sudden you look and see what you're doing and it's the first time, really. I'm going to divide this summer up in two parts. First part of this tablet is titled: RITES AND CEREMONIES. The first root beer pop of the year. The first time running barefoot in the grass of the year. First time almost drowning in the lake of the year. First watermelon. First mosquito. First harvest of dandelions. Those are the things we do over and over and over and never think. Now here in back, like I said, is DISCOVERIES AND REVELATIONS or maybe ILLUMINATIONS, that's a swell word, or INTUITIONS, okay? In other words you do an old familiar thing, like bottling dan-

delion wine, and you put that under RITES AND CEREMONIES. And then you think about it, and what you think, crazy or not, you put under DISCOVERIES AND REVELATIONS. Here's what I got on the wine: *Every time you bottle it, you got a whole chunk of 1928 put away, safe.* (26, 27)

His entries in his tablet are, of course, the most "safe" bottles of all, destined to preserve the summer beyond the coming winter as a more permanent vintage of *Dandelion Wine*. Though Doug himself frequently disappears from view, the process of discovery he describes, connecting public ceremony to private illumination, also describes the organizing principle of a book that is not exactly a novel, though it does develop a central theme. Like *The Martian Chronicles, Dandelion Wine* records the large-scale experience of a community through a patterned collage of vignettes and stories. Doug's perceptions give shape and meaning to the individual dramas that, woven together, record the summer of 1928. Essentially, the book integrates the rhythms of communal and personal life with the larger patterns of the season, opening with celebrations of exuberant vitality but increasingly dramatizing encounters with loss and death as the summer advances toward autumn. By the end Doug, initiated into the mysteries of both life and mortality, is prepared for the new season.

This basic pattern, moving from celebration of vitality to acceptance of loss and death, structures even those episodes that do not deal directly with Doug.[5] *Dandelion Wine*'s first major episode describes Doug's sudden "illumination" while picking fox grapes, the inner awareness that seizes him and shakes him fully to life (4–11). And subsequent episodes in the early weeks of summer celebrate similar "discoveries," though even here premonitions of the ravine's dark power (particularly in the episode originally titled "The Night," 37–45) anticipate more sobering events to come.

In the first half of *Dandelion Wine* each key episode celebrates the vitality of Green Town's "RITES AND CEREMONIES," sometimes by ironically contrasting true rituals with "modern" mechanical substitutes, the failed "Happiness Machines" which actually destroy communal life in the name of progress. Each story dramatizes a "discovery": the magical power of new tennis shoes, as Doug "looks down at his feet deep in the rivers, in the fields of wheat, in the wind that was already rushing him out of town" (25); Leo Auffmann's "Happiness Machine," built on the mistaken premise that machinery can replace the ceremonial magic of family ritual (33–36, 46–47, 53–

63); grandfather's joy in the ritual of mowing lawns, almost destroyed by Bill Forester's new-fangled grass that stays green yet never grows (another misconceived "happiness machine," 48–52); the pleasure of beating winter out of the rugs (64–67); the revelation that Colonel Freeleigh is a Time Machine, and that old people are romantic "far-travellers" (making them true "happiness machines," 80–89); and finally, the elegiac pleasure of the last ride on the trolley, at once a celebration and an anticipation of the stories of loss and mortality that dominate the second half of the book.

The themes of late summer are introduced in a curiously happy story about old Mrs. Bentley's ultimate relief when she accepts that her past no longer exists, that the ridiculous children who insist she was never young are essentially right (originally titled "Season of Disbelief," 68–77). But this whimsical mood of acceptance shifts dramatically in the pivotal central story (originally titled "Statues," 102–11), in which Doug's sudden loss of his most admired friend, John Huff, transforms his celebratory mood into despair at the inescapable fact of change. Confronted in this episode with the futility of his attempt to preserve the present through prolonging the childhood game of "statue," Doug begins a series of increasingly serious encounters with loss that finally blend quiet wisdom with his youthful vitality.

As the summer draws to a close, *Dandelion Wine* expresses the more sombre moods evoked by the coming season, dramatizing the mysteries of loss and mortality, of evil and sickness. Colonel Freeleigh dies, taking his magic window on the past with him (129–35). A young reporter and an aged lady discover they are born to be lovers, but are absurdly separated by their unsynchronized life cycles (140–54). The Lonely One strikes viciously and inexplicably from the ravine, gruesomely murdering young women, haunting everyone's shadows (158–76). Doug's great grandmother dies a natural death, showing how a full life reduces the terror of mortality (180–84). And Doug attempts once more to freeze time by possessing a mechanical "Tarot Witch" (188–204) before succumbing to deathly illness himself, until he is finally revived by a shamanistic junk man's magic potion, a "vintage" (221) blend of air from invigorating climates that revives Doug's will to live.

Finally recovered, having experienced the mysteries of life and mortality, having learned to accept and recover from loss, Doug himself proves healer in a family crisis. Aunt Rose, another well-intentioned but destructive "happiness machine," organizes the creative disorder of Grandmother's kitchen, destroying the source of her gourmet magic in the process. An unobtrusive shaman now himself, like the junk man who restored him to life, Doug sneaks down at night to recreate the magic pattern of chaos that can restore Grandmother's powers. Quietly hidden, he observes her reappear at two in the morning to practice her mysterious arts once again, "half blind once more, her fingers groping instinctively in the dimness, shaking out spice clouds over bubbling pots and simmering kettles, her face in the firelight red, magical, and enchanted as she seized and stirred and poured the sublime foods" (233). The festive, spontaneous meal of the entire household that ensues at three in the morning restores the celebratory ceremonial spirit of earlier episodes as Doug, his awareness extended now to anticipate appropriate rituals for the coming season, prepares to bottle the last dandelion wine and ceremonially end the season as it began (235–39).

The "magic" in Grandmother's kitchen is only the final manifestation of the magic that provides Bradbury's essential subject in *Dandelion Wine,* the magic of intuitive human wisdom preserved and expressed in ceremony. Child to the artist he will become, just as his prophetic tablet inscribed with his "yellow Ticonderoga pencil" (26) will develop into the book we read, Doug encodes the system of Green Town magic for later generations to contemplate and rediscover. And his central revelations concern the difference between human "magic," created through deeply felt symbols and sometimes mysterious resources of consciousness, and "happiness machines," which actually destroy life by substituting mechanical systems for organic processes. As these symbolic "Happiness Machines" and "Time Machines" suggest, Bradbury's autobiographical fantasy reworks in a more personal medium many of the central themes of his science fiction.

Appropriately, *Dandelion Wine* ends in the ceremonial spirit with which it begins, deepened, saddened, but also enriched by Doug's summer experience. The book opens with Doug's ceremonial inauguration of the summer from the enchanted bedroom in the cupola of his grandparents' home, the "sorcerers' tower" where he sleeps "with thunders and visions, to wake before the crystal jingle of milk bottles and perform his ritual magic" (2). And he officially ends the season from the same place of power, as the rituals for ending summer merge with those that prepare for school and the eventual winter. When he reflects thoughtfully on the end of summer he thinks of dandelion wine stored in the cellar until he falls asleep, and "sleeping, put an end to Summer, 1928" (239). Thus, he concludes his ritual orchestration of this last summer before the Crash, Green Town's unrecognized shaman ceremonially completing the transition from one life cycle to the next, from Green Town's innocent vitality to the future in which we read.

Something Wicked This Way Comes

Bradbury's second Green Town book, *Something Wicked This Way Comes,* dramatically confronts the themes of age, mortality, and evil introduced in the second half of *Dandelion Wine.* The shift in season takes us from summer celebration to the "October Country" that has always fired Bradbury's imagination, from Fourth of July ceremonies to Halloween. The brooding background presence of the ravine is replaced by a more active emblem of evil, the carnival that fuels itself on despair and balked dreams. Doug's preadolescent innocence still is represented in an older Will Halloway, but he is paired with a "best friend" representing the disturbing new impulses of adolescence—Jim Nightshade, fatherless and tough beyond his years, eager to experience the forbidden pleasures of adulthood, impatient to leave childhood behind. And the two boys representing the polarities of adolescence are now complemented by a third figure, Will's father Charles, embodying the despair of age and failing energy, who finds himself battling with them against the destructive allure of evil. Most fundamentally, Bradbury's shift of genre creates a profound shift of atmosphere. Whereas *Dandelion Wine* employs fantastical symbols to express the inner magic of Green Town life, *Something Wicked* transforms the magical realism of the earlier book into allegorical gothic fantasy. After the sunlight "illuminations" of the summer of 1928, we encounter the dark secrets of the carnival.

Always a master of the lyrical cadenza of description, Bradbury has never written with more unrestrained abandon than in this gothic fantasy, whose highly wrought fabric of imagery has received a mixed critical reception. Orville Prescott, an admirer of Bradbury's earlier work who labels him "the uncrowned king of science fiction writers," wrote when the novel first appeared that "it is my painful duty to report that *Something Wicked This Way Comes* . . . is a stupefying bore," blaming the effect on "festoons of purple rhetoric" and "pseudo-poetic prose" which make the story "pompous, pretentious, and exasperating."[6] Similarly, evaluating the novel in light of Bradbury's overall achievement, Gary K. Wolfe credits the novel with "occasional power generated by the sheer wealth of invention" only after introducing it as a "highly self-conscious work . . . [which] suffers from an artificially inflated style and barely controlled wealth of imagery and incident."[7] Wayne L. Johnson, on the other hand, describes it a book in which "Bradbury uses all of his talents to their fullest advantage," resulting in "a thoroughly polished work of entertainment."[8] Bradbury himself has a special affection for the novel, and has referred to it as "my favorite of all the books I've written."[9] The ornate richness of style in Something Wicked This Way Comes will undoubtedly continue to delight some readers while exasperating others.

Bradbury gives full rein to his descriptive powers in Something Wicked This Way Comes to explore several of his favorite themes—boyhood innocence, the ennobling and destructive effects of man's thirst for immortality, and the macabre symbols of Halloween brought to life in his most elaborate "dark carnival." The boys and father provide an effective point of view from which to dramatize the sinister appeal of evil, which assumes protean forms, all suggestive of allegory, all hypnotically fascinating, appealing to hidden obsessions and fantasies even as they inspire dread. Itself a motley assemblage of grotesques, freaks, and magical devices, the carnival, whose central metaphor is its Mirror Maze, refracts back powerful fragmented self-images to observers. Like the Maze, Mr. Dark binds his followers to him by evoking their deepest fears, as well as by promising fulfillment of their most furtive desires.

Bradbury embodies this vision of evil, the true lyrical center of the novel, both in the "autumn people" themselves and in the "entertainment" they provide. The autumn people represent dark powers and obsessions: Mr. Dark, the Illustrated Man reconceived as master of the carnival, whose very body projects an imagistic maze of desires and despairs; his grim assistant Cooger, reshaped through the carousel first as an unnatural young boy, then as the impossibly aged Mr. Electrico; the Dust Witch, with eyes and ears sewn shut, but feeling her way with preternatural sensitivity toward her prey; Mr. Skeleton and the hordes of nameless other freaks trapped through the centuries in the carnival's web of evil. Most frightening of all to the boys, perhaps, because they knew them, are the carnival's newest additions—

the crazed dwarf with idiot camera eyes who once was the lightning rod salesman, Tom Fury; and the demented little girl who days earlier was their teacher, Miss Foley.

The seductive power of evil manifested in the autumn people also attracts new victims to their "entertainments," which appeal to the hidden side of human nature. The Mirror Maze captures souls by exaggerating and fragmenting images of the self, so that Miss Foley's obsession with recapturing her youth imprisons her in her own projected image of herself as a little girl. The carousel can add years when run forward and subtract them when run backward, promising both immortality (to Will's father) and premature adult experience (to Jim Nightshade). The carnival's source of power, of course, is the power of temptation, the dark side of human nature which lusts for unnatural control. After researching the history of the carnival's appearances, Will's father reads from a nineteenth-century tract describing the "autumn people," then explains how the book's underlying seasonal metaphor applies not just to cycles of history, or to life cycles of individuals, but to ever-present potentialities in the human spirit as well:

"They sift the human storm for souls, eat flesh of reason, fill tombs with sinners. They frenzy forth. In gusts they beetle-scurry, creep, thread, filter, motion, make all moons sullen, and surely cloud all clear-run waters. The spider web hears them, trembles—breaks. Such are the autumn people. Beware of them."

After a pause, the boys exhaled at once.

"The autumn people," said Jim. "That's them. Sure!"

"Then—" Will swallowed—"does that make us . . . *summer* people?"

"Not quite." Charles Holloway shook his head. "Oh, you're nearer summer than me. If I was ever a rare fine summer poem, that's long ago. Most of us are half-and-half. The August noon in us works to stave off the November chills. We survive by what little Fourth of July wits we've stashed away. But there are times when we're all autumn people."[10]

The novel's allegorical narrative dramatizes this central metaphor, which identifies summer sun and autumn gloom with fundamental polarities of human nature. Ultimately, darkness is defeated by light though, as the seasonal metaphor suggests, the victory is necessarily transitory. The carnival's power is associated with the most vulnerable and threatening phases of life cycles: with autumn, when falling leaves and cold winds anticipate the coming winter; with adolescence,

when boys are alternately disturbed, excited, and frightened by a new
sexual awareness and imminent adulthood; with late middle age,
when vitality fades and brings horror at old age; with three in the
morning, when the soul is at low ebb between sunset and dawn,
when the dark carnival arrives, when Charles Halloway's skin becomes
"lizard's skin," as his "blood turned to rust" and his "mouth tasted
of night damps" (40). But opposed to these miasmic powers in nature
and men's souls are the restorative powers associated with summer
sun—with love, with respect for tradition and ceremony (represented
in this novel by the library where the crucial confrontation between
light and dark occurs), and ultimately, with laughter and good humor, which magically dispel the carnival's dark powers like sun dis-
perses fog. Each of the novel's three sections, "Arrivals," "Pursuits,"
and "Departures," depicts a stage in this cyclical opposition between
light and dark.

"Arrivals" (5–86) opens with premonitions of a coming storm and
closes with Will and Jim huddled in the back of a police car, enthralled and terrified at what they have witnessed, aware that they
will be pursued by dark powers in which no reasonable person would
believe. The opening lines establish the atmosphere of imminent danger and ominous vitality: "The seller of lightning rods arrived just
ahead of the storm. He came along the street of Green Town, Illinois,
in the late October day, sneaking glances over his shoulder" (5). Foreshadowing the action to follow, Tom Fury, a salesman whose origins
seem as exotic and mysterious as those of the carnival itself, gives Jim
Nightshade a lightning rod engraved with ancient pictographs and
symbols, warning him his house is in danger.

By the time the storm has passed and the carnival has settled in
behind it, Mr. Dark has transformed Tom Fury into a crazed dwarf
for his sideshow. Jim and Will, thrown out of the carousel which is
marked "Out of Order," spy that night from a tree. There they observe the carousel run backward, turning Mr. Cooger into an eerie
man-boy who returns to Miss Foley's and poses as her visiting
nephew. Cooger breaks a window and frames the boys for burglary.
Returning to the carnival to stop Cooger from becoming a man again,
the boys accidentally jam the carousel controls while he rides, then
watch in horror as he becomes an impossibly old, dying man. They
call the police, then watch as Mr. Dark artificially sustains Cooger's
life by propping him in an electric chair and displaying him as part

of the show—Mr. Electrico, an ancient Frankenstein's monster. The boys return to town with the police, unable to explain their danger, but certain that something wicked will soon come their way.

In "Pursuits" (89–170) the boys escape from the Dust Witch's first pursuit, hide beneath grates in the downtown sidewalk as the carnival parades through town looking for them, and finally enlist Will's father as their ally, culminating in a confrontation in the library that night. Initially, the Dust Witch employs her preternatural powers to track them home in a balloon, but Will succeeds in slashing the balloon with a toy arrow, creating a "wide ripping smile" (111) in the fabric which careens the suddenly helpless witch away. This "smile" is the novel's first association between mirth and the restorative powers of the embattled "summer people."

The more elaborate confrontation that night in the library further develops this theme. Will's father shows the boys accounts in the town records of the carnival's earlier appearances, reads from a religious tract about the sinister corruption of the autumn people, and speculates with them about the ancient origins of the carnival. Mr. Dark arrives. The boys hide in the stacks as he unsuccessfully tempts Will's father with an offer to restore his youth on the carousel, then crushes his father's left hand in his grip. When he finds the boys the Dust Witch places them in a trance under Mr. Dark's control, then stays to stop Charles Halloway's heart as Mr. Dark takes the boys to the carnival. But as he feels his heart slowing, Halloway suddenly perceives the entire scene as absurd and laughs, discovering to his surprise that the witch retreats in fear. Laughing fullheartedly, he drives her from the library, then embarks on a quest to save the boys. His hand maimed, his heart weak, he nevertheless feels the thrill of a first victory, knowing now he has powers of his own.

"Departures" (173–215) presents the final confrontations at the carnival, during which Will's father rescues the boys from Mr. Dark's control. In the process he kills the Dust Witch by inscribing a smile on a bullet she holds in her mouth during one of the acts (she apparently literally chokes to death on his smile). Surrounded by images of himself dying of age, he shatters the Mirror Maze with laughter. He recognizes a small boy appealing for help as Mr. Dark, transformed by the carousel, attempting to lure him into ambush, and destroys the boy by hugging him with relentless affection ("Evil has only the power that we give it. I give you nothing. Starve. Starve. Starve."

[204]). And finally, he helps Will rescue Jim Nightshade from the carousel where, still under Dark's influence, he frantically attempts to grow up. When Will begins crying next to Jim's prostrate body, the father tells him to laugh and sing instead, makes faces, and plays a silver harmonica in an impromptu soft-shoe routine until Jim revives. Summer sun, represented by smiles, laughter, and merriment, has at last dispersed the autumn mists.

But even in victory the father steers the boys to a sobering revelation. The carnival may never reappear in the form they encountered, but it will be back: "God knows what shape they'll come in next. But . . . they'll show. They're on the road" (213). Most disquieting of all, he and Jim look longingly at the carousel, each feeling the attraction of its unnatural power, promising both maturity and youth. They vigilantly destroy the machinery, but not before realizing that they too could decide to take only one ride, then another, until they might in turn end up proprietors of a carnival show, addicts enslaving freaks. They read the most disturbing moral about the "autumn people" in each other's eyes. "*Maybe*, said the eyes, *they're already here*" (214). "Exultantly" completing a race to town Charles Halloway discovers he still can run with the boys. As the novel ends they leave the "wilderness" behind as they "walked into town" (215). Having weathered the storm, they relax to enjoy the season, newly aware of dark powers within and around them, but feeling pride as well in their own warm vitality.

Exploring Bradbury's most sinister associations with magic and carnivals, *Something Wicked This Way Comes* takes its title from the witches' chant in *Macbeth*: "By the pricking of my thumbs, / Something wicked this way comes" (4.1.44–45). They refer to Macbeth himself, prototype of Mr. Dark, a potentially noble man murderously corrupted by ambition. Indeed, the tragedy's atmosphere of corruption describes as well the climate that accompanies Bradbury's autumn people: "Fair is foul, and foul is fair. / Hover through the fog and filthy air" (1.1.10–11). Like the witches, Bradbury's carnival captures souls through tempting prophecies, offering instant gratification of suppressed dreams. The Mirror Maze, like the witches' incantations, entraps victims in their latent obsessions, imprisoning their souls in its surfaces like monstrous stillborn fetuses: "Far away, in the meadow, shadows flickered in the Mirror Maze, as if parts of someone's life, yet unborn, were trapped there, waiting to be lived"

(41). This image of entrapment echoes imagery associated with Mildred in the world of *Fahrenheit 451* where, like the carnival's gothic Mirror Maze, the science-fictional "walls" entrap souls.

These ambivalent associations with magic and wonders, reflected in Bradbury's science fiction through his ambivalence about the impact of new technologies, originate in his earliest childhood associations. Though he was enthralled by magic shows and circuses as a child, his earliest memories of carnivals are intensely fearful, mingling associations of entrapment on the carousel, the sinister odor of the lion cages, and the sensed corruption of "carny people":

> When I was about three or four years old my mother took me on a carousel for the first time, and it terrified me. The horse was leaping up and down, and circling, and there was no way to get off, of course, once this thing got started. . . . Well, that's got to be locked into *Something Wicked*, doesn't it? The carousel as a symbol of early terror. And especially when you think of [it] sending [you] backward or forward [in time]. . . . Carnivals are a combination. I could always smell the lion house behind the carnival, the fantastic ammonia odor of the lion house. . . . The smell of the jungle is the smell of something primitive and dangerous—not always evil, but dangerous. And you sense carny people are not nice people. They get out of town just after they've done something dreadful. But you don't know what it is because you're ten, eleven, or twelve. Only when you're older do you get some of the sexual overtones of carnivals. All these people are kinky and strange and unhappy wanderers of the earth. Now that's not quite true of circus people. . . . But carnivals—they're seedy, fleabag things that live off the edges of people's lives, off of cheap thrills.[11]

If Bradbury associates the carnival with the dark side of magic and spectacle, he also associates it with the dark side of adolescence—the disturbing new power of sexuality, the knowledge of death that accompanies a new sense of selfhood. Between them *Dandelion Wine* and *Something Wicked This Way Comes* symbolically explore this time of painful and exciting transition. And Bradbury subliminally establishes an analogy to a similar transition in Green Town itself, home town of the American Dream, when the old ceremonies of celebration and evil begin to fade, preparing the way for the as yet unrecognized forms of a new age. For as the strong thematic parallels between Bradbury's autobiographical fantasies and his science fiction suggest, the basic patterns of such ceremonies always endure, celebrating both life and death.

Both in his autobiographical fantasy and in his science fiction, Bradbury seeks to reveal mythological truths through private discovery and vivid presentation of detail. His Green Town myth has its origins in personal "illuminations" about growing up, in the "special days" that reveal fundamental relationships which inform mythology in any era:

When I was around ten all of a sudden it was that glorious day when you look at the backs of your hands, at your wrists and your feet, and you say, "Oh my God. Why didn't someone tell me I was inside here looking out?" And that's happened to everyone, too, except again that hasn't been described often enough in fiction. I tried to take inventory of all those special days: the day you discover you're alive for the first time; the day you discover you're going to die for the first time—that comes later, for most people. . . . First there's the discovery that you're alive and that you're looking out of this skull and you're trapped in this wonderful experience—it's glorious and it's terrifying too. Then when I was about thirteen I discovered I could die, and that scared the hell out of me. And I thought, "How do you escape *that* knowledge? Well, I'll *kill* myself." Then you say, "Wait a minute. You're playing into its hands! You can't do that! You've got to stick around, make do." But the very thought that one day you've got to give it all up—my God, that's terrifying when you're thirteen.[12]

Impatient with the kind of reductionist "realism" he identifies with "reportage," Bradbury seeks, like Doug connecting revelation to ritual in his tablet, to discover the mythological meaning in such "special days." Without creating a symbolic and ceremonial context for such illuminations, he would miss the truth of the experience: "Mere reportage generally lies. The mythological is generally truer than reportage. Because reportage only looks at what it's looking at; it doesn't look beyond."[13] Because of this mythological treatment of memory, Bradbury's fantastical Green Town reminiscences reveal how tennis shoes and carnivals embody ancient dreams and despair. Through myth he discovers in his American childhood symbols evoking the ever-present mysteries of life and death which, properly understood and appreciated, balance and harmonize with each other. "But even in my brighter stories, of course, everything is played off against death—which is not negative, it's just a fact. And it gives meaning to everything, and it etches everything very clearly, and makes everything beautiful."[14] Thus the summer illuminations of *Dandelion Wine* play off dramatically against the foreboding autumn storm of *Something Wicked This Way Comes,* finally harmonizing momentarily the opposition of light and darkness in Green Town, Illinois—where American "innocence" survives another dreaded encounter with ancient "experience," before it must grow up to enter a complex new age.

Chapter Ten
Realist Fiction: Metaphors, Relationships, and Local Color

Though Bradbury is best known as a science-fiction and fantasy-fiction writer, he has also written extensively in other genres. The covers of his Bantam anthologies all are emblazoned with the phrase "the world's greatest science fiction writer" (to which Bradbury himself has objected without success); yet the volumes' actual contents, especially in the later anthologies, present more realist fiction than science fiction. And some of the realist fiction is among Bradbury's best. Indeed, several of his earliest prizewinning publications are realist stories: "The Big Black and White Game" (*GA*), selected for *The Best American Short Stories of 1946,* a sensitive study of middle-American racial attitudes in the forties, presents a child's view of a supposedly friendly baseball game between white vacationers and the black staff at a resort hotel; "I See You Never" (*GA*), in *The Best American Short Stories of 1948*, portrays deportation of an illegal alien; and "Powerhouse" (*GA*), in *Prize Stories of 1948: The O. Henry Awards,* creates a transcendentalist metaphor out of a woman's experience while trapped in a powerhouse during a storm.

The term "realism" can mean many different things in different contexts, and attempting to distinguish Bradbury's essentially "realist" fiction from his genre fiction illustrates how uncertain such distinctions can be. Indeed, because of his highly metaphorical style Bradbury's fiction has never fit comfortably into traditional categories, so that many science fiction readers continue to classify his science fiction as "fantasy," while a book like *Dandelion Wine* creates a borderline reality between fantasy and autobiography. Bradbury has, however, written many works of fiction that are probably most accurately described as "realist." These range from eerie psychological vignettes such as "The Town Where No One Got Off" (*GA*) to bizarre reminiscences such as "The Inspired Chicken Motel" (*ISB*) to the numerous local color pieces set in Mexico and Ireland to character and relationship studies such as "A Flight of Ravens" (*MF*) and "Heavy-Set" (*ISB*). In addition, Bradbury has written numerous tributes in fictional form to such admired figures as Lincoln, Picasso, Shaw, Wolfe, and Hemingway. Though some of this fiction is occasional, sentimental, and overwritten, Bradbury's best realist writing has been perhaps unduly ignored because he has been labelled a "fantasy" writer. A survey of some of the more effective realist stories can at least indicate the range of effects he has achieved in this medium.

Two early Bradbury stories, one clearly "fantasy" and the other a kind of hybrid "realism," illustrate how Bradbury's essential method and stylistic texture tend to blur traditional genre distinctions. "The Fog Horn" (*GA*), one of his best early fantasy pieces, could have been a pulp chiller (a potential that is visually realized in *The Beast from 20,000 Fathoms*, which transformed the story into a simpleminded monster movie). But Bradbury's imagery weaves the monster into a titanic metaphor for loneliness and loss, a physical embodiment of emotions evoked by the sound of a foghorn, which the monster mistakes for the mating call of another survivor from its own unfathomably distant past: "a voice like all time and all the fog that ever was . . . like an empty bed beside you all night long, and like an empty house when you open the door, and like trees in autumn with no leaves. A sound like the birds flying south, crying, a sound like November wind and sea on the hard, cold shore" (3). The fantasy premise symbolically expresses this overwhelming central emotion, finally represented in the monster's anguished death when it finds itself still unutterably alone, and sinks at last into oblivion.[1]

Similarly, "Powerhouse" (*GA*), an early "realist" story, if the central event is interpreted symbolically rather than literally, develops an extended mystical metaphor from its setting. A couple return on horseback to their desert home. Preoccupied by her first direct confrontation with mortality, her mother's imminent death, the woman reflects that she and her husband share everything except religion, which she has always found alien and irrelevant. A desert storm approaches and they take shelter overnight in a powerhouse. That night she feels the humming of the walls inside her body, and suddenly she feels herself psychically extended through the vast electric power system, so that "she descended gently like a widely filamented spider web upon a thousand square miles of desert" (117). Experiencing the world as "one pattern encompassed and held by the pulsing electric

web" (117), instantaneously perceiving the vast harmonious network
of life and death, joy and despair, she emerges from her vision with
a newly religious awareness. "Humming" a "strange soft tune" (119)
now herself, she suggests to her somewhat mystified husband that
they return some Sunday. Though "Powerhouse" appears to present a
transcendentalist spiritual experience rather than a fantasy reality, the
central metaphor is visualized as powerfully as that of "The Fog
Horn," and both stories illustrate Bradbury's musical, metaphorical
style at its best.

Just as "Powerhouse" illustrates a "magical" dimension to Bradbury's realism, so one of his best psychological stories, "Interval in
Sunlight," (*LAM*) effectively reworks the theme of an earlier weird
story, "The Next in Line" (*OC*), without the gothic background provided by the Guanajuato mummies. As in the earlier story, a poisonously unhappy American couple vacation in Mexico, and once again
the husband is manipulative and aloof. But in this story the wife,
whose emergence as a successful writer has helped finance the trip,
appears to gain the upper hand. She realizes how sick she is of his
constant complaints, of the humiliating games he plays which require
that she literally "pay" for her "mistakes," of his disguised hatred of
her success. Indeed, the story appears to dramatize female liberation
as she finally walks out in disgust, takes a taxi, then a bus—only to
freeze suddenly with horror, frantically catch a ride back to town, and
hopelessly return, as under a spell, to the man she has come to de-
spise. Without the grinning horror of the Guanajuato mummies, "Interval in Sunlight" artfully evokes a similar suffocating atmosphere of
entrapment, culminating in her final futile gesture of enraged desperation, which symbolizes her own self-destruction: as she listens to
a pianist in the patio, she reaches out and crushes two butterflies in
her fist.

Other realist treatments of relationships dramatize similar patterns
of desperation, or celebrate new acceptance and understanding. "A
Flight of Ravens" (*MJ*) reveals the shattering impact of alcoholism
through the point of view of a writer visiting old friends in New
York. Expecting to walk into the cozy home of the Piersons he remembers, he instead walks into a drunken arena of garbled escape
fantasies and grotesque explosions of irrational violence. He is un-
nerved first by the wife's afternoon tipsiness, then by her supposedly
cute story about the husband throwing his last birthday cake down

the ventilator shaft with the candles still lit, then by the shouting phony chumminess of his ex-boss and friend, who breaks his glasses congratulating him aggressively on his new book. Finally drunk himself, about to be sick, he senses that his old friends have departed forever, leaving behind a presence of ravens and tormented ghosts who occupy their bodies: "Williams felt as if a great flight of ravens were beating upon the hot air of the room. This was not Paul anymore. This was the husband of the strange woman who had moved in after the Piersons moved away" (196).

"The Better Part of Wisdom" (*LAM*) also dramatizes a visitor's initially shattering revelation, with very different consequences. A grandfather unexpectedly visits a favorite grandson, realizes his grandson's "roommate" is really his lover, then finally communicates his acceptance and understanding by telling the grandson about his own memories of a passionate (though platonic) twelve-year-old friendship with a traveling circus boy.

Some of Bradbury's realist stories essentially characterize unusual personality types. "The Little Mice" (*MM*) deftly captures the curious logic of an alcoholic couple's lifestyle. The couple renting them the addition to their tenement house refer to them as mysterious "mice" because they make no noise, avoid conversation, and have no lights except a small blue lamp. When their roof appears to catch on fire the landlord bursts in to see that their home is literally stuffed with empty bottles, among which they sit quietly every evening, drinking in the darkness. The "mice," their burrow invaded, scurry out the next morning with their few belongings and disappear forever.

"Heavy-Set" (*ISB*) presents a more extended portrait of an emotionally regressive bodybuilder, now thirty years old and living with his mother. Massively muscular and attractive physically, pursued avidly by teenage boys and girls until they outgrow him or he rejects them, he is dressed in a small boy's outfit, licking on a lollipop—his costume for the coming Halloween party. His mother, equally concerned and possessive, both hopes and fears he will finally meet someone who will lure him away from home. Dejected, he returns early from the party charging that everyone just wanted to talk with their girlfriends, pounds his punching bag until three in the morning, then walks into his mother's bedroom and rigidly lies next to her, squeezing his exercise balls, still in his little boy's costume, as she waits for morning to come. An example of Bradbury's psychological realism at its most effective, "Heavy-Set" uses precisely observed detail to dramatize its central character as well as to evoke an ominous atmosphere of balked energy.

Bradbury's fiction set in Mexico and Ireland tends to utilize local color as atmosphere, with mixed results. His best stories set in Mexico create an exotic, threatening atmosphere. He associates Mexico with colorful ritual, dangerous yet exciting vitality, and death, a background that provides an effective setting for the chilling effects of "Interval at Sunlight" (*LAM*) and "*El día de muerte*" (*MJ*), yet also provides a setting for colorful whimsy in "The Lifework of Juan Diaz" (*MJ*) and "*En la noche*" (*GA*). After living in Ireland while working on the script for John Huston's *Moby Dick*, Bradbury wrote a series of reminiscent sketches about the Irish, most of which are affectionately droll: "The Terrible Conflagration up at the Place" (*ISB*), "The Great Collision of Monday Last" (*MM*), "The First Night of Lent" (*MM*), and "The Anthem Sprinters" (*MJ*) all work this vein of light humor. "The Cold Wind and the Warm" (*ISB*) combines Bradbury's Irish impressions with a whimsical treatment of gay sexuality, while "The Beggar on O'Connell Bridge," the most moving of these stories, mingles comic exaggeration with poignant irony about an American's confrontation with the ambiguous plights and emotional con-games of Dublin beggars.

Bradbury has written numerous difficult-to-classify stories which essentially pay tribute to geniuses he admires. "In a Season of Calm Weather" (*MM*) projects an art lover's fantasy. George Smith, a devoted admirer of Picasso's, vacationing in Europe, stumbles upon the artist himself on a deserted beach, just as he concludes a mural he spontaneously carved in sand. Entranced, Smith absorbs the mural's beauty until the light fades, then listens to the tide that night as it obliterates the Picasso masterpiece only he and the artist will ever share. "The Kilimanjaro Device" (*ISB*) expresses Bradbury's shock at the manner of Hemingway's death. The protagonist (obviously a surrogate for Bradbury himself) drives all night to Ketchum, Idaho, in Sun Valley in his big-game truck Time Machine. He finds "Papa," gives him a ride, hints that there was a better time and place to die, more in keeping with his style, and with Hemingway's implicit agreement takes him back to die on the slopes of Kilimanjaro. Other such stories of tribute include "The Parrot Who met Papa" (*LAM*), a comical tribute to Hemingway; "Forever and the Earth" (*LAM*), in which Thomas Wolfe is transported from his deathbed through time to compose the true epic about space travel; and "G.B.S. Mark V" (*LAM*), and "Downwind from Gettysburg" (*ISB*), one presenting a robot that embodies the spirit (and talkativeness) of Shaw, the other a Lincoln robot assassinated again.

As this brief survey suggests, like his "fantasy" stories Bradbury's "realist" stories vary widely in theme and effect, illustrating his broad range of enthusiasms, his appetite for experimentation, and his persistence. He has always had "catholic tastes," and his writing career reveals his attempt to write stories like all those he likes most to read: "If it is at all possible, over the years each of us should develop many facets, many interests, many loves. I don't mean to be a jack-of-all-trades because in moving in too many directions you can never focus; but it is great fun to have very catholic tastes in reading, if you do like poetry and essays, and if you do enjoy reading detective stories and are not snobbish." Admitting that carrying such catholicity into his own writing ambitions means floundering sometimes and making "mistakes," he nevertheless identifies constant experimentation with meeting necessary challenges: "Only when you're making lots and lots of mistakes do you feel challenged."[2]

The result of such constant stylistic experimentation, stories such as "The Big Black and White Game," "Powerhouse," "Interval in Sunlight," and "Heavy-Set" demonstrate Bradbury's mastery of mainstream realist techniques, which at least partially explains the originality of his contribution to genre fiction. Though Bradbury's imagination seems to work most powerfully when unrestricted by the conventions of realism, his ability to generate a sense of wonder about contemporary realities has helped him flesh out characters, relationships, and background in science-fiction and fantasy settings as well.

Chapter Eleven

Other Genres, Other Media: Film, Drama, and Poetry

In addition to his extensive and varied body of fiction, Bradbury has also written numerous screenplays for television and film, adapted many of his stories for the stage and even financed productions of them, and published three volumes of poetry. As early as 1953 he began writing professionally for film studios, composing the treatment for *It Came From Outer Space*, the first science-fiction horror film in 3-D. In the sixties and seventies he published three volumes of drama, *The Anthem Sprinters and Other Antics* (1963), *The Wonderful Ice Cream Suit and Other Plays* (1972) and *Pillar of Fire and Other Plays* (1975). And his three volumes of poetry have now been combined into *The Complete Poems of Ray Bradbury* (1982). In addition to writing in these genres, Bradbury has written essays and reviews throughout his career on a wide variety of subjects, ranging from space travel to Walt Disney Studios to redesigning downtown Los Angeles. And his more adventurous forays working in new media including designing a musical comedy version of *Dandelion Wine*, writing lyrics for his cantata, *Christus Apollo*, and designing an opera based on his space age adaptation of *Moby-Dick, Leviathan 99*. Though Bradbury's reputation undoubtedly will continue to be sustained primarily by his fiction, his achievements in other areas are varied and impressive.

Film

A devoted movie lover from early childhood, Bradbury has worked with film productions in two major capacities—as the author of fiction translated into film, sometimes with and sometimes without his participation; and as a screenwriter both for major movie productions and for television drama. Despite his enthusiasm for film, however, he deliberately waited until he had established himself as a fiction writer before beginning film work. In 1961, after a decade of active screenwriting, including the treatment for *It Came from Outer Space*

(1953) and the screenplay for *Moby Dick* (1956), he reflected on the healthy fear that kept him from film work earlier in his career:

> When I look back over the seventeen-year period since I came to Los Angeles in 1934 with my love for motion pictures, the remarkable thing is how long I was able to hold off being tempted by them. I don't want to look upon this as a supreme act of will or integrity or anything, because I imagine it was just fear. Fear can be a very constructive element in one's life, if you are afraid of the right things. . . . I was afraid of the studios; and luckily, I had some good friends who advised me to learn how to write first and then go into the studios later in life. I found this good advice.[1]

His film career actually began with a bizarre experience in 1952, when Warner Brothers Studio called to see if he was interested in working with his friend, visual effects technician Ray Harryhausen, on a monster movie. He agreed, then discovered to his amazement that the studio had stolen the idea for the script from his story "The Beast from 20,000 Fathoms" (later retitled "The Fog Horn") which had appeared a year earlier in *The Saturday Evening Post*. Having forgotten the source of the idea, the studio then called Bradbury to work on the film, *The Beast From 20,000 Fathoms* (1953). After he pointed out the similarity between his story and the film concept, he received a telegram offering to buy the rights, to which he agreed. Essentially, they bought "the title, plus . . . one idea, which was only used for about two minutes"—and ignored the story's underlying metaphor, which might have given the film genuine emotional impact. Bradbury's comments on how the film should have been done illustrate his approach to translating fiction on to the screen. Rather than reducing the story to a clichéd monster movie, he would create a human drama to visually represent the monster's meaning, as a symbol of loneliness and unrequited love:

> You could do a parallel story that would really tear your heart out. You know, you can just imagine a mariner, and a girl that he leaves somewhere in the world, and at the same moment the monster comes in and tears down the lighthouse the man loses the girl too. . . . But finally the monster and the man are the same. . . . And the very last thing you see and hear is maybe the man standing on the shore and hearing, way out at sea, the dinosaur crying for his lost mate. And he doesn't have to say a thing. You know what the man is thinking and you don't need music or anything to jar you or to be overly sentimental. It could be great. Well, I'll do it someday. I've got the rights and I can do it over as a short sometime.[3]

Bradbury's first extended filmwriting experience followed shortly afterward, when he was asked to do a treatment for a film called *The Meteor*, finally issued as *It Came from Outer Space* (1953). Not only did he write an unusually elaborate treatment of over one hundred pages, but he also volunteered to write two different versions of the opening to convince the studio his concept of the movie was better than theirs. "So I did both versions and handed them in and lo and behold, they had enough brains to pick my way, and I won my point."[4] As it turned out, the movie rather successfully develops two of the themes that permeate Bradbury's own Mars stories—projection of fears onto the alien, and metamorphosis. Indeed, though he sees the film's limitations, Bradbury recalls with pride that when he congratulated Stephen Spielberg for *Close Encounters of the Third Kind* (which he loves) he received an unexpected tribute in return: "He [Spielberg] says, 'Well, how do you like your film?' And I say 'What?' And he says, 'Sure, it's yours. You know without *It Came from Outer Space*, I would never have made this film'—because he had seen it when he was, I don't know, twelve or thirteen."[5]

But Bradbury's most dramatic experience as a screenwriter was still to come, fulfilling one of his longstanding dreams which proved in reality—as such dreams often do—to be disillusioning as well as fulfilling. He developed a deep admiration for John Huston in the forties, and for years claimed he would take up screenwriting seriously only when Huston offered him work: "So, when friends used to write to me in my late twenties and early thirties and ask, 'Hey, Ray, when are you going to write your first screenplay?' I always wrote back half seriously, half humorously, 'when John Huston offers me a job.' "[6] After publication of *The Martian Chronicles* (1950) and *The Illustrated Man* (1951), Bradbury decided he was ready and asked his agent to contact Huston. When they met for lunch he gave Huston copies of his books and told him he was interested in working with him on a film.

Two years later Bradbury's dream came true when Huston offered him the screenwriting job for *Moby Dick*—a job which he accepted only after spending the night reading the novel (one that he hadn't gotten to yet) and discovering that he was "totally absorbed" by Melville's style. Subsequently, he spent six months in Ireland working with Huston, a time which was alternately exhilarating and maddening. Though the film itself is a mixed success (partially because Gregory Peck is not "mad" enough as Ahab), Bradbury's screenplay effectively compresses the action of the novel while preserving its spirit. But if his film experience was rewarding, his personal experience was trying and ultimately disillusioning. He discovered that his hero's flamboyant lifestyle could be highly destructive, and relations between them ended in furious controversy when Huston subsequently claimed half-credit for a screenplay Bradbury insists he wrote himself:

> I went over to the Screen Writers' Guild immediately. I said he didn't write the screenplay and couldn't ask for it. I was furious. I was murderous at that point. . . . It was thievery. So I filed through the Screen Writer's Guild. We had readings of the scripts by three people, who then judged and I won. I got sole credit on all the early ads for *Moby Dick*. Then John came back from Europe . . . and said he wanted the case reopened because he wasn't there when the decision had been reached and he had new evidence. And they reopened the case. Now that's not allowed! . . But they did reopen, and John submitted, as his evidence of what he had done, a copy of my screenplay with my name on it, in which he had gone through with a red pencil and indicated sections that he had supposedly written. What kind of evidence is that? Against my 2000 pages of corrected script. . . . Plus all my notes and outlines. But I lost. I saw the letters from the second group of judges, which said: "If judged on the material alone we would have to give the credit to Bradbury. But the fact that Huston is such a famous director makes us lean over backward."[7]

Throughout the late fifties and sixties Bradbury wrote television screenplays—some originals, some adapting his own stories to film—including many for Alfred Hitchcock, whom he admired intensely both professionally and personally. But despite his experience he left the first major film of his own work entirely in the director's hands. Truffaut invited Bradbury to write the screenplay and observe the filming of *Fahrenheit 451* (1966), an offer which Bradbury declined, partially because he had adapted the novel for the theater earlier and felt he lacked a fresh view of the material. In his enthusiastic response to the film, published in *Los Angeles Times,* he called it an experience for which "I shall be grateful . . . for the rest of my life," and claimed that the film was undoubtedly better because of his decision to leave it entirely in Truffaut's capable hands: "By keeping my mouth shut, I gave him license to purify the intention of my book." Commending Truffaut for his decision to reject many of the book's "technological and science fictional devices," he argued that by doing so Truffaut focused without distraction on the essence of the novel, Montag's anguished love affair with books. By rethinking the book on his own terms, Truffaut effectively translated Bradbury's message into the medium of film: "Our parallel loves had, by an optical illusion, somehow joined out there at the edge of tomorrow."[8] Other major productions based on Bradbury's fiction have been less successful. Jack Smight's *The Illustrated Man* (1969) includes some effective material, but the overall effect is confusing and out of focus. As Bradbury observes, "it is not a good film, but it has a lot of good stuff in it. . . . Everything is there except the film." Bradbury himself was not consulted on the project, and in this case the production surely would have benefited from his assistance, since the movie falls apart most glaringly where it departs from Bradbury's texts to develop a melodramatic frame narrative about the Illustrated Man. Though in general he respects the film industry and loves the film medium, Bradbury shares the frustration of many writers at unimaginative film translations of their fiction, and his frustration is compounded by his own screenwriting background, since he views the final product both as disappointed author and as frustrated screenwriter. His comments on how "The Veldt" could have been filmed illustrate his own detailed vision of how the story should be translated onto the screen:

The director [of *The Illustrated Man*] was a bad director and the producer wrote the screenplay and never showed it to me. If they'd asked me to do certain sections over I could have corrected the script in one day. But they never *asked* that. They were arrogant. They thought they knew everything. I went on the set one day to visit and they had this *beautiful* all-white set, like the inside of a mammoth's mouth, with white teeth. And I looked at it and I watched Steiger and his wife acting and I said to Jack, "Can I make a suggestion?"—very gingerly, you know, because I don't want to step on anyone's toes. "My *God,* this is a great set. I don't know what you plan, but in order to get a sense of suspense, why not have your camera prowl around the house at night? All by itself. No one's there. The camera prowls around the living room and you hear all the machines humming—tchh . . . tchh . . . —and the house is asleep. Then you peer into the parents' bedroom and they're asleep and maybe little machines are singing to them, quietly. And you go into the kids' room and their voice clock is singing [quietly], 'Tick tock, twelve o'clock.' And you move down the hall and into the playroom and into the center of the playroom and [whispering] *there are lions in there.* You wait a moment, then you pull back and fade out. . . . " [loudly] And that sets you up for the next *day*, doesn't it? But they didn't *do* it. *I* know more about directing than they do.[9]

The mini-series television production of *The Martian Chronicles* (1980) suffers from similar problems: though individual episodes are effective, the overall production drags, losing the brisk, vivid pacing of the book. By creating a plodding frame narrative in an attempt to integrate the chronicles into a more unified story, the production substitutes a lethargic narrative for the lyrical, kaleidoscopic effect created by Bradbury's collage of images and counter-images.

Something Wicked This Way Comes (1984)—directed by Jack Clayton, based on Bradbury's own screenplay, and produced by Walt Disney Studios—effectively captures the spirit of the book, though it has not proved a major commercial success. Yet those who are impatient with the novel's ornate style might well prefer the movie, which alters and simplifies the book's Byzantine complexity, providing a clean, clear exposition of the action. In part Bradbury translated from page to screen by introducing new material to clarify motivation and character. A new story line has been added to explain the father's (played by Jason Robards) melancholy—he suffers from a heart problem, and he is obsessed with his failure as a father in a specific incident, when Jim Nightshade's father saved his drowning son because he himself had never learned to swim. More fully than the novel, the film sketches in Jim Nightshade's father as a contrast to Charles Holloway, which helps to explain Jim's edge of surly desperation, his need to live up to a romantic image of manhood like that which haunts Will's father. The screenplay emphasizes what is only suggested in the novel—that Will's father and Jim, apparent opposites, both identify the carousel with an alluring but destructive image of manliness.

But essentially Bradbury's screenplay simplifies the story, dropping scenes that do not translate effectively into film, fusing characters and events in new combinations to advance the narrative more efficiently. Rather than becoming a small girl, Miss Foley gains youth and beauty but loses her sight. Tom Fury, rather than Cooger, becomes Mr. Electrico. The battle with the Dust Witch in the balloon, which could easily look ridiculous on screen, has been eliminated, as has the scene in which Will's father hugs to death the eight-year-old Mr. Dark. By having the father reach through the Mirror Maze to grab the hand of his drowning son, Bradbury effectively re-imagines in vi-

sual terms a key scene which is merely abstract in the novel. The
weakest scenes dramatize the novel's fundamental premise: that Will's
father defeats Mr. Dark and the Dust Witch, then revives Jim Nightshade, with mere laughter and merriment—an idea that may be too
simple dramatically even in the novel, which is even less convincing
on screen.

The screenplay of *Something Wicked This Way Comes* demonstrates
that Bradbury can apply his screenwriting talents effectively to adapting his own fiction. This partially results from Bradbury's longstanding interest in technical and theoretical problems presented by
translating from one medium to another. Over the years he has developed an experienced perspective on the strengths and limitations of
the printed word and the film image. Because print actually utilizes
the boundless resources of the imagination, the "theater" of the mind
itself, it can create special effects and meanings which are not limited
by technology, acting talent, or budgets. Yet what film lacks in flexibility it gains in overwhelming sensory immediacy. Used imaginatively, film can create visual effects similar to the effect of vivid
poetry, by "rendering down" language and narrative into compressed
imagery. As true film artists are aware, film constantly runs the risk
of limiting and constricting the imagination, because of the very
power of the medium:

> They're such *different* art forms, actually. You can do anything in a novel,
> and most of it you can't do on film because it's too expensive. It's very hard
> to transfer a whole novel over: you've got to render it down. What I love in
> working the various forms is the challenge of doing a thing one way here,
> another there. After all, a book doesn't really exist, does it? It's just symbols
> on paper and you've got to stuff those funny-looking little symbols in your
> head, and when they get in there it's like putting chemicals on litmus paper,
> it turns into something else . . . into fabulous words and images . . . and
> everything becomes a theater inside your head. . . . But the screen is totally
> realistic. It's not fantastic at all. Everything is right *out* there. You are totally
> in control of all the images, and it *constricts* the imagination if you're not
> careful. You have to find ways . . . allowing us to float free from what you've
> constricted us with.[10]

Though he recognizes fundamental differences between the media
in which he works, Bradbury also emphasizes the common element
in what he loves. Both books and films communicate "dreams,"

which can expand our sense of what is desirable and possible. Common to all his enthusiasms is a love of "romance": "Romance is what makes us grow. We have to romance ourselves into living. We have to have a dream of some sort, somewhere to go."[11] Different as they are, both the theater of the mind and the screen can project images that show not just what we are, but what we might be. In Los Angeles, capital of dreams both shoddy and inspired, Bradbury has learned how to project romance in all theaters available.

Drama

Bradbury's passion for "romance" in all forms includes a lifelong passion for theater. He traces his love of the stage back to his boyhood excitement at assisting Blackwood the Magician during his show. Bradbury went on to participate in many different aspects of theater before writing and producing his own dramas in the sixties. At the age of twelve he managed to secure a Saturday spot reading comics to children on radio station KGAR in Tucson. Active in the drama club in high school, he served as assistant producer, director, and master of ceremonies for the 1937 *Roman Review* at Los Angeles High School, then went on to participate for two years as a fledgling playwright in Laraine Day's Wilshire Players Guild, until he decided to concentrate full time on writing fiction. His radio drama, "The Meadow," was selected for *Best One-Act Plays of 1947–1948*. But his first major stage play, an adaptation of *Fahrenheit 451* for Broadway he worked on with director Paul Gregory and Charles Laughton, was never produced. Gregory and Laughton finally broke the news to him that the play just wouldn't work, an experience that confirmed Bradbury's fear that he wasn't yet ready for the theater. But the experience also established a relationship with Charles Laughton which deeply influenced his thinking about drama, helping him formulate his goals as a playwright:

In 1955 Charles Laughton and Paul Gregory asked me to adapt my novel *Fahrenheit 451* to the stage. I came up with a bad play. Laughton and Gregory gave me drinks one night at sunset and told me just how bad, but told me kindly. A few months later, Charles had me up to his house. He stood on his hearth and began to talk about Moliere, about the Restoration playwrights, but particularly about Shaw and Shakespeare.[12]

Bradbury became a frequent guest of Laughton, whose influence confirmed Bradbury's fascination with the power of the spoken word in theater, as well as his love of the playwrights he refers to most frequently as his ideals—Shakespeare and Shaw, who represent to Bradbury the tradition of "theater of ideas" he seeks to reactivate. Impatient with modern realism, naturalism, and absurdism, he seeks to bring romance, pageantry, and poetry to American theater. Fundamentally, his approach to drama springs from impatience with the predominant tone of contemporary drama. "I . . . cannot . . . accept a theater that is devoid of ideas and poetry."[13] Having discovered his gift for poetic lyricism in fiction, Bradbury finally made a plunge into theater in the sixties, attempting to translate his gift of language into the kind of theater he envisioned. Writing in the *Los Angeles Times* after his first major production (which ran for five months) and introducing a second (which ran for six months), he clarified his goals as a dramatist: "We have heard too little language on the American stage in its brief history. . . . I beg a small space on the far stage-apron to try out not only ideas which concern the space age, but the way these ideas find their best form in words."[14]

Bradbury's objectives here sound similar to those he achieved as a science-fiction writer, yet his dramas are as diverse as his fiction, presenting a wide variety of types of stories. His first major production, *The World of Ray Bradbury* (1964–65), did feature three science-fiction dramas—*The Veldt, The Pedestrian,* and *To the Chicago Abyss*—all adapted from earlier stories. But his next major production, *The Wonderful Ice Cream Suit* (1965), featured the poignant Mexican-American comedy of the title piece (generally regarded as one of Bradbury's most successful theater pieces) as well as the romantic fantasy of *A Device Out of Time* (dramatizing Colonel Freeleigh, the "Time Machine" from *Dandelion Wine*), and *The Day It Rained Forever* (about an old woman whose music brings rain to a southwest desert town).

After the early collapse of his New York production of *The World of Ray Bradbury* (1965), which received unfavorable reviews and was a financial disaster, Bradbury has confined himself to publishing selected dramas and to more limited productions, varying widely in spirit and genre. He presented a musical drama of *Dandelion Wine* in Lincoln Center in New York (1967), followed by a California production of his Irish plays (1967–68) which included *The Great Collision of Monday Last, The First Night of Lent, A Clear View of an Irish Mist,* and the title play, *The Anthem Sprinters.* Though he went on to pre-

sent other drama and branched into space age musical composition—
Christus Apollo, a musical cantata (1969); *Leviathan 99,* a radio drama
(1972); and *Madrigals for a Space Age* (1973)—Bradbury has not produced major theater productions since the sixties. His drama has
never been a resounding critical or commercial success, but it has
generated several successful California productions. And Bradbury believes that the quantity of royalty payments, the sales of his published
drama, and word of mouth all indicate that his drama is performed
extensively in schools and in local theater productions.[15]

For all his enthusiasm and occasional success in the theater, Bradbury's talents have thus far proven less suited to the stage than to
fiction and film. His prescription for a "theater of ideas" rich in poetry describes an admirable ideal, but ironically Bradbury's "poetic"
muse seems to function most effectively when offstage, rather than
in the limelight. The lyrical textures of Bradbury's best fiction create
evocative atmosphere and emotional resonance, gifts that as a screenwriter he effectively translates into the visual poetry of film. A more
verbal medium than film, drama sometimes allows Bradbury's descriptive powers to function effectively, but the stage also depends
upon strong characters to project poetry. And as Bradbury himself realizes, characterization has never been his strong point: "That's quite
often missing from a lot of my work—. . . real and believable
characters. . . . I'll have to be satisfied with putting my personal
fears, hopes, and dreams into the mouths of these characters who are
all really myself."[16] In the introduction to his latest collection of
drama, *Pillar of Fire and Other Plays,* he addresses this subject directly, formulating an aesthetic in which character is properly subor-
dinated to "Ideas":

> What you have in most of my stories and plays then is rarely a highly
> individualized character (I blunder into these on occasion) but Ideas grown
> super outsize; Ideas that seize people and change them forever. So, I should
> imagine, in order to do my plays at all, you must become the Idea, the Idea
> that destroys, or the Idea that prevails.[17]

Thus conceived, Bradbury's "theater of ideas" risks becoming
merely rhetoric and stage effects, and indeed such charges appear consistently in evaluations of Bradbury's drama. As Ben P. Indick observes, "The problem with this otherwise admirable ideal is that
audience identification with Ideas is more difficult than identification

with characters."[18] Writing as a disappointed fan of his fiction, John
Boland dismisses Bradbury's drama as "of little consequence," illustrating only that a gifted and enthusiastic artist who is "unable to
communicate in that medium" should "go back to short stories . . .
and continue to panic, horrify, and enthral me."[19] Characterizing
most of Bradbury's drama as "portentous" and "sentimental," B. A.
Fussell singles out *The Wonderful Ice Cream Suit* as the most effective
piece precisely because it dramatizes character and relationships rather
than inflated "poetry and ideas": "When Bradbury forgets poetry and
ideas, he creates the delightful title play which is about relations
among real people."[20] Similarly, Wayne L. Johnson concludes that
"with the possible exception of 'The Wonderful Ice Cream Suit,' the
quality of Bradbury's plays does not measure up to his fiction."[21]
Though the world of Ray Bradbury has been visualized effectively on
the printed page and in film, it has translated less dramatically into
live theater.

Poetry

Bradbury's fascination with poetry dates from an early love of
Shakespeare and membership in the Poetry Club in Los Angeles High
School. Since publishing "In Memory to Will Rogers" in the *Waukegan News-Sun* at the age of sixteen he has continued throughout his
career to publish poetry in a wide variety of publications, ranging
from local papers to journals and slick magazines. But not until the
seventies did he gain the confidence, "the strength, some might say
the *chutzpah*"[22] to unabashedly publicize his verse. Since then, many
of his new publications have been poetry collections. His first major
poetry anthology, *When Elephants Last in the Dooryard Bloomed* (1973),
presents some new material along with many of his poems from previous decades. And subsequently he published two similar volumes,
Where Robot Mice and Robot Men Run Round in Robot Towns (1977) and
The Haunted Computer and the Android Pope (1981), which emphasize
his more recent work. All three volumes are now collected in *The
Complete Poems of Ray Bradbury* (1982).
Bradbury's verse ranges widely in subject matter, fusing his central
preoccupations into incantatory celebrations. Ironically, however, his
lyrical gifts as a prose stylist have thus far translated less effectively
into poetry than into any other medium. He seems never to have applied to his poetry the lessons about a "clean" style he learned early

in his career as a fiction writer. Much of his verse illustrates the dangers of his romantic conception of the creative process carried to an extreme, dangers evident perhaps in the style with which he describes the origins of his poems: "This catch-all anthology gives me a chance to glance over my shoulder and dare to intrigue you with the accidents that knocked me flat downstairs into a poem."[23]

Unfortunately, such explosive "accidents" translate on the page into inflated rhetoric, artificial diction and syntax, and imprecise metaphor too often modulating into cliché. Because it reworks a theme developed in prose in *Dandelion Wine*, the title poem of *When Elephants Last in the Dooryard Bloomed* illustrates with particular clarity the results of this effusive "poetic" style. Though Bradbury's prose in *Dandelion Wine* constantly runs the risk of overwriting and sentimentality, it succeeds in linking rich tapestries of metaphor to concrete observation, illuminating a "magical" dimension in common things. Describing the ceremony of Beating the Rugs in spring, Bradbury fuses the ornate patterns in the rugs, the tidal rhythms created by the wire flails, into an exotic ritual with whimsically mystical overtones. His prose description moves wryly from concrete observation to implicit symbol, transforming the motion of the rugs into an oceanic image evoking timelessness: "Showers of lint, tides of sand, golden flakes of pipe tobacco fluttered, shivered on the exploded and re-exploded air. Pausing, the boys saw the tread of their shoes and the older people's shoes pressed a billion times in the warp and woof of this rug, now to be smoothed clean as the tide of their beating swept again and again along the oriental shore" (*DW*, 64).

Through similarly exotic imagery the verse description in "When Elephants Last in the Dooryard Bloomed" captures some of the same opulent atmosphere, but precise observation of the ritual is replaced in the poem by development of the awkward metaphor punned on in the title, identifying "white elephants" with the actual animals. The poem proceeds to free associate on this initial metaphor, losing in the process the playful tension between fact and symbol which invigorates the prose description. And the logic of the metaphor evaporates as well. The rugs, with their exotic oriental associations, must now be visualized as "elephants" with "faded . . . roses on their flanks," which in turn, in an abrupt shift of figures, become "pelts . . . in the sight of the sun / Which glorious made the panoplies of thread."[24] This initial development of the central metaphor, with its awkward diction and inverted syntax, leads to a resounding cliché contrasting

degenerate "modern" times with the past. Though the passage opens
with clever echoes of Whitman (also alluded to in the title), the metaphor which expresses this central contrast requires that we envision
contemporary rugs as made for "snails," as well as contemporary men
who eat only "the safe, sure, ever-recurring marshmallow." By this
point the poem has lost contact with anything except its own sono-
rous voice echoing (satirically?) the final lines of "Dover Beach":

> Old creatures, slung upon a wire in wind and light
> And years' ebbtide
> I beat you gently with my howdah wire-racket beater,
> Search tigers in the shade of your deep hills
> And stand, a monarch made, along your blind
>   impatient old
> And slumbrous side,
> And know that modern carpetings and rugs, so bland,
>   so broad,
> So nothing, and so shallow
> Were made for snails
> And men who breakfast, lunch, and dine
> Upon the safe, sure, ever-recurring marshmallow.
>
> (164)

Critical reaction to Bradbury's verse has varied from modest praise
to vehement criticism. Praising his variety of subject matter, the
"sheer force" of his style and the occasional "tenderness" of the domestic poems, *Kirkus Review* nevertheless concludes that "as poetry
the collection [*Where Robot Mice and Robot Men Run Round in Robot
Towns*] makes few new statements," before recommending it to
"Bradbury fanatics" who seek "a well-rounded picture of the man behind *The Martian Chronicles.*"[25] But the *Library Journal,* pointing to
"artificial inversions," "forced rhymes," and "poetic diction" that
"oozes with sentimentalized views of youth, age, and destiny itself,"
gives a similar recommendation in a less favorable tone: "it's hard to
imagine any audience at all for this volume [*When Elephants Last in the
Dooryard Bloomed*] other than the most die-hard of Bradbury buffs."[26]
Similarly, Gary K. Wolfe refers to Bradbury's "inflated diction that
calls to mind an uncomfortable blend of Whitman and Genesis."[27]
And Wayne L. Johnson, noting that "it is difficult at first to understand why Bradbury's poetry doesn't measure up to the quality of his
fiction," goes on to describe the curiously toneless abstraction of his

expansive style: "Bradbury also has a tendency to bring together in the same poem subjects so vast and frequently unrelated that even the most epic treatment is insufficient to tie the subjects together, let alone move on to some poetic synthesis."[28]

As the more favorable evaluations point out, many of Bradbury's poems present potentially interesting concepts and symbols, and they all contain glimpses of the vivid imagery characteristic of his descriptive prose. But the process of free association, of following his "muse," that generates rich metaphor and sure, clean rhythms in his prose has had the opposite effect in his poetry. Rather than illuminating its subjects, Bradbury's poetry more frequently obscures them in declamatory fog. The subjects themselves appear promising: there are poems about Green Town memories, about deep space and Mars, about domestic trials and joys, about football, Ty Cobb, Satchmo, and Egyptian railroads fueled by burning mummies. There are passages of mythic, cosmic imagery which, extracted from their fulsome surroundings, might generate a genuine sense of wonder, as in "We March Back to Olympus," which describes mankind as "once at the hub of the wakening / And vast starwheel / . . . Driven forth to grassless gardens."[29] But even here, Bradbury's early essays present such imagery with more sustained clarity and power.

Like the early pulp stories that Bradbury rewrote after he learned the magical effect of a clean style, many of these poems would benefit from thorough pruning and revision. But as is, the effect of Bradbury's poetic style is curiously monotonous: his most vivid images and fantasies blur together, so that nothing has distinct shape, color, or rhythm. A writer who brought authentic "poetry" into the conventions of genre fiction, Bradbury's actual poetry lacks the music and subtlety of his best prose.

Chapter Twelve
Detective Fiction:
A Memory of Murder and
Death Is a Lonely Business

In his sixties Bradbury seems to be emphasizing fiction once again. Publication of *A Memory of Murder* (1984), which presents previously uncollected early stories from the pulp detective magazines, prepared for publication of his first major novel in two decades, *Death Is a Lonely Business* (1985). Back in 1980, when he was just beginning to write again in a genre he has always loved but never felt he had mastered, Bradbury speculated that he might be "entering a new phase, depending on [the success of] this murder-mystery, suspense novel I'm doing in my sixtieth year. If it turns out well, God knows, I may do some more."[1] Because of his fascination with the mystery novel form, and because he has been encouraged by the generally favorable critical reception of his new novel, Bradbury greets this new phase of his career with delighted enthusiasm. Interviewing him about *Death Is a Lonely Business,* a *Wall Street Journal* reviewer found him well underway with his second mystery novel, *Falling Upward:*[2] "After his long absence from the novel form, Mr. Bradbury says he's fired up to continue writing detective stories. He has already completed 200 pages of a second detective novel, set around the old Hollywood studios, near where he lived as a boy. He says he wakes every morning with his mind churning with ideas, and he rushes to his typewriter."[3]

This brief description suggests that *Falling Upward,* like *Death Is a Lonely Business,* utilizes the California tradition of detective fiction to integrate personal memories with a mythical sense of time and place. Just as he adapted fantasy and gothic conventions to symbolically interpret his transition from boyhood in Waukegan, Illinois, so Bradbury now adapts the conventions of detective fiction to interpret his transition to adulthood during a vanished era in Los Angeles, his second "home town." In this sense Bradbury's detective fiction expands his earlier explorations of "autobiographical fantasy" into a new era of his life, creating yet another mythical landscape. The most vivid landscapes of his earlier fiction—October country, Green Town, and Mars—are now complemented by a mythically conceived California, at once a graveyard of losers and fading dreams and a vital center of creativity, where imagination (embodied in *Death Is a Lonely Business* in the fervent aspirations of Bradbury's hero) struggles to be free of the deathly hand of despair. As he has done earlier with weird fiction, fantasy, and science fiction, Bradbury in his new phase adapts the conventions of detective fiction to express his distinctive personal vision.

A Memory of Murder

The title of Bradbury's introduction to *A Memory of Murder* indicates that he presents this collection of early mystery tales with some misgivings: "Hammett? Chandler? Not to worry!" After reconstructing the context in which they were written—during the mid-forties, late in his apprenticeship period when he still met weekly with Leigh Brackett at Muscle Beach to compare their week's work—he concludes that "perhaps this collection is only of historical interest" and asks the reader to "judge kindly, and let me off easy."[4] His apprehension here is to some degree justified, since many of these mystery stories lack the originality and intensity of his previously collected stories from this era. These early tales from pulp magazines—*Dime Mystery Magazine, New Detective Magazine, Detective Tales, Flynn's Detective Fiction*—certainly never threatened the preeminence of Bradbury's favorites: Hammett, Chandler, Cain, and Macdonald. Some suffer from stilted execution, labored style, and unconvincing premises. Yet many readers will find the collection entertaining and often rewarding, not only because the stories do indeed have "historical interest" for those interested in the genre of detective fiction, but also because the better stories exhibit qualities characteristic of Bradbury's best fiction—vivid description, haunting atmosphere, and flamboyant characterization.

As Bradbury observes, the rationalistic conventions of detective fiction inhibited somewhat the intuitive lyricism he was beginning to express in other genres: "My weird, my fantastic, my science fiction concepts came as lightning bolts. . . . The detective tales, because they required hard thinking, prevented my flow, damaged my ability to use my intuition to the full" (*MoM*, 8). As might be expected,

Bradbury's best detective tales, like his weird and fantasy fiction, focus not on complexities of plot and motive but on striking characterization and macabre atmosphere. Given his lack of interest in elaborate plot structure and ratiocination Bradbury adapts mystery conventions to suit his temperament, and his viewpoint characters illustrate his struggle to write from his own strengths. Rather than utilizing the "cool" detective of vast experience and insight, the Sam Spade hero, Bradbury often presents the action through the perceptions of sensitive outsiders, even grotesques: a writer in "A Careful Man Dies" (anticipating his strategy in *Death Is a Lonely Business*, though this early story unconvincingly endows his writer with hard-boiled toughness), a perceptive street kid in "The Long Night," a circus freak in "Corpse Carnival," an outraged, still-conscious corpse in "It Burns Me Up!," a henpecked husband in "The Long Way Home," a not-so-dumb village idiot in "I'm Not So Dumb!," a sensitive boy in "The Trunk Lady." Even Bradbury's ex-cop hero, Douser (in "Half-Pint Homicide" and "Four-Way Funeral"), always successful in his battles with criminal thugs, is whimsically conceived: tiny in stature, unarmed, he destroys his sinister opponents with his genius for provocation, for simply bugging them until they self-destruct. A hero whom Bradbury's ingenuity cannot entirely save from silliness, Douser consciously parodies the prototype hero from which he departs: "Douser drew out cigarette papers and a tobacco bag. He began to make a cigarette quietly. He got half through rolling, fixing it into a rut to pour tobacco in when he said, 'Some damn guy in some damn detective novel did this all the time. Every time there was a lull in the conversation he did this. I can't for the hell of it figure why. Called the guy Sam Spade, I think' " (*MoM*, 60). Though Douser always gets his man, his cigarettes never stay rolled.

Many of these early mystery stories illustrate Bradbury's struggle to adapt his talents to fit the genre, and the most successful succeed in projecting vivid imagery, evocative atmosphere, and interesting character revelation. Though the political background to "The Long Night" is a bit muddled, the fast-paced narrative succeeds because of the tough street dialogue and the richly detailed barrio atmosphere (both the murder plot and Fannie Florianna, the monumentally fat ex–opera singer, reappear in another context in *Death Is a Lonely Business*). "Corpse Carnival" creates a disturbing, macabre setting, though it is difficult to imagine the beautiful tightrope walker's affair with a Siamese twin, and impossible to believe the narrator would turn her in for murdering his odious brother to set them free. "The Trunk Lady" presents a harrowing family drama from the viewpoint of a neglected rich child who insists on exposing the family skeleton in the attic. "The Candy Skull" utilizes the sinister background of the Guanajuato mummies and the Mexican *el día de muerte* (day of the dead), artfully weaving together the mystery plot with the American protagonist's acceptance of mortality. And "Yesterday I Lived!," perhaps the finest of these stories, creates a moving elegiac tribute to a betrayed movie star, effectively evoking gothic atmosphere in the film studio where she was destroyed by her cameraman. Bradbury uses realistic detail here to establish mood and metaphor:

> They walked over into the film laboratory to get the film. Steve was frankly afraid of the place. Always had been. It was a huge dark mortuary building with dead-end passages and labyrinths of black walls to cut the light. You stumbled through pitch dark, touching the walls, careening, turning, cursing, twisting around cutouts; walked south, east, west, south again and suddenly found yourself in a green-freckled place as big as the universe. Nothing to see but green welts and splashes of light, dim snakes of film climbing, winding over spools from floor to high ceiling and back down. The one brilliant light was a printing light that shot down from a projector and printed negative to positive as they slid by in parallel slots. The positive then coiled over and down into a long series of developing baths. The place was a whining morgue. Jake Davis moved around in it with ghoullike movements. (*MoM*, 153)

As Bradbury's introduction suggests, *A Memory of Murder* illustrates that in the forties his detective fiction rarely achieved the eloquence of his best fiction in other genres. Yet these early stories are not without their successes, and some of the concepts and characters from the early fiction reappear, reconceived and transposed, in *Death Is a Lonely Business*. When he returned to detective fiction many years later, Bradbury observed that "I've loved it for forty years and I've always wanted to do it and for some mysterious reason my subconscious says, 'Hey, this is the year.' "[5] In his first detective novel, dedicated "to the memory of Raymond Chandler, Dashiell Hammett, James M. Cain, and Ross Macdonald," Bradbury makes his own original contribution to a literary tradition he has always loved.

Death Is a Lonely Business

In a 1970 review in the *Los Angeles Times,* "Ross Macdonald Socks
It to the Eastern Mob," Bradbury defined some of the values he associates with the detective novel. As the title suggests, his defense of
Macdonald is part of an attack on a literary establishment ("the Eastern Mob") that enshrines cynical reductionist realism as art and deval-
ues the metaphorical power of popular culture forms. Thus,
Bradbury's tribute to Macdonald characterizes both detective fiction
and science fiction as similarly undervalued genres. Both deal with
threatening realities as Perseus deals with Medusa; that is, they refract grim reality off a magic shield of metaphor, so that it can be
recognized and destroyed. "The head of Medusa is best seen on a
bronze shield. Looking ahead into that shield, you reach behind to
decapitate." Whereas science fiction uses the shield to ward off future
dangers, the detective novel refracts disturbing realities in past and
present: "We see the reality of death, murder, greed, sex, time and
growing old, years and growing sad, landscapes from which people
vanish never to return. But it is reality distilled. There's the point."[6]
    Bradbury loves detective fiction because it is an implicitly mythical
medium that, like horror fiction, allows us to confront unacceptable
realities in symbolic form. And, like his quasi-allegorical gothic
novel, *Something Wicked This Way Comes, Death Is a Lonely Business* develops the symbolic potential of its genre to an extreme. Though the
plot deftly builds from murder to murder to the final confrontation
with wretched "Death" himself, the action is often subsumed within
the highly wrought asides, the lyrical atmosphere of rain and despair.
Finally finding his own voice as a detective writer, Bradbury invests
the hard-boiled detective tradition with his own distinctively sump-
tuous prose—fused here with a new vein of nostalgic humor—and an
overtly symbolic theme.
    This richly textured prose is not uniformly successful and not to
everyone's taste, yet most reviewers, with some reservations, concur
in Earl Gottschalk's conclusion that "by the end of the tale, it is clear
that Mr. Bradbury has moved successfully from fantasy to detective
fiction."[7] Less favorable reviews tend to agree with Geoffrey O'Brien
that Bradbury's ornate, dreamy style is inappropriate to detective fiction: "Unfortunately, the hardboiled genre demands a minimal aura
of reality to achieve its effects, whereas Mr. Bradbury's book is so
dreamy and fog-laden we never get our bearings."[8] But others, like

Stefan Kanfer, comment on the novel's "overload of sunstruck prose," yet find the overall effect evocative and richly mythical: "The hero is soon dwarfed by the ancient archetypes who save the story by running away with it."[9] As Gottschalk observes, the tough heroes of Bradbury's predecessors would hardly recognize as one of them the rhapsodic narrator in *Death Is a Lonely Business*. But it is the voice of this narrator, who is modeled closely on Bradbury himself in his early years as a writer, that gives the novel its distinctive tone and theme: "Instead of producing a tough detective yarn in their [Chandler, Hammett, Cain and Macdonald] tradition, Mr. Bradbury has written a relaxed, nostalgic story, laced with humor and set in the foggy, oceanfront community of Venice, California in 1950. Unlike most detective stories, this one takes place in a world where the system isn't corrupt and one person can make a difference."[10] This treatment of the viewpoint character makes Bradbury's detective novel a vehicle for his own style of mythicized autobiographical fantasy, and it also helps shape the murder-mystery plot into a symbolic fable about the process of achieving a creative adult identity.

The novel's opening descriptions establish an atmosphere of dilapidated decay, as well as the poignant wry lyricism of the narrative voice:

> Venice, California, in the old days had much to recommend it to people who like to be sad. It had fog almost every night and along the shore the moaning of the oil well machinery and the slap of dark water in the canals and the hiss of sand against the windows of your house when the wind came up and sang among the open places and along the empty walks.
> Those were the days when the Venice pier was falling apart and dying in the sea and you could find there the bones of a vast dinosaur, the rollercoaster, being covered by the shifting tides.
> At the end of one long canal you could find old circus wagons that had been rolled and dumped, and in the cages, at midnight, if you looked, things lived—fish and crayfish moving with the tide; and it was all the circuses of time somehow gone to doom and rusting away.[11]

The haunting mood established here expresses loss and regret, but it is not simply nostalgic. The imagery evokes both entrapment in antiquated dreams and intimations of a natural cycle of decay and replenishment. New life flits among the bars of the abandoned lion cages, but they will soon contain corpses as well—and the narrator comes perilously close to becoming one of them. This vanishing world of Venice may have its dilapidated beauty, but it also threatens to destroy the emerging new life of the narrator, who is just beginning to taste success after years of struggling to become a professional writer. The novel's title encodes the threat: "Death" has literally made it his "business" to murder "Lonelies," and the narrator appears to be on his list of potential victims. To survive, he must both differentiate himself from and protect as best he can his "Lonely" friends, including some appealing grotesques who are already doomed by their own despair before Death begins taking their destruction out of their own hands. As the primeval oil machinery relentlessly displaces old structures, this California landscape—like the Lonelies' lives—has become littered with the architecture of failed and exhausted dreams— the abandoned roller coaster, the submerged lion cages, the movie house about to be torn down, the trolley station where old men endlessly bicker. To survive, the narrator must endow his own dreams with life.

Ultimately, to defeat Death the narrator must overcome his own despair, his inner suspicion that perhaps he is indeed just one of the Lonelies, doomed to pursue an unreal dream of becoming a real writer while his life turns hollow. Death is both the nightmare that stalks him and his friends—and his alter ego. His love of books is mirrored inversely in Death's gloomy library. For Death is a pretentious, reclusive little fellow named A. L. Shrank, whose library and name both suggest the origins of his malevolence: his library is a mausoleum dedicated to death and despair, and his name, suggestive both of excessive self-analytical therapy and diminished stature, parodies the morbidly self-conscious intellectualism Bradbury associates with the literary establishment ("the Eastern Mob"). Unaware during their initial meeting of Shrank's hidden identity, the narrator recognizes with some distaste a peculiar affinity between them. As he searches fruitlessly for a cheery book, he finds his own image oddly refracted in Shrank's mannerisms and style: "He was imitating my banter. His thin smile was a weak-tea duplicate of my own. I felt it would vanish if I, in turn, shut my mouth" (68).

But the narrator has another alter ego, an ally—Elmo Crumley, detective-turned-writer as he is writer-turned-detective—whose tough-minded experience helps the narrator survive, even as the narrator revitalizes him by inspiring him to create fiction of his own. Indeed, both writer-detectives work at novels based on their experience, and it is never clear which (if either) writes the novel we read. But this reflexive relationship between the writer-protagonists and the novel itself is both a zany joke and a central metaphor, for thematically the novel's central conflict contrasts attitudes toward the past and toward "dreams" (fictions): the doomed Lonelies are imprisoned by inadequate or faded dreams or merely dying of old age, while the survivors creatively embrace their past to build new dreams for the future. Symbolically, the writing process represents a creative approach to loss and despair, the capacity to grow and change with experience.

The narrator and his friends survive because they recognize and ward off the reality of Death, both in their inner selves and in the outer world. Because they finally reveal Death's true identity, they can survive the encounter with despair and proceed with their lives as a creative process. For Death himself is revealed to be the archetypal Lonely (so that death is not only a business concerning Lonelies, but the business of a Lonely), whose power comes only from his victims' despair, as becomes clear in his final confrontation with the narrator: "He's quit, I thought. He knows he must be the last one. He knows he can't kill me" (275). Finally, Death's body—the wretched, small frame of A. L. Shrank—floats limply in the submerged lion cage, mirroring the image that begins the story, freeing the narrator to leave his own despair behind. As the novel closes he and his survivor friends drive back through the mythical landscape that opens the book. But now the rain has stopped, and the narrator is no longer sad, but reflective, observing the debris of dilapidated dreams with quiet thoughtfulness as images from his own past come clearly into focus:

> And more cars arrived and police were getting ready to dive in to get whatever that was out of the cage . . . and we drove along the middle of the night coast among the big, sighing derricks, leaving behind a strange, small apartment where I worked and leaving behind the dark, small lean-to [Shrank's home] where Spengler and Genghis Khan and Nietzsche and a few dozen old candy wrappers waited and leaving behind the shut trolley station where tomorrow some lost old men would sit again waiting for the last trains of the century.
>
> Along the way, I thought I saw myself passing on a bike, twelve years old, delivering papers in the dark morn. Further on, my older self, nineteen, wandering home, bumping into poles, lipstick on his cheek, drunk with love. (278)

Now he possesses his own past and looks ahead to professional success and to marriage, to dreams rendered true in fiction and in life. Secure at last in his adult identity as a successful creator, he can lightheartedly follow Henry, the blind black man who helped show him the way to his personal illumination, into his future—which at the moment is a celebration with fellow friends and survivors. Bradbury has successfully integrated his lyrical style with the conventions of the detective novel, though some fans of the hard-boiled genre may find Bradbury's first mystery novel overwritten and ephemeral. Certainly none of the writers to whom the novel is dedicated has written in quite this vein, in prose so saturated with digression and metaphor, about a murder plot so overtly resonant with personal and cultural mythology. But fans of Bradbury's earlier fiction will recognize that he has finally written detective fiction in his own voice, and in the process forged a new landscape and a new style. For *Death Is a Lonely Business* does not merely recapitulate Bradbury's earlier themes in a new setting: the new location in time, place, and tradition has inspired a new theme, consistent with earlier work but significantly different in emphasis. The poignant imagery of loss and decay recalls the landscape of October country, and the magical evocation of personal memory recalls earlier Green Town dramas. But the tone evoked by this California setting is more wry, more humorously ironic, occasionally more grittily profane, than the tone of Bradbury's earlier fiction.

Along with the haunting atmosphere of loss and doom, *Death Is a Lonely Business* provides witty hyperbole and sly observation: one of the principal clues is a corpse's awful haircut from the world's worst barber, a Lonely who flees the country leaving mangled heads in his wake when a phony photograph of himself playing piano with Scott Joplin is exposed; Constance Rattigan, whom local legend has typecast as a tragic movie-star recluse broken in spirit, turns out to be delightfully raunchy and alive, savoring her addictions to old movies, frivolous sex, and exercise; one of the novel's pleasures is the intricate tapestry of allusions, from echoes of Bradbury's early story "The Foghorn" in the opening descriptions (3, 16), to the goofy but suggestive reworking of Thomas Mann's title *Death in Venice* (47), to the invocation of Ishmael's famous opening lines of *Moby-Dick* as the narrator sets off to be shorn by the notorious barber (62). In *Death Is a Lonely Business* Bradbury utilizes his symbolic shield, his style, to reveal the Medusa of Death and Despair as both lonely and entertaining. He has at last fashioned the California detective genre into a medium in which he can communicate with grace, distilling reality into his own distinctive mythology.

Chapter Thirteen

"Nostalgia for the Future": The Myth behind the Life

Like his own writing, Bradbury's career is remarkable for its diversity and intensity. Beginning as an ambitious youth with wild dreams, boundless energy, and a talent he could only trust was there, he established himself not only as a writer but as a paradoxical symbol of the space age. In a life filled with "Discoveries and Revelations" (to use Doug Spaulding's terms in *Dandelion Wine*), his crucial "discovery" was his distinctive literary style. With it he created a vivid mythology from standard popular culture images, exploring the ambivalent fears and desires generated by an age of great transitions. Shaping symbols that interpret our transition from Green Town to the early stages of the space age, his own public image has come to embody the contradictory impulses of the times. The "uncrowned king of science fiction"[1] in popular imagination, no matter how much he and others point to the diversity of his actual writing, his public image expresses the irony of his best fiction: dreaming of rockets and man's destiny in space, he rides a bicycle because he hates cars; fervently recording innocence vanishing in the past, he dramatizes it vanishing again on fresh new worlds.

Perhaps Willis McNelly's phrase, "nostalgia for the future,"[2] best evokes the central emotions generated by Bradbury's art. His best work is "mythical" in the positive sense of the term, generating symbols that interpret the relationship between memory and desire, past and future, hopes and fears. And to survey Bradbury's career is to discover that, like such writers as George Bernard Shaw and H. G. Wells, Bradbury himself represents the themes of his creations. To the generation that grew up reading his early Bantam paperbacks, at least, he is subliminally and perhaps irrevocably identified with the image on the covers—there is the thoughtful contemporary man in dark-rimmed glasses, surrounded by a collage of dinosaurs and rockets, vampires and robots, alien landscapes and architecture. Like the Illustrated Man, the carnival, Mars—like all the central symbols in

Bradbury's writing which refract back to observers their latent fears and desires—Bradbury himself has become an icon of our ambivalent response to future shock and change. Embodying a myth in one's own life presents dangers as well as rewards, and in some ways Bradbury may have become captive to his own image. Most of his work since the early sixties lacks the subtlety and vitality of the fiction that established his reputation. Prolific and energetic throughout his career, he seems nevertheless, while emerging as a popular and successful public figure, to have lost the magical intensity that informs his best art. Readers seeking the poignant irony, bizarre terrors, and lyrical atmosphere of the earlier fiction may find much of the later fiction, the drama, and especially the poetry overwritten and diffuse by comparison. Yet Bradbury has continued to produce some excellent work throughout his career and in the eighties he has entered a productive new phase as a fiction writer; most important, his early achievements have been enhanced rather than diminished by time. As Gary K. Wolfe observes, whatever the mixed success of many of Bradbury's recent experiments, his reputation as a significant and original American artist rests on a secure foundation:

Bradbury [is assured] a permanent place in the history of the American short story, just as his introduction of stylistic sophistication and metaphorical use of science fiction concepts in the late 1940s earn him a significant place in the history of science fiction. . . . Much of the early criticism of his science fiction for its scientific unsoundness has abated as the genre broadens its scope to make room for metaphor and poetry, but it is increasingly being replaced by a feeling on the part of many readers that Bradbury's best work remains his early work . . . that he has increasingly turned away from the areas of his greatest strength in favor of forms in which he is less comfortable. . . . Bradbury has always been a resourceful artist, and any final conclusions about the value or direction of his later work would be premature. Of his earlier work, however, there can be little doubt: for all its eclecticism and occasional stylistic excesses—perhaps even because of these—it stands as one of the most interesting and significant bodies of short fiction in modern American literature.[3]

Now that Bradbury has successfully returned to writing fiction, Wolfe's warning about premature evaluation is especially apt. In any case an artist should be judged, finally, by his achievement in his best work, and Bradbury has written several books that seem destined to survive as provocative and enduring expressions of the American imagination. As is evidenced both by their continued popularity and by the steadily increasing volume of critical commentary they evoke, *The Martian Chronicles* and *Fahrenheit 451* are securely established as American science-fiction classics. And numerous of Bradbury's other books seem certain to survive as minor classics in their genres, most notably *Dandelion Wine* (and perhaps *Something Wicked This Way Comes* and *Death Is a Lonely Business*) as well as the best short-story collections: *The October Country, The Illustrated Man,* and *The Golden Apples of the Sun.* A pioneer who blazed a trail from the genre magazines to mainstream publication, who has helped salvage the best of the past to carry into a problematic future, Bradbury's most fundamental achievement has been to express the challenges of an exciting and disconcerting new age.

Notes and References

Preface

1. "Drunk, and in Charge of a Bicycle," introduction to *The Stories of Ray Bradbury* (New York, 1980), xiv.
2. Orville Prescott, "Books of the Times," in *The New York Times*, 21 October 1953, 27.
3. "The Inherited Wish," introduction to William F. Nolan's *The Ray Bradbury Companion* (Detroit, 1975), 3.

Chapter One

1. *Dandelion Wine* (New York, rev. ed., 1976 pb.), 9.
2. "The Inherited Wish," 5.
3. *Dandelion Wine*, 6.
4. "The Inherited Wish," 5–6.
5. 1980 interview with Bradbury.
6. Nolan, *Bradbury Companion*, 40.
7. Interview with Craig Cunningham, Oral History Department, University of California at Los Angeles, 1961; transcript in UCLA Special Collections; hereafter referred to as the Cunningham interview.
8. "Los Angeles is the Best Place in America," *Esquire*, October 1972, 176.
9. Ibid., 117, 174.
10. This subject is treated in Bradbury's short story "Heavy-Set," in *I Sing the Body Electric!* (New York, 1959 pb.), 229–40.
11. Cunningham interview.
12. "W. C. Fields and the S.O.B. on Rollerskates, A Remembrance," *Producer's Journal*, June 1973, 22.
13. Ibid., 23.
14. Bradbury reconstructed this relationship in some detail during his 1980 interview with me (hereafter referred to as the Mogen interview). It illustrates that his years "running with . . . these sad strange people" ("W. C. Fields and the S.O.B. on Rollerskates," 23) were also exciting and creative times:

> My friend and I wrote scripts for them every week and turned them in every Wednesday night, and the following week George would tell us how great the scripts were. But I'm sure he never read them. Now why should he? Because they were dreadful. But he pretended that he did, which shows what a nice man he was. And they actually did use one of my routines in one of their broadcasts in 1935. Every

one of their broadcasts had a little skit which ended the show. I wrote this thing for them which has Gracie saying, "Oh! Oh! Ooooh!" And George says, "Oh Gracie, Gracie, what's *happened*? Are you fainting? *Say* something to me. *Speak* to me, Gracie." She says, "Oooh. Oooh." He says, "Oh Gracie. *Say* something." She says, "This is the Columbia Broadcasting System." And that was the end of the show.

15. Mogen interview.
16. Cunningham interview.
17. Ibid.
18. Ibid.
19. Ibid.
20. Ibid.
21. See the *Writer,* October 1958, 5–10.
22. During his 1980 interview, Bradbury reminisced about the time when he and Leigh Brackett recognized his transition from accomplished hack to original writer:

> Once I got through the apprenticeship with Leigh and could break free she recognized the moment of breaking free and said, "Oh yeah. Well, this isn't like me anymore and God bless, you know, you're at last free of the influence. Go that way." And then, of course, I got all kinds of rejections because the conventional stories were easier to sell, but they were a bore. So "The King of the Grey Spaces," which was my pivotal breakthrough story in science fiction, was rejected by three or four magazines. . . . And finally the editor of *Famous Fantastic Mysteries* read it and had enough brains to publish it. And it's just about boys, that's all, who wanted to be rocket men.

23. Mogen interview.
24. Ibid.
25. Ibid.
26. Ibid.
27. Nolan, *Bradbury Companion,* p. 56.
28. See his interview, "Ray Bradbury on Hitchcock, Huston, and Other Magic of the Screen," *Take One,* 26 September 1973.
29. Mogen interview.
30. Ibid.

Chapter Two

1. Michael Franklin, Martin Last, Beth Meacham, Baird Searles, eds., *A Reader's Guide to Science Fiction* (New York: Avon, 1979), 24–25.
2. Bradbury remembers his first encounter with Isherwood as an exciting and pivotal moment in his career:

> It was all accidental. I bumped into him in a bookstore about thirty years ago and handed him my copy of the book [*The Martian Chronicles*] and his face sank. I

realize he received books every day of his life, just as I do now. He thanked me very tepidly, then left. But two or three days later he calls me on the phone and says, "My God, what have you done?" And I say, "What do you mean?" He says, "Well, this is a beautiful book. I'm going to review it for *Tomorrow*." So that really was a changing point in my life. And then he brought me to meet Aldous Huxley and Gerald Heard and all those people told me that I was good. And we all need that, don't we? At a certain age you don't really believe because no one's told you: and it doesn't help if your friends tell you or if your wife tells you. . . . They love you and they're prejudiced. But when strangers tell you that, that's so important (Mogen interview).

3. Christopher Isherwood, *Tomorrow*, October 1950, 56–58.
4. J. B. Priestley, "They Come From Inner Space," *New Statesman and Nation* 46 (5 December 1953):712.
5. Orville Prescott, *New York Times*, 21 October 1953, 27.
6. Angus Wilson, *Science Fiction News*, May/June 1953, 2.
7. Kingsley Amis, *New Maps of Hell* (New York: Harcourt Brace, 1960), 105.
8. Ibid., 106.
9. Joseph Kostoletsky, "Science, Yes—Fiction, Maybe," *Antioch Review* 13 (June 1953):237.
10. Quoted from "Ray Bradbury" in the *Wilson Library Bulletin* 39, no. 3 (November 1964):268.
11. "What Can a Writer Say," *Weird Tales*, 1 January 1945, 93.
12. *Famous Fantastic Mysteries*, October 1949, 119.
13. *Current Biography*, June 1953, 9.
14. In *The Ray Bradbury Review*, ed. William F. Nolan (San Diego: Nolan, 1952), 34.
15. *Thrilling Wonder Stories*, November 1953.
16. Nolan, *Bradbury Review*, 40.
17. Edward Wood, *Journal of Science Fiction* 1, no. 1 (Fall 1951): 8–12.
18. William Atheling, Jr. [James Blish], *The Issue at Hand* (Chicago: Advent, 1964), 48.
19. Damon Knight, *In Search of Wonder* (Chicago: Advent, 1967), 282.
20. Ibid., 112.
21. Anthony Boucher, *Magazine of Fantasy and Science Fiction*, February 1956, 95.
22. L. Sprague de Camp and Catherine Cook de Camp, *Science Fiction Handbook, Revised* (New York: McGraw-Hill, 1975), 49.
23. Knight, *In Search of Wonder*, 109.
24. Thomas M. Disch, *New York Times Book Review*, 26 October 1980, 14, 32.
25. "Why Science Fiction?" *Nation*, 2 May 1953, 364.
26. Ibid., 365–66.

27. See his science articles in the sixties, and his Aviation-Space Writers Association Award in 1968.

28. Isherwood, *Tomorrow*, 57.

29. See Steven Dimeo's "Man and Apollo: Religion in Bradbury's Science Fantasies," in *Ray Bradbury*, ed. Martin Harry Greenberg and Joseph Olander (New York, 1980), 156–64.

30. Russell Kirk, *Enemies of the Permanent Things* (New York: Arlington House, 1969), 119.

31. Mogen interview.

Chapter Three

1. Gary K. Wolfe, "Ray Bradbury," in *Twentieth-Century American Science Fiction Writers, Dictionary of Literary Biography* (Detroit, 1981), 8:62.

2. Willis McNelly, "Ray Bradbury," in *Science Fiction Writers: Critical Studies of the Major Authors from the Early Nineteenth Century to the Present Day*, ed. E. F. Bleiler (New York, 1982), 171.

3. Two aspects of Bradbury's style are treated extensively in the Taplinger anthology of critical essays, *Ray Bradbury*. Sarah-Warner J. Dell surveys his use of imagery in "Style is the Man: Imagery in Bradbury's Fiction"; and Eric S. Rabkin's "To Fairyland by Rocket: Bradbury's *The Martian Chronicles*" is an interesting stylistic analysis of Bradbury's fusion of science-fiction and fantasy verbal conventions.

4. "I went through the imitative period, which is very important. It has to be part of your life and you actually no more than plagiarize, right and left. You just go through and study people's work. I know I came up against problems in writing where I would want to say a certain thing in a certain way, or I wanted to put over a certain mood. Quite often, I would go to a magazine and get a copy of *Colliers* or *The {Saturday Evening} Post* or sometimes an old copy of writers like Edgar Allan Poe and Nathaniel Hawthorne. I would sometimes cut out the paragraph I needed and paste it right into my story, or sometimes retype it into my story, and then try to find ways of paraphrasing this or writing it on my own. I think this period lasted from the time I was seventeen until I was nineteen. Then I began . . . to be able to do these things without copying directly, but the mystery of how these people did what they did and why I was not able to do the same thing was always there. So, in frustration, I ripped the pages out of these books and inserted them into my own stories" (Cunningham interview).

5. Cunningham interview.

6. "How to Keep and Feed a Muse," *Writer* (July 1961).

7. Dorothea Brande, *Becoming a Writer* (New York: Harcourt Brace, 1934), 123.

8. Mogen interview.

9. See his series of articles for the *Writer*: "The Joy of Writing" (October 1956); "Zen and the Art of Writing" (October 1958); "How to Keep

and Feed a Muse" (July 1961); and "The Secret Mind" (November 1965). This is also a common theme in interviews with Bradbury.

10. Brande, *Becoming a Writer*, 74.
11. "The Inherited Wish," 5.
12. Mogen interview.
13. Ibid.
14. Ibid.
15. Ibid.
16. Ibid.
17. Ibid.
18. Judith Merril, "Books," in *Fantasy and Science Fiction*, October 1965, 95.
19. Ibid., 95.
20. Mogen interview.
21. "Marvels and Miracles—Pass it On," *Galileo*, no. 1, 1976, 12–14, reprinted from the *New York Times Magazine*, 20 March 1955.
22. Wolfe, 8.
23. Ibid.
24. Reprinted and revised in *The Martian Chronicles* as "The Third Expedition."
25. Wayne L. Johnson, *Ray Bradbury* (New York, 1980), 5.
26. Cunningham interview.
27. Both versions are reprinted in Nolan's *Bradbury Companion*, 100–2.
28. Cunningham interview.
29. Mogen interview.
30. Compare to this passage in "A Sound of Thunder" (in *The Golden Apples of the Sun* [New York, 1954 pb.], 94), an excellent illustration of what Bradbury means by an aside:

It came on great oiled, resilient, striding legs. It towered thirty feet above half of the trees, a great evil god, folding its delicate watchmaker's claws close to its oily reptilian chest. Each lower leg was a piston, a thousand pounds of white bone, sunk in thick ropes of muscle, sheathed over in a gleam of pebbled skin like the mail of a terrible warrior. Each thigh was a ton of meat, ivory, and steel mesh. And from the great breathing cage of the upper body those two delicate arms dangled out front, arms with hands which might pick up and examine men like toys, while the snake neck coiled. And the head itself, a ton of sculptured stone, lifted easily upon the sky. Its mouth gaped, exposing a fence of teeth like daggers. Its eyes rolled, ostrich eggs, empty of all expression save hunger. It closed its mouth in a death grin. It ran, its pelvic bones crushing aside trees and bushes, its taloned feet clawing damp earth, leaving prints six inches deep wherever it settled its weight. It ran with a gliding ballet step, far too poised and balanced for its ten tons. It moved into a sunlit arena warily, its beautifully reptile hands feeling the air.

. . . .

The Thunder Lizard raised itself. Its armored flesh glittered like a thousand green coins. The coins, crusted with slime, steamed. In the slime, tiny insects wriggled, so that the entire body seemed to twitch and undulate, even while the monster itself did not move. It exhaled. The stink of raw flesh blew down the wilderness.

31. *Dinosaur Tales* (New York, 1982), 20.
32. "The Next in Line," in *The October Country* (New York, 1956 pb.), 28.
33. Ibid., 19.
34. *The Martian Chronicles* (New York, 1951 pb.), 1.
35. Bradbury is very conscious of this aspect of his style, the ways in which vivid imagery helps to sustain a reader's suspension of disbelief:

These are some of the literary tricks you learn, over a period of time. That is, if you describe a thing well enough, vividly enough, through the senses—sense of smell, sense of taste and color, sense of hearing—if I can involve you with all these senses then you'll believe anything I tell you, just anything. You can make anything happen in a fantasy, the most improbable things, if you attack people through their senses. Then they've got to believe. Logic may say, "Gee whiz, that can't happen." But the logic of the senses says otherwise (Mogen interview).

36. *Dandelion Wine* (New York, 1959 pb.), 9–10.

Chapter Four

1. *The October Country* (New York, 1956 pb.), acknowledgment. Subsequent parenthetical page references, indicated by the abbreviation *OC,* refer to this edition.
2. Nolan, *Bradbury Companion,* 40.
3. Hazel Pierce, "Ray Bradbury and the Gothic Tradition," in Greenberg and Olander, *Ray Bradbury,* 171.
4. Wolfe, "Ray Bradbury," 8:65.
5. Nolan, *Bradbury Companion,* 54.
6. During our interview, Bradbury described meeting the model for this sinister character decades later. Ironically, it was the "vampire" who returned late in life to confirm his memories of making dandelion wine:

I was back visiting in Waukegan a few years ago, and I walked into the town barber shop, and I didn't know who would be there. Originally one of the barbers had been my grandma's boarder, who owned the barber shop when I was a kid. He'd come in and have lunch every day, and he became a character in "The Man Upstairs," the vampire who lived and boarded in my grandma's house. So I walked in the barber shop about three years ago, and the barber took one look at me and threw his comb and scissors on the floor and said, "My God, I've been waiting for you to come through that door for forty years."
It turned out he had total recall of that period when he lived in my grandma's boarding house when I was one or two years old. So he was out here visiting about

two years ago, and I sat him down here with a tape recorder and we started going back over that period, and he says, "Oh, I have a memory of you and your grandad and your brother. There used to be a big field of dandelions right across the street there, an empty lot, and your grandfather would send you over there with paper sacks, and you'd make the wine." And I said, "Oh, thank God! What year was that?" And he said, "1923." It was so precious to have that given back to me. He's going to become a good friend now. Of course, he was around twenty at that time and now he's getting on toward eighty years old.

7. Knight, *In Search of Wonder*, 113.
8. *The Halloween Tree* (New York, 1972 pb.), 61. Subsequent parenthetical page references, indicated by the abbreviation HT, refer to this edition.
9. Pierce, 184.
10. Ibid.
11. "Death Warmed Over," *Playboy*, January 1968, 252.
12. Ibid., 102.
13. Ibid., 253.

Chapter Five

1. See David Mogen, *Wilderness Visions*, Science Fiction Westerns, vol. 1 (San Bernardino, Calif., 1981); also *New Frontiers, Old Horizons*, Science Fiction Westerns, vol. 2 (San Bernardino, Calif.: Borgo Press, forthcoming).
2. See especially "Day After Tomorrow: Why Science Fiction?" *Nation* (2 May 1953); "A Serious Search," *Life* (24 October 1960); "Cry the Cosmos," *Life* (14 September 1962); "Remembrances of Things Future," *Playboy* (January 1965); "An Impatient Gulliver Above our Roofs," *Life* (24 November 1967); "From Stonehenge to Tranquility Base," *Playboy* (December 1972); "On Going on a Journey," foreword to *Mars and the Mind of Man*, ed. Bruce Murray (New York: Harper and Row, 1973); "The Life Force Speaks—We Move to Answer," introduction to *Colonies in Space*, ed. T. A. Heppenheimer (Harrisburg, Pa.: Stackpole Books, 1971); "Beyond Eden," *Omni* (April 1980).
3. Willis McNelly, "Bradbury Revisited," *CEA Critic* 31 (March 1969):6.
4. "Marvels and Miracles—Pass It On!", *New York Times Magazine*, 20 March 1955.
5. Ibid.
6. Mogen interview. Bradbury has apparently confused Billy Buck here with the grandfather, though all three of Steinbeck's central characters—the grandfather, Billy Buck, and Jody—represent the "westering" spirit surviving into an era without meaningful challenge.
7. Ibid.

8. Reprinted as "R is for Rocket," in *R is for Rocket* (New York, 1965 pb.). Subsequent parenthetical references to *RR* refer to this edition.

9. In *The Illustrated Man* (New York, 1952 pb.). Subsequent parenthetical references to *IM* refer to this edition. For an interesting analysis of this passage as "American surrealism," see William F. Toupence, "Some Aspects of Surrealism in the Work of Ray Bradbury," *Extrapolation* 25 (Fall 1984), 234–38.

10. In *A Medicine for Melancholy* (New York, 1960 pb.). Subsequent parenthetical references to *MM* are to this edition.

11. In *The Golden Apples of the Sun* (New York, 1954 pb.). Subsequent parenthetical references to *GA* refer to this edition.

12. Both in *Long After Midnight* (New York, 1976 pb.). Subsequent parenthetical references to *LAM* refer to this edition.

13. "Remembrances of Things Future," 99.

14. Ibid.

15. Mogen interview.

16. "Remembrances of Things Past," 103.

17. In *I Sing the Body Electric!* (New York, 1969 pb). Subsequent parenthetical references to *ISB* are to this edition.

18. The Old Ones' actual doctrine is quite traditionally Christian, however, in its emphasis on attaining perfection of the spirit by escaping the sins of the flesh.

19. In *The Machineries of Joy* (New York, 1964 pb). Subsequent parenthetical references to *MJ* are to this edition.

20. "Beyond Eden," *Omni*, April 1980, 116.

Chapter Six

1. Eric Rabkin, "To Fairyland by Rocket: Bradbury's *The Martian Chronicles*," in Greenberg and Olander, *Ray Bradbury*, 123–24.

2. Mogen interview.

3. Franklin et al., *Reader's Guide to Science Fiction*, 25.

4. Mogen interview.

5. Cunningham interview.

6. See Johnson's *Ray Bradbury*, 112–19; also, in Greenberg and Olander, *Ray Bradbury*, see Wolfe's "The Frontier Myth in Ray Bradbury" and Gallagher's "The Thematic Structure of *The Martian Chronicles*."

7. See especially Wolfe's excellent analysis, "The Frontier Myth in Ray Bradbury" in the Greenberg and Olander anthology cited above. My own treatment of this theme also appears in another context in *New Frontiers, Old Horizons*.

8. *The Martian Chronicles* (New York, 1951 pb.), 49. Subsequent parenthetical page references to *MC* are to this edition.

9. This association is explored in detail in Eric Rabkin's "To Fairyland by Rocket: Bradbury's *The Martian Chronicles*," in the Greenberg and Olander anthology cited above.

10. Mogen interview.

Chapter Seven

1. In Greenberg and Olander, *Ray Bradbury*.

2. Wolfe, "Ray Bradbury," 8:62.

3. J. B. Priestley, "They Come from Inner Space," *New Statesman and Nation* 46 (5 December 1953):712.

4. Ibid.

5. "The Joy of Writing," *Writer,* October 1956, 294.

6. Ibid.

7. This phrase is taken from the title of Kingsley Amis's 1960 book on science fiction (which makes ample reference to Bradbury's work), *New Maps of Hell* (New York: Harcourt Brace, 1960).

8. Mogen interview.

9. "A Portrait of Genius: Ray Bradbury," interview in *Show,* December 1964, 55.

Chapter Eight

1. Orville Prescott, "Books of the Times," *New York Times,* 21 October 1953, 27.

2. *Fahrenheit 451* (New York, 1953 pb.), 97. All subsequent references are to this edition.

3. "At What Temperature do Books Burn?" *Writer*, July 1967, 19.

4. In Greenberg and Olander, *Ray Bradbury,* 195–213.

5. "At What Temperature do Books Burn?" 19.

6. Ibid., 20.

7. Amis, *New Maps of Hell,* 109.

8. Donald Watt's essay, "Burning Bright: *Fahrenheit 451* as Symbolic Dystopia" in Greenberg and Olander, *Ray Bradbury,* provides an excellent analysis of the ways Bradbury's central symbols structure the novel.

9. "At What Temperature Do Books Burn?" 19–20.

10. Amis, *New Maps of Hell,* 109.

11. McNelly, "Ray Bradbury," 174.

12. Mark R. Hillegas, *The Future as Nightmare: H. G. Wells and the Anti-Utopians* (New York: Oxford University Press, 1967), 158.

Chapter Nine

1. Cunningham interview.

2. Mogen interview.

3. Robert O. Bowen, "Summer of Innocence," *Saturday Review,* 7 September 1957, 18.

4. *Dandelion Wine* (New York, 1959 pb.). Subsequent page references are to this edition.

5. Marvin E. Mengeling provides an excellent analysis of structure and theme in "Ray Bradbury's *Dandelion Wine*: Themes, Sources, and Style," *English Journal* 60 (October 1971), 877–87.

6. Prescott, "Books of the Times," 27.

7. Wolfe, "Ray Bradbury," 8:72–3.

8. Johnson, *Ray Bradbury,* 104.

9. Mogen interview.

10. *Something Wicked This Way Comes* (New York, 1963 pb.), 142. Subsequent page references are to this edition.

11. Mogen interview.

12. Ibid.

13. Ibid.

14. Ibid.

Chapter Ten

1. Bradbury recalls that he became conscious of the power of the underlying metaphor only after he wrote the story: "The dinosaur in love with the lighthouse is a terrific metaphor for unrequited love. I didn't know I was writing it, but there it is, and people read that story and it haunts them, it makes them sad, because of a time in their own life when they called out to someone and no one answered" (Mogen interview).

2. Cunningham interview.

Chapter Eleven

1. Interview, Arnold R. Kunert, "Ray Bradbury on Hitchcock, Huston, and Other Magic of the Screen," *Take One,* 26 September 1973, 16. Much of my information in this section on film comes from this excellent interview, as well as from my own interview and the Cunningham interview at UCLA.

2. Mogen interview.

3. Ibid.

4. Ibid.

5. Ibid.

6. Kunert interview, 16.

7. Ibid., 19–20.

8. "*Fahrenheit* on Film," *Calendar,* in the *Los Angeles Times,* 20 November 1966, 16.

9. Mogen interview.

10. Ibid.

11. Ibid.
12. Introduction to *The Wonderful Ice Cream Suit and Other Plays of Today, Tomorrow, and Beyond Tomorrow* (New York, 1972 pb.), ix.
13. Ibid.
14. "What I Learned as My Own Producer," *Calendar, Los Angeles Times*, 28 February 1965, 28.
15. Mogen interview.
16. Cunningham interview.
17. Introduction to *The Pillar of Fire and Other Plays for Today, Tomorrow, and Beyond Tomorrow* (New York, 1975 pb.), xi.
18. Ben P. Indick, *The Drama of Ray Bradbury*, privately printed pamphlet, T-K Graphics, 1977.
19. John Boland, *Books and Bookmen* 19 (November 1973):122.
20. B. A. Fussell, "On the Trail of the Lonesome Dramaturge," *Hudson Review* 26 (Winter 1973–74):755.
21. Johnson, *Ray Bradbury*, 142.
22. Introduction to *The Complete Poems of Ray Bradbury* (New York, 1982 pb.), 4.
23. Ibid., 1.
24. Ibid., 164.
25. *Kirkus Review* 45 (15 November 1977):1258.
26. Peter Dollard, *Library Journal* 99 (15 February 1974):491.
27. Wolfe, "Ray Bradbury," 8:74.
28. Johnson, *Ray Bradbury*, 144–45.
29. *The Complete Poems of Ray Bradbury*, 16.

Chapter Twelve

1. Mogen interview.
2. This tentative title was provided by Bradbury in correspondence.
3. Earl C. Gottschalk, Jr., "Ray Bradbury Achieves His Own Fantasy," *Wall Street Journal*, 28 October 1985, 18.
4. Ray Bradbury, *A Memory of Murder* (New York, 1984), 9. Subsequent page references in the text identified *MoM*.
5. Mogen interview.
6. Ray Bradbury, "Ross Macdonald Socks it to the Eastern Mob," *Los Angeles Times*, 5 July 1970, 11.
7. Gottschalk, "Ray Bradbury Achieves His Own Fantasy," 18.
8. Geoffrey O'Brien, *New York Times Book Review*, 3 November 1985, 26.
9. Stefan Kanfer, "Dwarfed by Ancient Archetypes," *Time*, 28 October 1985, 90.
10. Gottschalk, "Ray Bradbury Achieves His Own Fantasy," 18.

11. Ray Bradbury, *Death Is a Lonely Business* (New York, 1985), 3. Subsequent page references in the text.

Chapter Thirteen

1. Prescott, "Books of the Times," 27.
2. McNelly, "Ray Bradbury—Past, Present, and Future," in Greenberg and Olander, *Ray Bradbury*, 19.
3. Wolfe, "Ray Bradbury," 8:75.

Selected Bibliography

PRIMARY SOURCES

Page references in my text are to the Bantam and Ballantine paperback editions, since they are most accessible both to general readers and to scholars.

1. Novels

Dandelion Wine. Garden City, N.Y.: Doubleday, 1957; New York: Bantam, 1959 pb.

Death Is a Lonely Business. New York: Alfred A. Knopf, 1985.

Fahrenheit 451. New York: Ballantine, 1953; Ballantine, 1953 pb.

The Halloween Tree [juvenile]. New York: Alfred A. Knopf, 1972; New York: Bantam, 1972 pb.

The Martian Chronicles. Garden City, N.Y.: Doubleday, 1950; New York: Bantam, 1951 pb.

Something Wicked This Way Comes. New York: Simon & Schuster, 1962; New York: Bantam, 1963 pb.

Switch on the Night [children's book]. New York: Pantheon, 1955; London: Rupert Hart-Davis, 1955.

2. Short-Story Collections

Dark Carnival. Sauk City, Wis.: Arkham, 1947.

Dinosaur Tales [juvenile]. Toronto, New York, London, Sydney: Bantam, 1983 pb.

The Golden Apples of the Sun. Garden City, N.Y.: Doubleday, 1953; New York: Bantam, 1954 pb.

I Sing the Body Electric! New York: Alfred A. Knopf, 1969; New York: Bantam, 1971 pb.

The Illustrated Man. Garden City, N.Y.: Doubleday, 1951; New York: Bantam, 1952 pb.

Long After Midnight. New York: Alfred A. Knopf, 1976; New York: Bantam, 1978 pb.

The Machineries of Joy. New York: Simon & Schuster, 1964; New York: Bantam, 1965 pb.

A Medicine for Melancholy. Garden City, N.Y.: Doubleday, 1959; New York: Bantam, 1960 pb. Revised as *The Day it Rained Forever.* London: Rupert Hart-Davis, 1959.

A Memory of Murder. New York: Dell, 1984 pb.
The October Country. New York: Ballantine, 1955; Ballantine, 1956 pb.
R is for Rocket. Garden City, N.Y.: Doubleday, 1962; New York: Bantam 1965 pb.
S is for Space. Garden City, N.Y.: Doubleday, 1966; New York: Bantam, 1970 pb.
The Stories of Ray Bradbury [Bradbury's selection of one hundred favorite stories]. New York: Alfred A. Knopf, 1980.
Twice 22 [collecting *The Golden Apples of the Sun* and *A Medicine for Melancholy*]. Garden City, N.Y.: Doubleday, 1966.
The Vintage Bradbury. New York: Vintage Books, 1965 pb.

3. Poetry
The Complete Poems of Ray Bradbury [collection of the three earlier volumes]. New York: Ballantine, 1982.
The Haunted Computer and the Android Pope. New York: Alfred A. Knopf, 1981.
When Elephants Last in the Dooryard Bloomed: Celebrations for Almost Any Day in the Year. New York: Alfred A. Knopf, 1973.
Where Robot Mice and Robot Men Run Round in Robot Towns. New York: Alfred A. Knopf, 1977.

4. Drama Collections
The Anthem Sprinters and Other Antics. New York: Dial Press, 1963; Dial Press, 1963 pb.
Pillar of Fire and Other Plays. New York: Bantam, 1975 pb.
The Wonderful Ice Cream Suit and Other Plays. New York: Bantam, 1972 pb.

5. Edited Anthologies
The Circus of Dr. Lao and Other Improbable Stories, edited by Bradbury. New York: Bantam, 1956 pb.
Timeless Stories for Today and Tomorrow, edited by Bradbury. New York: Bantam, 1952 pb.

SECONDARY SOURCES

1. Bibliographies
The single most helpful source on Bradbury's career still is William F. Nolan's book-length illustrated bibliography, *The Ray Bradbury Companion* (Detroit: Gale Research, 1975). However, Wayne L. Johnson's *Ray Bradbury* (New York: Frederick Ungar, 1980), Joseph D. Olander's and Martin Harry Greenberg's anthology of critical articles, *Ray Bradbury* (New York:

Taplinger, 1980), and Gary K. Wolfe's entry on Bradbury in *The Dictionary of Literary Biography*, vol. 8 (Detroit: Gale Research, 1981) all include helpful, more up-to-date selected bibliographies. The Popular Culture Center at Bowling Green State University possesses the largest and most accessible collection of Bradbury's work (including what originally was William F. Nolan's private collection), which includes over 2500 items and over 50 manuscripts.

2. Books

Dimeo, Richard Steven. *The Mind and Fantasies of Ray Bradbury*. Ph.D. dissertation, University of Utah, 1970. Hardcover facsimile, 1976. A well-researched thematic interpretation of Bradbury's life and career.

Greenberg, Martin Harry, and Joseph D. Olander, eds. *Ray Bradbury*. New York: Taplinger, 1980. A helpful and interesting anthology of critical articles treating major themes in Bradbury's work. See entries below under Dimeo, Gallagher, Mengeling, Rabkin, Watt, and Wolfe.

Johnson, Wayne L. *Ray Bradbury*. New York: Frederick Ungar, 1980. A useful survey of Bradbury's life and career, organized thematically.

Slusser, George Edgar. *The Bradbury Chronicles*. San Bernardino, Calif.: Borgo Press, 1977. A monograph-length analysis of Bradbury's major themes, with much emphasis on the Calvinist overtones of his fiction.

Toupence, William F. *Ray Bradbury and the Poetics of Reverie: Fantasy, Science Fiction, and the Reader*. Ann Arbor, Mich.: UMI Research Press, 1984. Application of reader response theory to selected Bradbury texts, especially *Fahrenheit 451*.

2. Essays

Dimeo, Steven. "Man and Apollo: Religion in Bradbury's Science Fantasies." In *Ray Bradbury*, edited by Greenberg and Olander (see principal entry above), 156–64. An informed analysis of an interesting dimension of Bradbury's work.

Isherwood, Christopher. Review of *The Martian Chronicles*. *Tomorrow*, October 1950, 56–58. An important historical document because it helped establish Bradbury's mainstream reputation in the 1950s.

Gallagher, Edward J. "The Thematic Structure of *The Martian Chronicles*." In *Ray Bradbury*, edited by Greenberg and Olander (see principal entry above), 55–82. A convincing description of the structural design of *The Martian Chronicles*.

McNelly, Willis E. "Ray Bradbury." In *Science Fiction Writers: Critical Studies of the Major Authors from the Early Nineteenth Century to the Present Day*, edited by E. F. Bleiler (New York: Scribner's, 1982), 171–78. A perceptive short overview of Bradbury's career.

Mengeling, Marvin E. "The Machineries of Joy and Despair: Bradbury's Attitudes toward Science and Technology." In *Ray Bradbury*, edited by

Greenberg and Olander (see principal entry above), 83–109. A convincing argument that Bradbury's reputation as a "technophobe" is fundamentally inaccurate.

————. "Ray Bradbury's *Dandelion Wine*: Themes, Sources, and Style." *English Journal* 60 (October 1971):877–87. Perceptive interpretation of Bradbury's achievement in *Dandelion Wine*.

Nolan, William F. "Ray Bradbury: Prose Poet in the Age of Space." *Magazine of Fantasy and Science Fiction* 24 (May 1963):7–22. The first extended interpretation of Bradbury's achievement.

Priestley, J. B. "Thoughts in the Wilderness: They Come from Inner Space." *New Statesman and Nation* 46 (5 December 1953):712,714. Another review illustrating Bradbury's reception by mainstream critics in the 1950s.

Rabkin, Eric S. "To Fairyland by Rocket: Bradbury's *The Martian Chronicles*." In *Ray Bradbury*, edited by Greenberg and Olander (see principal entry above), 110–26. An original and convincing analysis of Bradbury's lyricism as a "parametric center" in the *Chronicles*.

Sisario, Peter. "A Study of Allusions in Bradbury's *Fahrenheit 451*." *English Journal* 59 (February 1970):201–5. A helpful gloss on some of the allusions in *Fahrenheit 451*.

Toupence, William F. "Some Aspects of Surrealism in the Work of Ray Bradbury." *Extrapolation* 25, no. 3 (Fall 1984):228–38. An intriguing argument that Bradbury "discovered surrealist territory on his own . . . spontaneously, manifesting a kind of native American surrealism" (230), focusing on Bradbury's description of his writing process and a lyrical passage from "The Rocket Man."

Watt, Donald. "Burning Bright: *Fahrenheit 451* as Symbolic Dystopia." In *Ray Bradbury*, edited by Greenberg and Olander (see principal entry above), 195–213. An analysis of the ways fire imagery structures *Fahrenheit 451*.

Wolfe, Gary K. "The Frontier Myth in Ray Bradbury." In *Ray Bradbury*, edited by Greenberg and Olander (see principal entry above), 33–54. A well-researched interpretation of Bradbury's treatment of one of his most eloquent themes.

————. "Ray Bradbury." In *Twentieth-Century American Science Fiction Writers*, vol. 8 of the *Dictionary of Literary Biography* (2 vols.), edited by David Coward and Thomas L. Wymer (Detroit: Gale Research, 1981), 61–76. An excellent chronological survey of Bradbury's career, including a helpful bibliography.

Index